POLITICS AND SOCIETY IN

Placing

POLITICS AND SOCIETY IN WALES SERIES
Series editor: Ralph Fevre

The Politics and Society in Wales series examines issues of politics and government, and particularly the effects of devolution on policy-making and implementation, and the way in which Wales is governed as the National Assembly gains in maturity. It will also increase our knowledge and understanding of Welsh society and analyse the most important aspects of social and economic change in Wales. Where necessary, studies in the series will incorporate strong comparative elements which will allow a more fully informed appraisal of the conditions of Wales.

Placing the Nation

ABERYSTWYTH AND THE REPRODUCTION OF WELSH NATIONALISM

By

RHYS JONES

CARWYN FOWLER

*Published on behalf of
the University of Wales*

UNIVERSITY OF WALES PRESS
CARDIFF
2008

British Library Cataloguing-in-Publication Data.
A catalogue record for this book is available from the British Library.

ISBN 978–0–7083–2137–9

Typeset by Columns Design Ltd, Reading, Berkshire
Printed and bound in Great Britain by Antony Rowe Ltd, Chippenham, Wilts

Contents

Acknowledgements

We are indebted to a range of individuals and organizations who have helped us in some way to complete this book. We break with academic tradition somewhat by thanking first of all our family and friends who have supported us, either directly or indirectly, throughout this project. Our parents, wives and family have been a constant source of support throughout our academic careers and have also provided a welcome antidote to the strains associated with producing a book such as this. *Diolch o galon a llawer o gariad i chi i gyd.*

Thanks also to colleagues and mentors within the Institute of Geography and Earth Sciences (IGES) in the University of Wales Aberystwyth, the School of European Studies in Cardiff University and further afield. The high levels of collegiality and academic endeavour within IGES, where the original project on which this book is based was conducted, provided us with a strong academic and social foundation from which to study the intricate geographies associated with nationalism. Thanks in particular to our colleagues, namely Tim Cresswell, Luke Desforges, Deborah Dixon, Bob Dodgshon, Bill Edwards, Kate Edwards, Mark Goodwin, Gareth Hoskins, Martin Jones, Gordon MacLeod, Robert Mayhew, Pete Merriman, Richard Phillips, Heidi Scott, Mark Whitehead and Mike Woods. Thanks also to Anthony Smith and Ian Gulley for producing the illustrations to a very high quality and to postgraduate and undergraduate students within IGES, who have provided inspiration and distraction in equal measure. In addition, other friends and colleagues from outside IGES have provided much support for this project. The book bears the stamp of Barry Jones, who acted as supervisor for Carwyn Fowler's PhD, but other individuals have also contributed in more subtle ways to the arguments that we propound within its pages. We think specifically of James Anderson, Pyrs Gruffudd, David Harvey, Mike Heffernan, James Mitchell, Anssi Paasi, Duncan Tanner and Colin Williams. Thanks to you all for your patience and guidance.

Many of the ideas discussed in the book have already seen the light of day in some form or other. We have presented conference papers and seminars in Aberystwyth, Bangor, Brighton, Cardiff, Glasgow, Leeds, Lincoln, Liverpool, London, New York, Pontypridd, Quebec City, Roskilde and San Francisco, which have discussed, inter alia, the geographies of the reproduction of nationalist discourse. Thanks very much for the questions and comments that various audiences have made in response to these papers. We would like to thank Murray Leith for organising conference panels that served as a forum for our work. By the same token, referees for a variety of different periodicals have helped us to hone our ideas concerning the geographies of nationalism over a number of years. Thanks to you for seeing something that was worth publishing in the majority of these papers.

More formally, we would also like to thank a number of organizations, which have provided financial support for our research on the geographies of nationalism. Aberystwyth University provided pump-priming money to support a research project in which Rhys Jones (along with Luke Desforges) began to examine the more local contexts within which nationalist discourses and practices were reproduced. We also extend our gratitude to the Social Science Committee of the Board of Celtic Studies, which funded the research project on which this book is based. The year-long project, for which Carwyn Fowler acted as a Research Assistant, produced an incredible amount of raw data with which we were able to interrogate the complex processes through which Welsh nationalism was reproduced on the streets of Aberystwyth. Rhys Jones would also like to thank the Arts and Humanities Research Council for its support of the project (Grant number: AH/E503586/1). The Research Fellowship, which it granted to Rhys Jones, provided much-needed space and time with which we were able to complete the book. Thanks also to Ralph Fevre, the Editor of the Board of Celtic Studies' 'Politics and Society in Wales' series, for his support and guidance, Andy Thompson, who, as Reader, provided illuminating and incisive comments on the earlier drafts of the various chapters, and Sarah Lewis, from the University of Wales Press, for making the publishing process as painless as possible.

Finally, we wish to thank warmly the various individuals who, in most cases, willingly gave of their time in order to answer our questions about their experiences in Aberystwyth. Their forbearance in doing so made this project possible and has also brought a more human and colourful perspective to the themes discussed in this book. *Diolch yn fawr i chi i gyd.*

It goes without saying that the mistakes, misrepresentations and omissions are ours.

Rhys Jones
Carwyn Fowler
2008

Series Editor's Foreword

A recent article by a Welsh novelist worried over the changing character of Cardiff. In a column in *Prospect*, John Williams expressed concern that the city was being changed by 'Welsh incomers, the Welsh-speaking government and media types from the north and west of the principality, while the monoglot speakers of Kairdiff English have started to feel like second-class citizens in their own city'.[1] A reader who knew little of Wales might have wondered what Williams was talking about. Was he alluding to a divide of language, or language and social class, or was he saying something about culture or even politics too? Readers with inside knowledge would certainly recognize the article was alluding to a cultural difference beyond language but how deep could that difference really go in an era of globalization? When the generally deplored, but assumed unstoppable, reality of world-wide cultural homogenization is received wisdom, what could be so different about the culture and politics that was native to Ceredigion and Gwynedd that Williams feels it to be literally *out of place* in the Welsh capital barely a hundred miles to the south?

Williams did not miss the irony of an anxiety over Welsh-speaking incomers and nor can we, because Chapter 7 of *Placing the Nation* is all about the politics of resistance to a perceived threat to the character of the Welsh-speaking communities of north and west Wales posed by English monoglot incomers. Over the years, groups like Adfer and Cymuned have made precisely the same point as the one John Williams: the culture of such incomers was literally *out of place* (in Y Felinheli or Pen Llŷn). I have learnt better than to provoke an argument about, as Jones and Fowler put it, 'the where of Wales' and this is not why I raise John Williams' idea that Pen Llŷn has somehow annexed Pontcanna. I do this to show that *Placing the Nation* has immediate relevance, and considerable significance, to a great many other places, and events, around the world.

The idea at the core of the book can be simply expressed: people have ideas but ideas also have people and, because of this, ideas also have places. If this sounds like another way of landing myself in the middle of an argument about which ideas belong where, I should make it clear that I am not making any claims about ideas belonging in, or being better fitted to, particular places. All I mean is that people come up with ideas when they are in a place. People then spread and elaborate these ideas together and they do that in places too. Ideas have to have a location but I would hesitate to say they have a birth-place. The backwaters of the Austro-Hungarian Empire would have a valid claim to be the cradles and nurseries of ideas about nation and community you will encounter in *Placing the Nation* but I would be reluctant to identify any of them as birth-places.

What Jones and Fowler have to tell us is no more an argument about which ideas start where than it is about which ideas belong where. The simple but significant fact they want us to grasp is that when the ideas of Welsh nationalism came to popular attention and were, over time, turned into the moving spirit of a social movement (providing the teleology of numerous parties and associations), the people who brought this about had locations, places you could fix using GPS or Galileo if they had been around at the time. And one of the most important fixes would have been on the seaside town of Aberystwyth in Ceredigion, approximate population 17,000 people of whom roughly 6,000 are students (a factor of some importance in *Placing the Nation*).

Aberystwyth in Ceredigion might sound a plausible, and possibly romantic, location for history-making if you hear of it in Arizona or North Carolina but there is just a chance that someone from the UK, or I suppose I mean England, might find Aberystwyth a bit of a parochial and mundane subject for a work of social science or history. Rhys Jones and Carwyn Fowler show them why they are wrong to feel this way and what they have to tell us here is as valid in Kiev and Rangoon as it is in Ceredigion. We can learn a lot from seeing how one (comparatively) little place was the location for the elaboration of a modern idea of nationhood.

Not that the mundane can be, or should be, exorcised from the story Jones and Fowler have to tell. At various points in it, the students of Pantycelyn Hall, the Welsh-medium hall of residence at the University of Aberystwyth, seemed to have been electrified by the excitement of feeling they were at the very heart of a new social movement. I have no doubt that for many of them this wild enthusiasm made them feel very much at the centre of things and far from mundane. But the everyday, and the very parochial, has a central role in *Placing the Nation*. Consider the girl getting a lift on the crossbar of a young man's bicycle on Marine Parade in Aberystwyth, after a party. This is as quotidian an event as you like, but Jones and Fowler show us it had a role to play in the development of a strand of civil disobedience in the Welsh nationalist movement.

The bicycle on the promenade reminds us that not all of those who were central participants in the movement were aware that they were doing anything of historical significance at the time. On the other hand, some of the figures interviewed by Jones and Fowler appear to look back on their younger selves with a mixture of wry amusement and frank amazement at the way their naive, haphazard and laughably small-scale efforts had such an impact in the longer term. The most obvious example of this being the Saturday afternoon in February 1963 when a small group of activists sat down in the middle of Trefechan Bridge, so blocking the southern route into Aberystwyth and, it transpired, provoking some local equivalents of the Kairdiff working class – in this case the Aberystwyth 'cardis' – into a punch-up.

The wry amusement of the movers and shakers looking back on what they did in their youth, wondering how on earth any of it ever worked, is as much a feature of this book as is the extraordinary excitement of a handful of key meetings. What it also makes us understand is the feelings of people who are engaged in a common campaign and whose enthusiasm is sustained by that shared experience as much as by tangible progress towards their goals. We understand so much about the movement because Jones and Fowler have done such a good job of their research. They give us the human stories behind all of this living history and of course, that means they tell us about all the quarrels and conflicts as well as the co-operation.

There is no doubt that *Placing the Nation* is an invaluable historical record as well as being cutting-edge social science on the geography of nation and nationalism. In my opinion, however, what makes the book most valuable is the way it helps readers with little knowledge of, and perhaps even less sympathy towards, Welsh nationalism to understand why it moves people. This, after all, is what a book like this sets out to do but the fact that *Placing the Nation* achieves this aim says a lot for the skill, empathy, good judgement and humanity of its authors.

Ralph Fevre
Cardiff/Kairdiff/Caerdydd
December 2007

NOTES

[1]   John Williams, 'These Islands – Cardiffs I have known', *Prospect*, August 2007.

Plates

Illustrations are reproduced by permission wherever possible. Every effort has been made to trace the copyright-holder in each case. Where this has not been possible, the publishers will be pleased to make the necessary arrangements at the first opportunity.

Tables

1

Introduction: place, scale and nationalism

Our aim in this book is to demonstrate the value of a geographically sensitive interpretation of the various processes that reproduce nationalism as a discourse. Studies of nationalism, to date, have to a large extent been preoccupied with understanding the historical, political and social aspects of nationalism. In terms of the history of nationalism, many classical theorists have sought to determine the modernity or otherwise of nations and nationalism. The debate between two intellectual giants in the field of the study of nationalism, Ernest Gellner (1983) and Anthony Smith (1986), in particular, has centred on ascertaining the time of the formation of nations and the ideology of nationalism. Others have examined the (ab)use of history (Hobsbawm 1983) and time (Anderson 1983; Bhabha 1990a) within the ideology of nationalism. Political scientists, on the other hand, have attempted to chart the ways in which nationalism is employed as an ideology that structures political action, most specifically with regard to the state. Work has been conducted, in this respect, on how nationalism can both reinforce (Tilly 1975; Mann 1995) or challenge (Hutchinson 1987) state power. More recently, a loose band of social constructivist theorists of nationalism have emphasized the numerous social contexts within which nationalism, as a discourse, is produced, reproduced and consumed. Social constructivists have shown how classical theorists' understandings of nations as monolithic and uniform social groups are misplaced, given the way in which all nationalisms and national discourses are complicated and fractured by a variety of other gendered (Enloe 1989; Yuval-Davis 1997) and ethnic (Chatterjee 1986; Yuval-Davis 1997) identities. Of course, we have oversimplified the characteristics of the intellectual projects that are bound up in the work of these various authors; the boundaries between studies of the historical, political and social aspects of nationalism are blurred. And yet, we would argue that our main point holds true; namely that the majority of studies of nationalism conducted within the social sciences have focused on the historical, political and social characteristics of nations, nationalisms and national discourses. As a reflection of this emphasis, we may note that the vast majority of studies of national-ism have been conducted within the disciplinary confines of history, political science and sociology.

Running parallel to – or maybe trying to catch up with – this large and impressive body of research has been the work conducted on nationalism by geographers. Research on nationalism within geography experienced a substantial fillip with the publication of a seminal paper by Williams and Smith (1983) in which the authors outlined a variety of different contexts within which geographical concepts, such as location, scale and territory, impinged on the processes through which national-ism was promoted and reproduced. As we show in Chapter 2, a variety of geographers have taken forward the baton from Williams and Smith and, at present, studies of nationalism comprise a relatively large and lively grouping within the discipline, particular within the context of political geography. But despite the substantial amount of work that has been conducted by geographers on nations and nationalism over the past thirty or so years, we would contend that there is considerable scope to augment this research. In the first place, geographers, we would argue, have tended to examine how nations are *represented* above all else or, in other words, how nationalist ideas are communicated or transmit-ted through a variety of media. Although there have notable exceptions to this trend, we suggest that there is a need for geographers to take more seriously the way in which a geographical perspective – emphasiz-ing themes such as space, place, scale, territory, mobility, nature, spatial-ized performance and so on – can provide additional insights into the complex ways in which nations are *reproduced*. The reproduction of nationalism refers to the ways in which various individuals, institutions and processes help to produce, transmit and consume national dis-courses that are part of the group-making project of the nation. In refocusing on this issue, geographers would be able to contribute to broader debates within studies of nationalism, in which there have been numerous studies of the ways in which nations and nationalism are reproduced. In the second place, we maintain that geographers need to take on board in a more systematic way the insights provided by social constructivist accounts of nationalism. Certain geographers have, admit-tedly, begun to address the complexities inherent in all nationalisms by showing how all national identities are cross-cut with other forms of social categorization (with regard to gender, see Nash 1996; for race, see Radcliffe 1999). We contend, nonetheless, that there is considerable scope to show how specific geographical concepts are implicated in – and indeed can further – the more nuanced and complex portrayal of nationalism that is contained within social constructivist theories.

Our aim in this book, therefore, is to further a geographically-sensitive take on a social constructivist understanding of nationalism. The benefits of promoting such an approach are threefold and we have already hinted at some of them in the above paragraph. The first benefit is a largely parochial and disciplinary one. We suggest that geographical understandings of nations and nationalism will be enriched by engaging in a more systematic way with the broader insights that have been provided by social constructivist accounts of nationalism. By taking heed of these insights, we believe that the 'voice' of geography and geographers will be heard within broader debates in the social sciences concerning the processes that seek to form and reproduce nations and nationalism. In this respect, we believe that geography's 'voice' is one that is potentially worthy of note within this debate. A potential second broader benefit, therefore, might well arise from advocating a more explicitly geographical take on social constructivist interpretations of nationalism. Geographers' focus on and understanding of particular geographical concepts, we would argue, places them in an ideal position from which to shape and steer social constructivist debates concerning nationalism. We maintain that the concepts of place and scale, which form the substance of the discussion in this book, are appropriate means of showing geographers' ability to influence social constructivist inter-pretations of nationalism. The value of focusing on these two key geographical concepts as a means of contributing to a social constructiv-ist project is clear. By interrogating the ways in which nationalism is produced, reworked and contested within particular places, we aim to illustrate the way in which nationalism is inherently fractured; not just socially but also spatially (Agnew 2004). By the same token, an explora-tion of the connections between places – as the locations within which nationalist sentiment is produced, reworked and contested – and the nations, national organizations and/or national territories within which they are emplaced has the potential to illustrate a further set of scalar tensions, which, once again, show the multiplicity of forms taken by any one nationalism. The third benefit arising from advancing a geographi-cal interpretation of the social construction of nationalism is that it may extend the object of enquiry of the social constructivist project. Social constructivists' interrogation of how different marginalized groups either engage with, or are excluded from, dominant nationalist dis-courses, while an eminently laudable and worthwhile academic and political project, may well tend to underestimate the ways in which other individuals and groups, which are more closely aligned to the dominant national project, may also contribute to the plurality of nationalism. We want to suggest that an ethnographic focus on the reproduction and reworking of nationalist discourse within certain places is one particularly powerful way of excavating the variegated 'archaeology' of dominant nationalist projects (Foucault 1970 [1966]).

We have bandied about a number of different terms and concepts in the opening paragraphs of this chapter and have been remiss in not explaining them in any great detail. What is most crucial at this stage is to explain carefully our understanding of nationalism as a concept. We follow the precepts of social constructivist accounts of the nation by considering nationalism as a discursive formation, which was first promoted on a large scale during the late eighteenth century and which has been reworked in a variety of different contexts since this time (Calhoun 1997: 9–12). Nationalism, as such, is a socially constructed discourse or, in other words, 'a way of speaking that shapes our consciousness' (ibid: 3). Adopting such a definition possesses many implications. First of all, thinking of nationalism as a discursive formation should make us wary of ascribing a degree of ontological reality or agency to nations as such. Nations do not exist to be reflected in and through an ideology of nationalism. Rather, we need to think about the way in which a discourse of nationalism seeks to promote the 'groupness' of a particular nation (Brubaker 2004). The degree to which a particular nation assumes a degree of reality within the broader socio-spatial consciousness is not determined by the vitality or cohesiveness of the nation in question but is, rather, contingent upon the effectiveness of the group-making project contained within a particular nationalist discourse. Second, conceiving of nationalism as a discursive formation alludes to its flexibility and heterogeneity as a concept; it can be employed as the basis for forms of cultural identity and political action in a wide variety of different contexts, as Calhoun (1997: 21–2) has argued:

> The common denominator among, say, Japanese economic protectionism, Serbian ethnic cleansing, Americans singing the 'Star-Spangled Banner' before baseball games, and the way the World Bank collects statistics is a discursive formation that shapes and links all of them, even though it may not offer a full causal explanation of any of them.

In this way, nationalism can be used as a principle with which different actors can seek to legitimate a broad range of different forms of political action. The value of such an approach becomes immediately apparent when one considers the particularities of how the nation-building project has been advanced in Wales over the past 150 so years, which is the main empirical focus for this book. As we show in Chapter 3, national discourse has been enlisted in a variety of ways by a wide range of organizations over this period; some organizations' claims have centred on issues of political sovereignty whereas others have promoted a Welsh nationalist discursive formation that has concentrated far more on the alleged cultural distinctiveness of Wales and Welshness (see Nairn 1977: 214). Similarly, conceiving of Welsh nationalism as a discourse also draws attention to the numerous actors that have been involved in promoting alternative and competing understandings of the characteristics of the Welsh nation. Taken together, therefore, an exploration of the social construction of a nationalist discourse is a valuable way of highlighting the pluralities of sentiments, identities and forms of political action that are subsumed under the banner of nationalism. Finally, in thinking about nationalism as a discourse, we are also encouraged to explicate the ways in which this discourse is embedded in a variety of more material practices and institutions of social, cultural and political life (Fairclough 2003). As Gregory (2000: 180) has noted, 'discourses are not free-floating constructions but are materially implicated in the conduct of social life'. Nationalist discourse, in this way, draws sustenance from pre-existing political and cultural institutions as well as contributing to the formation of, and the significance ascribed to, those selfsame institutions. It is because of this more material aspect which is inherent in all nationalist discourses that we prefer the term 'social production' to 'social construction', when considering the ways in which nationalist discourse is produced, transmitted and consumed. While social construction draws our attention – and rightly so – to the production and circulation of particular knowledges, it fails to take seriously the materiality of social and spatial life. The term social production, on the other hand, encourages us to consider both the ideas and knowledges that are produced and circulated concerning a particular thing, as well as the ways in which these ideas and knowledges are grounded within material relations. Lefebvre's (1991: 1) ideas, we believe, are a particularly useful way of conceiving of the productive connections and tensions between various kinds of discourse and the more material aspects of the human condition. According to Lefebvre, space is produced through a continual triple dialectic between *spatial practices*, which refer to the material forms of social spatiality; *representations of space*, redolent of spaces of ideological power, utopias and vision;

and *spaces of representation*, which refer to the more marginal or clandestine spaces of resistance promoted by the inhabitants or users of a particular space. We adapt Lefebvre's framework in this book as a way of thinking about how nationalist discourse produces, and is produced through, a threefold interaction between nationalist practices and institutions, dominant and more clandestine representations of nationalist 'groupness' (Brubaker 2004). In this way, for instance, national institutions – and the various practices contained within them – bring a degree of materiality to the existence of a nation. They are formed as a result of various kinds of nationalist discourse – both dominant and resistant – and also help to structure the kinds of nationalist discourse that can be furthered by various actors.

Our understanding of the geographical concepts of place and scale also needs to be clarified at this point. Both concepts have undergone considerable refinement in recent years, particularly within the disciplinary confines of geography and we discuss these various contributions at some length in Chapter 2. Suffice to say at this point that we understand place in two different ways in this book. First of all – and most straightforward – place refers to a relatively localized segment of the earth's surface that elucidates a sense of attachment amongst its inhabitants (Tuan 1977; Cresswell 2004). This does not mean that we conceive of these types of places as ones that are wholly spatially-circumscribed in character. Massey (1994) has shown that all places are constituted in large part as a result of various networks that connect them to a variety of other different places. The character of a particular place is shaped, therefore, through its relations to other, sometimes distant, places. The second meaning of place employed within this book is with regard to the way in which the national territory is conceived of as the 'place of the nation' within nationalist discourse (Taylor 1999). National territories, in this sense, are said to be places of meaning and attachment for members of the nation. Once again, the character of these national places is dependent on their networked connections with other places, within and outwith the borders of the nation. Referring to the connections between national territories and more localized places also draws our attention to the issue of scale. In this book, we understand geographic scale in relational terms. Scale, as many authors have argued recently, is relational in that each scale is constructed with regard to its relation to other geographic scales; one cannot understand the processes occurring at one geographic scale without also considering their connections with processes taking place at other scales (e.g. Swyngedouw 2003). Following on from such ideas, we seek to demonstrate how the reproduction of Welsh nationalist discourse – at the national scale – is intimately tied in with the politics of more localized places and scales. In addition, a common and significant theme that unites contemporary understandings of both place and scale is the emphasis that has been placed on the politicized character of both concepts. Politics are central to the processes that determine the character of particular places, as well as the particular kinds of scalar connections that are emphasized within specific socio-spatial discourses and practices. In this respect, we need to reflect on how certain kinds of nationalist discourse will be promoted within particular places and across different scales and how others become marginalized.

Up until this point, we have spoken largely of abstract places, scales and nationalisms but it is important for us to begin to ground the book in a more specific geography. Our empirical focus of enquiry, in this respect, requires some explanation and justification (see also Chapter 3). We chart the geographical contours exhibited within Welsh nationalist discourse in this book. The reasons for focusing on Welsh nationalism are numerous. First, it is a nationalism that has become increasingly vibrant, especially in the period between the 1960s and the present day. Second, it is a nationalism that has exhibited a significant amount of plurality and heterogeneity. Work by Williams (1999) with regard to race and Davies (1999) in the context of gender has shown how Welsh forms of national identity have been complicated in social contexts while others have sought to demonstrate the way in which it has also been qualified in more spatial terms. Dicks and van Loon (1999), for instance, have examined the different kinds of identity exhibited in industrial south Wales while Evans (forthcoming) has explored the various articulations of Welshness that can be found in north-east Wales. Even the more dominant forms of Welsh nationalist discourse display a large degree of heterogeneity. A large number of organizations have been associated with the main nation-building project within Wales but, as we show in Chapter 3, they have promoted slightly different nationalist discourses. This makes a study of the variegated contours of Welsh nationalism especially appealing for researchers and, hopefully, for the reader. Third, it is a nationalism in which the significance of particular places and scalar connections has been especially apparent. Different kinds of Welsh nationalist discourse have been promoted in different places within Wales and these have been connected in different ways to the broader political geographies of Welsh nationalism (Day 2002). Our immediate focus of enquiry is on the significant role that has been played by the town of Aberystwyth, located on the coast of west Wales, for the reproduction of Welsh nationalist discourse. Despite being a small town of some 15,000 inhabitants, it has been an extremely significant location within the political, cultural and social life of Wales (see Lewis 1980). Its importance derives largely from the location of two important institutions within the town, namely the University of Wales, Aberystwyth and the National Library of Wales. The town is dominated by the University since over 8,000 students study in Aberystwyth. In addition, the town has served as an important location for the development of various nationalist organizations, such as Plaid Cymru, Cymdeithas yr Iaith Gymraeg (the Welsh Language Society) and Cymuned (literally, Community). It has also been the location of the headquarters of a large number of other organizations, whose existence testifies to the distinctiveness of Wales as a political and cultural territory. Taken together, therefore, Aberystwyth can lay claim to being a key site for nationalist organizations of different hues in Wales since the 1960s. Some might criticize us, in this respect, for using a social constructivist (or productivist) perspective in order to examine the politics of place and scale that have contributed to the reproduction of a dominant Welsh nationalist discourse in Aberystwyth. As we argued earlier, we believe that such a venture is warranted and worthwhile since, in doing so, we are able to contribute to a broader post-modern agenda by showing how even a dominant nationalist discourse is actually fissured and variegated in character.

Following this introduction, we proceed in Chapter 2 to focus on some of the key concepts that help to underpin this book. We begin by justifying the value of a geographical approach for revitalizing social constructivist interpretations of nationalism. We maintain that the key geographical concepts of place and scale are important starting points within this intellectual project. Focusing on place enables us to show how politicized networks of people within particular localities help to produce, transmit and consume nationalist discourse. These networks are never uniform or simple in character; nor are the nationalist discourses that are reproduced by and within them. It is the nationalist discourses reproduced within networks such as these, nonetheless, that are refracted into a broader politics of nationalism existing at the national scale, being embedded in a variety of different nationalist institutions and practices. A relational politics of scale, as such, can help to explain the connections between the politics of nationalism within localized places and the broader politics of the nation. Place and scale, therefore, are key components within the production, circulation and consumption of nationalist discourses. The chapter finishes with a reaffirmation of the value of such a geographical approach as a way of energizing social constructivist accounts of nationalism that have become rather jaded (Brubaker 2004).

The remaining chapters explore more empirical issues. In Chapter 3, we commence by elaborating on some of the general trends that have affected the trajectories taken by Welsh nationalism over the long term. Since this is an enormous topic, we focus in particular on the ways in which geographical themes have been implicated within the broader shifts that have taken place within the reproduction of Welsh nationalist discourse. Key organizations have been crucial within this process at different points in time: for instance, the Liberal Party, Plaid Cymru, the Welsh Language Society and, more recently, Cymuned. We chart briefly, and contrast, the different nationalist discourses that have been promoted by these organizations. Doing so enables us to begin to show how variegated the dominant nationalist project has been in Wales. We conclude the chapter by introducing the town of Aberystwyth, drawing specific attention to the key locations within it, which have acted as anchor points or nodes for the networks of nationalists that have been based within the town. In this way, Chapter 3 acts as an empirical foundation for the more specific themes discussed in the following four chapters.

In Chapter 4, we move on to the first of our substantive case studies, which examines the politics of Welsh linguistic nationalism, particularly during the 1960s. The 1960s witnessed considerable soulsearching among Welsh nationalists concerning the status of the Welsh language, given the fact that it had undergone a sustained period of decline throughout the whole of the twentieth century. Numerous events and interventions at the beginning of the decade led to the formation of Cymdeithas yr Iaith Gymraeg, the Welsh Language Society, which has campaigned unceasingly since this time for an increased protection of and status for the Welsh language (see Phillips 1998 for an excellent review). What is significant in the context of our research is the way in which a complex politics of place and scale was at work in the formation of the Society, in its first campaigns during the 1960s, and in the Welsh Language Act of 1967, which came about – at least in part – as a result of its efforts. In this regard, the (re-)emergence of a Welsh linguistic nationalism during the 1960s was wholly dependent upon politicized practices and networks of people within the townscape of Aberystwyth, as well as a more complex scalar dialogue with processes taking place at a broader Welsh and British scale.

The nationalist significance of education is discussed in Chapter 5. The role played by education, at all levels, in reproducing Welsh speakers, as well as a Welsh cultural identity, has been a source of considerable debate over the past 150 or so years. Significantly, the provision of Welsh-medium education in different parts of Wales has come about through a complex interplay between national directives that have been, on the whole, supportive of the Welsh language and a more localized educational politics that has demonstrated extreme levels of either support for or antipathy against Welsh-medium education. Our empirical work in this chapter develops these themes by examining the contentious politics that surrounded the role played by the Welsh language within the University College of Wales, Aberystwyth and latterly the University of Wales, Aberystwyth. We begin by discussing the long-standing campaign for the establishment of a Welsh-medium hall in the University College during the late 1960s and early 1970s. This was a campaign that was played out largely within the confines of the College and town but also drew considerable succour from, as well as contributed to, the broader linguistic and educational politics that existed at the Welsh national scale at this time. The second half of the chapter moves on to discuss how the Welsh-medium hall that was established during the mid-1970s, Pantycelyn, has acted as a hotbed of nationalist discourse and practice until this day. Most notable, in this respect, have been the recent campaigns by students within the hall and the broader University to increase the institutional support provided for the Welsh language within the University itself, as well as in the higher education sector throughout the whole of Wales. Taken together, such themes illustrate how nationalist discourses concerning Welsh-medium education have been forged through intricate connections between highly localized practices within Aberystwyth and broader nationalist debates.

In Chapter 6, we change tack by focusing on the significance of electoral politics for Welsh nationalism. Ever since the 1920s, when Plaid Cymru began to contest elections, Welsh nationalists have exhibited something of a love-hate relationship with electoral politics. On the one hand, they have shirked away from engaging fully with electoral politics since many have argued that it is an unwelcome distraction from the more pressing needs of securing the future of the Welsh language and culture. Others have maintained that electoral success is necessary if a sound future is to be secured for the Welsh language and culture. Electoral politics, of necessity, illustrate strong connections and tensions between specific localities (as constituencies) and the broader politics of the state. Nowhere do we witness these connections and tensions more clearly than in the context of the electoral politics that took place in the constituency of Aberystwyth and Ceredigion North during the late 1980s and early 1990s. A particular set of localized and scalar personal, temporal and spatial contingencies were necessary for the formation of an electoral alliance at this time between Plaid Cymru and the Green Party, one which succeeded in winning the seat in the General Election of 1992. We argue, in addition, that the creation and subsequent success of the alliance within the constituency possessed important ramifications for the emergence of a new kind of ecologically informed nationalist politics in Wales, one that is still apparent today.

Our final substantive chapter examines the contentious nationalist politics relating to the need to protect Welsh-speaking communities from Anglicizing influences. The need to protect particular communities within a so-called Welsh-speaking heartland has been a major concern for a variety of different nationalist organizations in Wales for much of the twentieth century. These communities are deemed to be crucial to the reproduction of the Welsh language and culture since it is only in these specific locations that the Welsh language is spoken on a day-to-day basis as a community language. A complex politics of the Welsh 'national place' or territory has revolved around this issue. Some organizations have called for Welsh nationalist politics to focus solely on the needs of Welsh speakers within the heartland whereas others have attempted to navigate a more difficult compromise between acceding to the linguistic needs of Welsh speakers throughout the whole of Wales as well as seeking to protect the linguistic rights of Welsh speakers within the heartland. Significantly in the context of this book, this debate concerning the imagined territory that is contained within the Welsh nation-building project has been played out in the pubs and cafes of Aberystwyth. The formation of the organization Cymuned within the town in 2001, in particular, signalled a period of contentious debates between members of the new organization and members of the more established Welsh nationalist organizations, especially Plaid Cymru and Cymdeithas yr Iaith. Once again, in this case, a localized politics of place within the town of Aberystwyth shaped, and was shaped by, the nationalist debates taking place at a broader Welsh scale.

We seek to show in this book, therefore, how place and scale, and more broadly geography, matter for the reproduction of nationalism. In other words, our aim is to show the way in which a geographical perspective can advance and, indeed, re-energize, a constructivist inter-pretation of nationalism. More broadly, we believe our research reaffirms the value of geographical insights as a means of furthering the postmodern intellectual project. These broader implications of our work are taken up at greater length in the conclusion.

2

Nations, place and scale: a theoretical context

NATIONALISM: WHEN, WHO AND WHERE?

Studies of nationalism have undergone something of a transformation in recent years. Classical theories of nationalism have been augmented – though by no means replaced – by a series of social constructivist explanations. Geographers' voices, we would argue, have not been heard within this reconfiguration of ways of understanding nationalism and nationalist discourse. Our aims in this chapter are to begin to show how geographers might engage with social constructivist interpretations of nationalism. Encouraging a more meaningful dialogue between human geography and social constructivist accounts of nationalism, we maintain, will be of considerable benefit to both camps. At one level, social constructivist debates concerning nationalism and nationalist discourse may serve to invigorate geographical research on nationalism. Embracing the tenets of social constructivist interpretations of nationalism, specifically, should promote an increased focus on the geographies of the production and reproduction of nationalist discourse, and not merely the geographies of its representation. In another context, we seek to demonstrate the way in which an explicitly geographical approach can bring new insights to broader debates about nationalism throughout the whole of the social sciences. A geographical perspective, in this respect, can shed new light on some social constructivist debates about nationalism. In addition to these purely conceptual concerns, it should come as little surprise to the reader that the discussion contained in this chapter also acts as the theoretical foundation for the remaining chapters of this book.

As was touched upon in Chapter 1, classical studies of nationalism have, to a large extent, been dominated by a concern for explicating the important connections between nations, nationalism and the notion of time. Such a fascination with the timing or the history of the nation has been apparent over a number of years (*Nations and Nationalism* 2004). The debate has been manifest most clearly in discussions concerning the alleged modernity, or otherwise, of nationalism and has been based on the important contributions of a number of key scholars, such as Gellner (1983) and Smith (1986). Important distinctions can be drawn, in this respect, between those who see the nation, as well as the broader ideology of nationalism, as a product of the material and discursive transformations that characterized the modern period (Anderson 1983; Breuilly 1993; Gellner 1983; Hobsbawm and Ranger 1983), and perenni-alists or ethnosymbolists, who have sought to highlight the continuity between modern nations and earlier ethnic communities of people or so-called 'ethnie' (Smith 1986; see also Armstrong 1982; Connor 1990; Smith 2003). Such work shows how classical theories have become fascinated with the 'when of the nation': its time of formation; its use of time; its use of history (Connor 1990; Hobsbawm and Ranger 1983).[1] While numerous worthwhile contributions have been made from this perspective, they have increasingly been questioned in recent years by various authors whose accounts of nationalism are based on constructiv-ist ideals (Kornprobst 2005: 405). Classical theories of the nation have been criticized on many interrelated levels. One area of concern has revolved around the tendency for classical theorists of nationalism to conceive of nations as ontological social categories. Nations, within classical theories, have been viewed almost as agents in their own right, possessing the ability to affect social and spatial change (Brubaker 2004: 2–3, 8). Social constructivists such as Calhoun (1997: 3), however, have sought to counter such a viewpoint by arguing that nations and nation-alism should be viewed as 'a "discursive formation", a way of speaking that shapes our consciousness'. As Brubaker (2004: 9, original emphasis), has pithily put it, a nation 'is a key part of what we want to explain, not what we want to explain things *with*'. He develops his argument as follows:

> Ethnicity, race, and nation should be conceptualized not as substances or things or entities or organisms or collective individuals – as the imagery of discrete, concrete, tangible, bounded, and enduring 'groups' encourages us to do – but rather in relational, processual, dynamic, eventful, and disaggregated terms. This means thinking of ethnicity, race, and nation not in terms of substantial groups or entities but in terms of practical categories, situated actions, cultural idioms, cognitive schemas, discursive frames, organizational routines, institutional forms, political projects and contingent events (Brubaker 2004: 11).

The 'groupness' of nations is something, therefore, that needs to be forged through continual and iterative practice and explained by aca-demics rather than being taken as an ontological 'given'. Group-making is, therefore, a project that is based on a series of events – both extraordinary (Ignatieff 1993) and banal (Billig 1995). According to Calhoun (1997: 4–5), critical features of nationalist discourse or rhetoric, which help to constitute a nation as a 'group', include notions relating to boundaries, indivisibility, sovereignty, an 'ascending' notion of legiti- macy, popular participation, direct membership, culture, temporal depth, common descent and territoriality. While the exact combination of these discursive underpinnings of nationalist discourses may vary from one nation to the next, they are all key features of a broader discourse of nationalism. Nations, in this respect, are communities of people that are imagined through a series of nationalist discourses (Anderson 1983), rather than being actual communities of people, which are purposive in character. A second related concern is associated with the tendency for classical theories of nationalism to portray nations as unproblematic and homogeneous social categories. The focus within classical theories of the nation is to examine the production and circula- tion of dominant forms of nationalist discourse. In extreme examples of such a perspective, it is the viewpoints of a nationalist elite that solely matter (e.g. Hobsbawm 1983; Hroch 1985). The political and cultural desires and demands of the broader population feature little within such classical accounts. The exception, in this regard, is the work of ethno- symbolists or perennialists, who have attempted to draw attention to the cultures residing within the mass of the nation (e.g. Smith 1986). The danger within this work, nonetheless, is that it once again tends to reify a homogeneous nation – defined from the bottom up – which is, in fact, highly variegated in character. Following on from such comments, social constructivists have also criticized the tendency for classical theories of the nation conveniently to 'forget' the differing engagements of various marginalized and under-represented groups with the discourse of nationalism. Özkırımlı (2000: 192), for instance, makes clear that:

> None of these [classical] theories took account of the experiences of the 'subordinated', for example the former European colonies and their postcolonial successors, or women, ethnic minorities and the oppressed classes.

Influenced by a post-structural turn in the social sciences, contribu- tions by various authors have sought to rectify this deficiency by demonstrating the multiple ways in which a dominant nationalist dis- course can be complicated and problematized: Enloe (1989) and Yuval- Davis (1997), for instance, with regard to issues of gender; Bhabha (1990a) and Chatterjee (1986; 1993) with reference to the 'Westocentric' (Yuval-Davis 1997: 3) aspects of classical theories of nationalism; and

Billig (1995), whose focus has been on demonstrating the everyday and banal contexts within which nationalism is reproduced.

The various contributions made within this area of research are, of course, to be welcomed. They have acted as valuable correctives to classical accounts of the nation, which have been predicated upon male, Western and white ideals. But despite the value of these more contemporary understandings of the variegated processes whereby nationalist discourse is produced, circulated and consumed, we want to suggest that they can be criticized on two fronts. First of all, we contend that much of the social constructivist work conducted on nationalism has tended to concentrate on the alternative nationalist discourses promoted by marginalized groups that are far removed from the central and dominant nationalist discourse. There is an obvious emancipatory quality to such work that should not be underplayed or criticized. It is an important aspect of the post-modern project to 'give voice' to previously under-represented groups and individuals. At the same time, we believe that there is considerable scope to augment the parameters of such a project. It is almost too easy, in this respect, to show how a dominant nationalist discourse can be qualified by other external voices and viewpoints. Following Foucault (1969; 1977), it is more challenging – but also more powerful, we would argue – to illustrate how dominant nationalist discourses are characterized by internal tensions and inconsistencies, which are redolent of social patternings of power that are as important as those that exist between dominant and other marginalized groups. In the second place, social constructivist accounts of the nation have tended to focus on the *social* contexts within which a dominant nationalist discourse is problematized. In this respect, it is the existence of other social fractions, possessing alternative accounts and understandings of a dominant discourse of nationalism – or, alternatively, possessing alternative and equally valid discourses of nationalism – that has acted as the object of enquiry. Apart from the notable postcolonial accounts of the production of nationalist discourse, less attention has been directed within the social constructivist literature, we would argue, towards the *spatial* contexts, which help to complicate our understanding of dominant nationalist discourses. Nor has there been much of an effort within the social constructivist literature to comprehend how different spaces may lead to the production of alternative nationalist discourses. Ironically, it is the more classical theories of nationalism – and especially those concerned with explaining sub-state, ethnic or minority nationalisms – that has tended to emphasize the importance of such themes (e.g. Hechter 1977; Nairn 1977; Smith 1982). We do not advocate a return to more classical accounts of nations and nationalism in this book. Rather, we promote the need for an integrated understanding of how social *and* spatial processes and forms – the *who* as well as the *where* of nationalist discourse – may complicate classical accounts of the production of nationalism as a discourse. Doing so would also enable geographers and others to contribute to wider debates in the social sciences concerning the need to examine the spatial configurations of post-modern social formations (see Soja 1989; 1996). Our argument in the pages that follow in this chapter is that a geographically sensitive reading of the embeddedness of nationalist actors and ideas within particular places can provide a particularly useful method of charting the heterogeneity of a dominant nationalist discourse.

But while there may be a need for a more spatially sensitive reading of the social construction of nationalist discourse, it is unclear whether geographers, at present, possess the necessary skills to address this need. Admittedly, geographers – after a slow start – have increasingly sought to map out the spatial contours of nationalism. The clarion call for a more sustained interrogation of the manifold geographies of nationalism came, we would argue, in the form of an important paper published by Williams and Smith (1983). The paper, which represented an intellectual marriage between a geographer and a sociologist, outlined a number of different ways in which geographical themes could be woven into studies of nations and nationalism. Williams and Smith's (1983) paper possesses a further significance, since it succeeded in spurring on geographers in their studies of nationalism. Three geographical themes have been examined in greater detail as part of this work. Territories, the spatial foundations of nationalist discourse, have been the subject of considerable research, especially with regard to the idea of the national 'homeland' (e.g. Anderson 1986; 1988; Herb 1999; Hooson 1994; Murphy 2002; Paasi 1996; Penrose 2002; Jones and Fowler 2007a; 2007b). Territories or national homelands are viewed, in this respect, as the mechanism through which a nation is said to be: connected with the bureaucratic organization of the state (Taylor and Flint 2000: 233); contrasted with other neighbouring nations (Conversi 1995); connected to its history. The significance of territory as a way of connecting a nation's geography with its history within nationalist discourse is made clear in Anderson's (1988: 24) research when he argues that:

> the nation's unique history is embodied in the nation's unique piece of territory – its 'homeland', the primeval land of its ancestors, older than any state, the same land which saw its greatest moments, perhaps its mythical origins. The time has passed but the space is still there.

Some of the more important empirical research on the importance of a national territory has centred on Israel/Palestine. Territory has been used here as a mechanism for demonstrating an association between the Israeli and Palestinian nations and their respective states and, through the use of ever-more prevalent and impassable borders, as a way of defining one nation in opposition to the other. Finally, nationalist discourse in Israel/Palestine has portrayed a disputed territory as a national homeland, which provides ideological succour for their respective nationalist causes (Azaryahu and Kellerman 1999; Hooson 1994).

Another focus of geographical research has been on understanding how landscapes take on a particular status as means of representing national essences (e.g. Agnew 2002; Cosgrove and Daniels 1988; Daniels 1993; Gruffudd 1994; 1995; Johnson 1997). Shields (1991: 182–99), for instance, has focused on the importance of the Canadian North for the constitution of Canadian nationalism. For Shields (ibid: 198), 'the "True North" is a common reference "point" marking an invisible national community of the initiated'. Shields, for instance, describes the work of Canadian historian W. H. Morton, who maintained that an understanding of the Canadian North was imperative if people were fully to understand the nature of the Canadian identity (in ibid: 182). The rugged landscape of the north was totally distinct from the urbanized areas of southern Canada and was seen to represent the essence of Canadian nationalism. In addition to being a symbol of the purity of Canada within Canadian nationalist discourse, Shields also suggests that the landscape of the north of Canada has been used to distinguish the Canadian topography and nation from that of the US. A large proportion of the nineteenth-century literature that portrayed the Canadian North as a significant factor in the formation of the Canadian nation, for instance, was consumed by audiences in the US. The landscape of the Canadian North, in other words, came to be used as a symbol of the deep-rooted and significant differences that were said to exist between the Canadian and US nations. Indeed, the massive arctic hinterland that existed in the north of Canada, for many Canadian nationalists, enabled the Canada to identify with other northern states, such as Norway, rather than with the US (ibid: 198). In this study, along with other work that has been conducted in this area of research, landscapes are used within nationalist discourse as symbolic representations of the 'true' essence of particular nations. This is an important point to which we return below.

Finally, much recent work in geography has examined the importance of particular sites, such as statues, memorials and museums within nationalist discourse. Although the empirical focus of these studies has been wide-ranging, they have all sought to demonstrate how specific locations may take on the status of symbolic centrepieces of nationalist commemoration (e.g. Crang 1999; Heffernan 1995; Johnson 1995; Lorimer 1999; Whelan 2003). Sidorov (2000), for example, has examined the significance of the Cathedral of Christ the Saviour in Russia as a representation of key nationalist ideals within Russia. Originally designed as a memorial to the great Russian victory against Napoleon's French forces in 1812, it was viewed as a way of memorializing the 'unprecedented zeal, loyalty to and love of the faith and Fatherland' (quoted in Sidorov 2000: 557). The most interesting aspect of Sidorov's paper, nonetheless, is the way in which he is able to show how the materiality of the Cathedral reflected key changes in the broader political and nationalist makeup of Russia/Soviet Union. In this way, the Cathedral was seen to represent the fundamental political and nationalist changes that had taken place around it over the long term: from an imperialist Russia to a communist Soviet Union to a capitalist and highly nationalistic Russia. A specific location or site, in this respect, was seen to reflect the broader cultural and political shifts that had affected a particular nationalist discourse over time.

While the volume of work generated by geographers in a relatively short period of time has been impressive, we want to suggest that its thematic focus has been relatively narrow. In one context, the focus on territory, landscape and sites, while welcome, has meant that other key geographical concepts – such as scale, place and mobility, for instance – have not been examined to the same extent. In another context, we maintain that there has been a tendency within this work to explore, above all else, how nations are represented within nationalist discourse. To put it another way, we contend that the majority of geographical work conducted to date on nationalism has concentrated on how nationalist ideas are essentialized before being communicated or transmitted through a variety of media. The impressive work that has been conducted by geographers on the importance of particular landscapes within nationalist discourse can be used to illustrate this point. Daniels' (1993) study of the importance of particular types of landscape imagery for American and English nationalism, Gruffudd's (1994) exploration of the significance of rural landscapes as symbolic images of Welshness and Johnson's (1997) research on the importance of the rural landscapes of the west of Ireland for Irish nationalism, illustrate how geographers have shown an overarching interest in the spatial representation inherent in nationalist ideologies. The work conducted by geographers on the significance of particular locations or sites for nationalism illustrates a similar pre-occupation with issues to do with representation. In this work, particular sites – be they folk museums (Crang 1999; Lorimer 1999), war memorials (Heffernan 1995) or statues (Johnson 1995; Whelan 2003) – are viewed as material or concrete representations of national essences. The danger with such work is that it tends to fall into a classical mould in which nations are seen to be unproblematic and homogeneous in character as well as being social categories that are defined solely by a nationalist elite. One can almost get the impression that the designation of one form of nationalist representation – whether in landscape painting or statuary – by one set of elite individuals can lead to a singular vision of a national essence. There are obvious exceptions to this tendency, such as Johnson's (1995; see also 2003) discussion of the public response of Irish citizens to monuments in Dublin. In her work, Johnson was able to show how the inhabitants of Dublin were able to challenge the elitist meanings ascribed to the statue of Anna Livia Plurabella on O'Connell Street as they renamed it the 'floozie in the jacuzzi'. Work by the non-geographers, Kaufmann and Zimmer (1998), too, has illustrated the ways in which the embodied presence of people within the 'authentic' landscapes of the nation can lead to different interpretations of those landscapes and their importance for nationalist discourses.

As part of a social constructivist project, we believe that geographers would do well to broaden their object of enquiry in order to avoid an implicit essentializing of the nation. Geographers must follow the lead of other social scientists by considering the complex and sometimes conflicting ways in which nationalist discourses are produced and reproduced. In referring to the reproduction of nationalist discourse, we seek to draw attention to the various individuals, institutions and processes that help to produce national discourses that are part of the group-making project of the nation (Brubaker 2004: 13–14). By emphasizing the reproduction of nationalism, therefore, we conceive of nations as political and cultural processes in motion, rather than being static political forms (Zimmer 2003: 178). The use of the term reproduction also draws attention to the need to examine how nationalist discourses become a meaningful part of an individual's identity or, in other words, how nationalism is transformed into a national identity and becomes a national world-view (Dilthey 1924), episteme (Foucault 1970) or habitus (Bourdieu 1977). Taken together, the reproduction of nationalist discourse enables us to show how a particular politics is played out within nationalist discourse; with regard to its production, its circulation and its consumption.

One way in which we can highlight such themes is by examining the 'situated actions' (Brubaker 2004: 9) that help to produce the groupness of nations and other social categories. The particularities of place – and the practices of different kinds of nationalist activist or ordinary citizen within them – are of the utmost importance in delineating the contours of the group-making project associated with all kinds of nationalist discourse. Nationalist discourse, in this sense, is embedded within particular places and is shaped, in large measure, by the politics of place that exist within these places. The challenge, in this respect, must be to sharpen the geographical work that has been conducted to date on the role of place within the reproduction of nationalist discourse (e.g. Agnew 2002; Appleton 2002; Confino 1997; Confino and Skaria 2002a; Edensor 1997; 2002; Jones and Desforges 2003; MacLaughlin 2001). At the same time, this work must also be avowedly concerned with the notion of geographical scale in order to show how a politics of place – linked to the production of nationalist discourse – becomes reworked into a set of ideologies that are circulated throughout, and consumed by, the broader membership of the nation, as well as being embedded in and articulated through nationalist organizations of various types. The following two sections examine the significance of the two important geographical concepts of place and scale for the reproduction of nationalist discourse and, in so doing, begin to show how an explicitly geographical approach can enliven a social constructivist account of nationalism that has become, according to one significance commentator, 'complacent and clichéd' (Brubaker 2004: 3).

PLACING THE NATION IN THEORETICAL CONTEXT

The notion of place is one that possesses significant meaning in both lay and academic contexts. In lay contexts, it conjures up many different and sometimes contradictory ideas. Place evinces notions of possession, of difference and of meaning (Cresswell 2004: 1–12). The study of place within academic circles has occurred in the most sustained manner within the discipline of geography and it is significant that here, too, its meaning has been plural and contested (ibid: 15–51). Place has been alternatively defined by, and has acted as a key area of academic concern for: regional geographers, who have used the term as a shorthand way of describing the ideographic or the particular (e.g. Hartshorne 1939); humanistic geographers, who have sought to emphasize the experiential connections between places and different individuals (e.g. Relph 1976;

Tuan 1977); radical geographers, who have stressed the politics and conflicts that are constitutive of a continual process whereby places are produced (Anderson 1991; Cresswell 1996); structurationist geographers, who have emphasized the processual aspects of place as the producers and products of human action (Pred 1984; Thrift 1983); and a variety of other human geographers, who have advocated the need to think of places that are the product of networked associations that extend over a variety of different scales (Massey 1994).

The detailed differences between these various theoretical and epistemological perspectives need not detain us at present. Rather, we want focus on common themes that are manifest within them. Moreover, these are important themes that have implications for the topic of this book. First, there is an acceptance within contemporary human geography that places should not be viewed as localities that are purely small-scale and spatially circumscribed in nature. Tuan (1977), for instance, has argued that it is possible to think of places as spatial categories that range from a chair or bed to the scale of the globe. As alluded to above, Massey (1994), too, has maintained that places should be viewed as the meeting points for numerous socio-spatial networks that extend outwards to encompass other places in other parts of the world. The second theme that emerges from recent writings on place within human geography is that places, despite their superficial uniformity and homogeneity, are always highly politicized and contested in character. They are the locations in which certain powerful individuals, groups or institutions are able to promote their own material and ideological visions, whilst, at the same time, being resisted by other, less powerful groups, which possess potentially divergent visions of the past, present and future of that place (Cresswell 2004: 26–9; more broadly, see Sharp et al. 2000). Such a politics of place may derive from a combination of factors, including: the spatial division of labour; communications technology and access to it; the characteristics of local and national states; class, gender and ethnic divisions and the way in which they are linked to place-based identities; and the microgeography of everyday life and the way in which it structures social interaction (Agnew 1996: 132–3; see also Lefebvre 1991).

These two issues of are of great significance for the two different types of places examined in this book. One is a more conventional – almost common sense – interpretation of place, where place is viewed primarily as a relatively localized segment of the earth's area, which is characterized by certain feelings of attachment (Cresswell 2004).[2] In addition to this localized conception of place, we discuss another meaning of place within studies of nationalism, namely the way in which nations and national territories as a whole can be considered within nationalist discourse as places that are infused with national meaning (Taylor 1999: 102). Both a localized and national place are themselves the products of networks extending over a variety of different scales. The politics of place, too, is equally relevant within both types of place, being apparent in the struggle for power within a variety of localized places and national places. The networked connections between – along with the various politics and struggles that exist within – these two different types of place are discussed at greater length below.

Let us turn, first of all, to discuss the significance of what we may term localized places for nationalist discourse. In this respect, it is clear that there is a growing interest in studying the significance of localized places, localities and the local scale in the reproduction of nationalism. Agnew (2004: 228; for empirical studies, see Agnew 1987; 2002), for instance, has sought to clarify the character of this new emphasis. He argues that the focus of work in this area is on 'relating national identities to the geographical scales and contexts in which they are embedded'. Moreover, this alternative way of thinking about the importance of localized places for nationalist discourse conceives of the local as something that plays a constitutive role within nationalism. Nationalism, therefore, is not characterized by a 'nationalist "wave" that washes over a territory from either a center or the margins wiping out all other identities in its path' (Agnew 2004: 228). In this way, according to Agnew (ibid), 'the national is always forged in and through "the local"'. Furthermore, according to Agnew (2002: 3), it is only through understanding local politics that we are also able to make sense of nationalism. He argues that 'the identities, values and preferences that inspire particular kinds of political action therefore are embedded in the places or geographical contexts where people live their lives'.

Broadly speaking, therefore, Agnew's work affirms the fact that localized places should play an important role in our conception of how nationalism is reproduced. His work, furthermore, signals how a firm grasp of the significance of localized places is imperative if we are fully to comprehend the group-making project that is associated with nationalism. We maintain, however, that it is possible to distinguish a number of different ways in which such localized places are implicated in the reproduction of nationalist discourse (Agnew 2004: 228). First, and at a general level, a focus on the importance of places enables us to demonstrate that nations, despite their pretensions to uniformity (e.g. Smith 1991: 14), exhibit a profoundly heterogeneous character (see Brubaker 2004; Calhoun 1997). In this way, we can suggest that there are many ways of being a member of a nation (Bowie 1993: 190) and it is the particularities of place, amongst other factors, that inform the development of these heterogeneous national identities. Places are key sites in which individuals make sense of their relationship with nationalist discourse, for as Cohen (1982: 2) has cogently argued, 'the ethnography of locality is an account of how people experience and express their difference from others, and of how their sense of difference becomes incorporated into and informs the nature of their social organization and process'. As such, we would argue that a focus on localized places can enable us to further the social constructivist agenda by showing how national identities are contingent in nature as they are contested and reworked by different individuals and groups *in particular places* (Baker 1998; MacLaughlin 2001). Different people, living in different places, will make sense of the group-making project associated with nationalism in a variety of ways (see Agnew 1987; 1996). National identities are informed by other processes occurring within particular places. Thought of in another way, it is in particular places, where people live and work, that nationalist discourse is consumed or, in other words, becomes part of the mundane and day-to-day lifeworlds of the members of the nation (Billig 1995; Jones and Desforges 2003). It is arguable that it is only by examining places, therefore, that can we actually truly understand how national identities are accommodated within the world views of individuals.

Secondly, we need to think about how certain localized places become used as metonyms employed within nationalist discourse (Appleton 2002). This second context is closely related to the efforts made to illustrate the importance of landscape and particular places as ways of representing a nation within nationalist discourse. A good account of this process appears in Confino and Skaria's (2002a) work of the 'local life of nationhood' in both Germany and India. In Germany, for instance, they argue that it is possible to show how the idea of *Heimat* – or, alternatively, a notion of homeland that was predicated on a particularly local or regional *genre de vie* or way of living – acted as a key ideological focus for German nationalism, especially in the period after the Second World War (see also Applegate 1990; Confino 1997). *Heimat*, in this sense, became a symbol of a German people that had been wronged by national socialism and, significantly, the symbolism associated with *Heimat* was rooted in abstract localities. Abstract localities throughout Germany – popularized through film and literature – formed the basis of popular imaginations of the character of the German nation and, thus, took on the status of metonyms within German nationalist discourse in the post-war period. Confino and Skaria's discussion of the important role played by abstract localities in defining the essence of the Indian nation emphasizes cognate themes. Here, it is argued that Indian nationalism was constituted through a process of scalar refraction from the local to the national; in essence, Indian nationalism was viewed through a lens provided by different localities. A similar discussion appears in Appleton's (2002) account of the significance of the *Saturday Evening Post* for the reproduction of American nationalism. The *Saturday Evening Post* was a weekly magazine published in the US up until 1969. Significantly, Appleton shows how the magazine assumed a pre-eminent status as an 'artifact of a national ideology' (Appleton 2002: 425). For much of the twentieth century, the magazine used place and the 'local scale' as a way of articulating the key cultural facets of the American nation within nationalist discourse. Places such as a mid-west farmstead, replete with baseball-playing young people, for instance, were portrayed by the *Saturday Evening Post* as a 'crucible of national life', thus assuming the status of a geographical representation of some of the key essences of an American nation.

While this work on Germany, India and the US is to be complimented for its effort to examine the way in which places and the local scale are enlisted within nationalist discourse, we would argue that the focus on localities and the local scale solely as 'metonyms' within nationalist discourse is too limited. In the first place, by solely highlighting the metonymic qualities of place or, in other words, how 'nationalist imaginary deploys the trope of the local to articulate the specificity of the nation' (Confino and Skaria 2002b: 5), there is a danger in which geographic theory can serve implicitly to reinforce reified and essentialized accounts of nations within particular nationalist discourse. Various places – either abstract or concrete – can come to represent the alleged homogeneous and essential attributes of particular nations. Second, the focus within this work on the significance of the local scale in a generic and abstract sense also has the potential to underplay the ways in which actual places – and the politics and processes of contestation that exist within them – may contribute to a variegated and politicized reproduction of nationalist messages, symbols and discourse (in a related context, see Confino and Skaria 2002a). According to Appleton, it is an abstract tavern or church or farm that helped the readers of the *Saturday Evening Post* to make sense of their place within an American nation. In a similar vein, the role that *Heimat* played within German nationalism was based largely on its imagined and abstract status within German popular culture. There is obviously some value in emphasizing the importance of abstract places as representations of a nation's characteristics or ideals. This work, nonetheless, tends to underestimate the potential for actual places to contribute in an active and productive manner to the reproduction of nationalist discourse. In addition, the empirical and conceptual focus on the abstract and largely homogeneous places that exist as exhibitors of a national essence means that there is less of an opportunity to consider how the politics of actual places contribute to the reproduction of nationalist discourse. In Appleton's work, indeed, it is exactly during a period when real places begin to appear in the *Saturday Evening Post* during the 1960s – for example, with respect to the negative influence of organized crime in New England towns – that the role played by the local scale within the reproduction of American nationalist discourse was finally called into question within the pages of the magazine.

In the light of these criticisms, we argue that we need to emphasize a third context in which we can view the importance of localized places for the reproduction of nationalist discourse. Localized places of different kinds are not merely *tools* to be used by powerful agents within their nationalist discourses. Rather, localized places can also play an active role in the generation of ideas and sentiments that can ultimately reproduce nationalist discourse. We should view places as sites that may actively shape the production of nationalist ideology and sentiments rather than viewing them as sites that merely respond to nationalist messages or as sites that are impotent in the face of the national appropriation of local symbols and imagery. We would maintain that the adoption of such a viewpoint encourages us to move away from an abstract vision of place to one which is far more concrete in character.[3] Focusing on place in such a way enables us to highlight the politics and contestation that exists between different fractions of the nationalist movement as well as between different nationalist discourses. By addressing the active and constitutive role played by particular places in reproducing nationalist discourse, we can also begin to show how particular individuals, groups and discourses are chosen to be worthy of promotion while other individuals, groups and discourses are deemed to be of marginal use and value (cf. Miller 2000: xii). In other words, it is by examining the politics of place that we can illustrate the politics involved in the group-making project that nationalist discourse seeks to promote.

Let us be clear about one thing here. We are not advocating an argument in which agency is ascribed to place as such. We refer, instead, to the need to look at the practices, struggles and discourses produced by people living and working in particular places. What is important, we would argue, is the politics of place and how this might be rearticulated through a combination of processes into a politics of the nation. By the same token, such an approach necessitates us examining how real people, living and working in actual places, consume and rework nationalist discourses. As we indicated in the previous chapter, the work of the French sociologist, Lefebvre (1991: 1), is particularly useful when considering such a politics of place. Places and spaces, within his framework, are not viewed as static, pre-given or empty areas (Lefebvre 1991: 1; see also Soja 1989; 1996). Rather, we need to think of places and spaces as things that are produced through a combination of different processes that are combined together in a triple dialectic. Local or national places are produced through particular practices and material relations, and are represented by a combination of powerful individuals and organizations, as well as other, more marginalized, groups. Lefebvre's work encourages us to focus on discursive politics and material practices that help to produce and reproduce particular places and their associated identity politics. In broad terms, such an approach also implies a more agency-centred interpretation of nationalism or, as Thompson (2001: 21, original emphasis) puts it, a focus on how 'individuals actively employ their "common stock of knowledge" about nations and national identities' (see also Thompson and Fevre 2001).

Some research has begun to elaborate on these themes in empirical contexts. Brubaker's (2004: 20–27) recent work on the Transylvanian town of Cluj, for instance, has elaborated on the place-based production, circulation, reworking and contestation of Romanian and Hungarian nationalist discourse. By examining the particularities of place within Cluj, among other things, Brubaker is able to demonstrate the highly contingent consumption of nationalist discourses within the town. Despite the active production of nationalist discourse by a nationalist elite within the town – most notably, its Romanian mayor, Gheorghe Funar – the definition of Romanian and Hungarian groupness within Cluj has been low (ibid: 23). The contrast between Cluj and the neighbouring town of Târgu Mureş has been marked, where a different kind of localized politics of place has led to an extreme hardening of nationalist identities. In Brubaker's work, therefore, we see how a politics of place is both emplaced within, and is an active contributor to, nationalist discourse. Recent work on Wales, too, has begun to show how people, living and working in certain places – pubs, university campuses and local housing markets, for instance – help to shape national politics in an active way (Cloke et al. 1998; Desforges and Jones 2000; Jones and

Desforges 2003; Fevre et al. 1999; Thompson and Day 1999; in a more general context, see Thompson 2001). Fevre et al. (1999), for instance, demonstrate how national discourses are reproduced at small scales and in mundane social contexts. Their study discusses the way in which many people in north Wales use the processes that operate within the local housing market, in which Welsh speakers cannot afford to compete with English newcomers, in order to help them to reaffirm their sense of Welsh nationalism. A lack of housing in rural areas, therefore, is recast as a national issue, one which emphasizes a sense of opposition between English and Welsh speakers. Thompson and Day (1999), too, have noted the key role that individuals' experiences in pubs and bars – where people with varying linguistic abilities meet each other, and where arguments may take place – play in enabling them to shape their own interpretation of their national identity. Similarly, Jones and Desforges (2003) have examined the way in which the day-to-day practices of students on university campuses can act as mundane reproducers of nationalism. Banal instances of linguistic conflict in lecture theatres, halls of residence and bars, for instance, may be refracted into a far broader contentious national politics. Importantly, these are not merely discursive conflicts. They are also conflicts and divisions – generative of nationalist discourse – that are borne out of material practices, as different individuals choose to sit in either the bar or lounge area of a pub, or as students decide to sit in one linguistically homogeneous group in lecture theatres. The common emphasis in these studies is on how the discourses, practices and struggles of people within actual places may reproduce nationalist discourse in an active manner.

Of course, the purported product of the group-making processes occurring within these localized places is a nation, associated with a homogeneous national territory, to which all members of the nation feel a sense of attachment. It is in this context that the idea of a national homeland assumes great importance, for, as Agnew (2004: 227) has argued, 'the fusion of a piece of land with the symbolic and mythical history of the nation is what gives nationalism symbolic power' (see also Anderson 1988). Another way of thinking about the significance of national territories within nationalist discourses is to conceive of the way in which national territories can become places themselves. Taylor (1999: 102, emphasis added), in particular, has stressed the significance of such an argument by maintaining that 'by combining state and nation in nation-state, sovereign territory has been merged with sacred homeland to *convert space into a place*'. An important element within nationalist discourse, according to Calhoun (1997: 4–5), is the way in which it seeks to promote the connection between the members of the nation and a national territory, so that the latter assumes the status of a place that is imbued with national meaning and significance. National territories, therefore, are part of the group-making project of the nation and do not merely exist. They are the product of a series of territorial discourses and counter-discourses, as well as of particular organizations and practices that provide the national territory with a more concrete form.

But of course, such national territories or places are not necessarily characterized by unity or homogeneity. There is still considerable scope to examine the politics of such national places, as territorial practices, representations of territory and territories of representation (Lefebvre 1991: 1; Whitehead et al. 2007) are played out within the place of the nation. Taylor's (1991) research on England, for instance, has illustrated how the use of certain landscapes as a way of imagining Englishness and of its promoting its inherent values – particularly those rural landscapes of the south-east – has actually led to the disenfranchisement of other English people who do not identify with these particular landscapes. The individuals and groups who have been exempted from this vision of Englishness, most notably, are those living in English cities and/or in the north of England. Similar themes have been explored in Wales with regard to political efforts to define a Welsh-speaking heart-land by organizations such as Cymuned (see Jones and Fowler 2007a). Certain parts of Wales are deemed to be of greater importance to the cultural well-being of an imagined Welsh nation and this has the potential to lead to an invidious politics of national place within Wales. We examine this theme at far greater length in Chapter 7. These two brief examples show how a politics of national place is an important element within the reproduction of nationalist discourse.

Of course, a discussion of the significance of scalar connections between a localized politics of place and a nationalist discourse, existing at a broader national scale, can be construed to be misleading. After all, adhering closely to a spatialized social constructivist understanding of nationalism would seem to arouse suspicion in any type of overarching national body or group, which is the product of more place-based nationalist discourses. Indeed, if the focus of our attention is on the consumption of nationalist discourse, then there is room to argue that a sense of nationalism is constructed in very different ways by different people living and working in different places, making any talk of a broader community of the nation irrelevant. And yet, we believe that there is still some scope to think through the existence of a national group. As Brubaker (2004: 13, original emphasis) has argued, in thinking about group-making as a project, we need to focus on 'the dynamics of *group-making* as a social, cultural, and political project, aimed at transforming categories into groups or increasing levels of groupness'. In other words, the aim of a dynamic social constructivist account of nationalism must be to show how contingent temporal and spatial processes and projects can – and sometimes do not – lead to the sedimentation of nations as defined groups of people, rather than jettisoning the whole concept of the nation as group. It is a case, therefore, of not taking the nation as group for granted, rather than taking it out of the nationalist equation altogether. In this regard, the success or otherwise of the group-making project of nationalism may be measured in different ways. On the one hand, successful nationalist discourses may help to encourage a widespread popular belief in the relevance of an alleged national culture, history and territory for the target membership of the nation. In more material contexts, we argue that successful national discourses may also be indicated through the formation of different organizations, policies and strategies, whose existence is in some way related to the protection and enhancement of the status of a nation and its associated nationalist discourse. Similarly, particular practices can help to sediment and concretize national territories and organizations. Our argument in this book, therefore, is that localized places can contribute to emerging nationalist discourses, as well as the various national organizations that help to embed the nation in more material contexts (Lefebvre 1991: 1). What needs to be studied at greater length, we maintain, is the way in which a localized politics of place can be rearticulated and rescaled into a nationalist discourse – circulated and consumed at a broader national scale – in and through the practices and discourses of a group of key nationalist activists. But of course, such a contention necessitates a clear understanding of the concept of scale and scalar politics and it is to these themes that we turn in the following section.

GEOGRAPHIC SCALE AND NATIONALIST DISCOURSE

A discussion of the potential contribution of localized places to the process of reproducing nations as groups or national places, of necessity, draws our attention to the relationships that exist between practices and institutions operating over different geographical scales. The concept of scale has been a long-standing concern within human geography. While it is possible to think about cartographic scale, which refers to the level of abstraction used when producing maps, and methodological scale, which relates to the scale of enquiry chosen by a researcher when carrying out a research project, the most significant meaning of scale within current debates in human geography is with regard to the concept of geographical scale (see Smith 2000: 724–5). Geographical scale refers to the 'dimensions of specific landscapes' and processes (ibid: 725). For much of the twentieth century, geographical scale has been assumed to be relatively unproblematic. It has been viewed as a largely pre-given and static concept. The types of pre-existing scales that have structured most human activities have ranged from the body to the home, the neighbourhood, the city, the region, the nation state, the continent and the globe. Particular metaphors have been used to conceptualize this hierarchical layering of scale. Scales, from this more conventional viewpoint, have either been viewed as ladders, 'where one climbs up the scalar rungs from the local, through the regional and national to the global' (Herod and Wright 2002: 6) or concentric circles or Russian dolls, which are redolent of a series of nested hierarchies (ibid: 6–7). Metaphors such as these reinforce the idea that scales are pre-given and static entities. Furthermore, they give an impression of different scales being distinct one from the other. Although there may be some degree of interaction between different scales, each scale may be distinguished from another since they are either individual Russian dolls or separate rungs on the ladder.

Recent debates in human geography – arising predominantly as a result of an increased influence of Marxist ideals and social theory within the discipline – have sought to problematize the notion of geographical scale (see, for instance, Brenner 2001; Howitt 1998; Marston 2000; Marston and Smith 2001; Purcell 2003; Smith 1992a; 1992b; Swyngedouw 1996; 2000). The fundamental points made within this area of research are now well known within human geography and, indeed, their impact is beginning to be felt throughout the social sciences. Writers from various backgrounds have, broadly, emphasized three different themes as part of their efforts to promote a different conception of geographical scale. First, geographical scale should be viewed as something that is socially constructed or produced. In other words, scale is something that is not pre-given and static in nature but is rather the product of particular institutions and actors. As an illustration of this point, we can think of the increased significance of the notion and the scale of the neighbourhood within contemporary urban policy within the UK. As Whitehead (2003) has shown in a detailed study of the

implementation of urban policies in the West Midlands, while neigh-
bourhoods may well have pre-dated these urban policies, it is clear that
the implementation of the latter has given added meaning and relevance
to the neighbourhood scale as the most important scale for unfolding
mechanisms of urban governance in the West Midlands. Second, contemporary writers on geographical scale have argued that it should be
viewed as something that is relational in character or, in effect, something that is constructed through its relation to other geographical scales.
Rather than thinking about scales as things that are largely distinct from
one another, we need to appreciate how processes taking place over or
within one scale are necessarily associated with other geographical
scales. Brenner (2001: 600), in this respect, has argued for the need to
adopt a plural understanding of scale:

> In this plural aspect, the word 'of' connotes not only the production of
> differentiated spatial units as such, but also, more generally, their
> embeddedness and positionalities in relation to a multitude of smaller or
> larger spatial units within a multitiered, hierarchically configured
> geographical scaffolding.

Developing Howitt's (1998: 56) call for an interrogation of how
'various sorts of and scales of analysis might intersect and inform each
other', Brenner's focus on the plural understanding of scale elaborates
upon the mutual interpenetration of different scales, meaning that it is
difficult, at least at a conceptual level to separate out one from another.
One concrete way in which such thinking has been elaborated upon in
recent years is through the notion of 'glocalization' (Brenner 1998;
Swyngedouw 1996). 'Glocalization', a mingling of global and local,
refers to the way in which global processes and institutions are increasingly becoming embedded within particular localities. While the significance of such a process may well be apparent in a range of different
locations (Massey 1994), it is noticeable that the debate about 'glocalization' has tended to centre on the so-called global cities (Sassen 1991).
Here, local and global politics intertwine in complex ways so that it is
difficult, at face value, to separate out the global from the local. The
urban policies being implemented in London, for instance, are as much a
testament to a need to preserve its status as a financial centre of global
importance as they are of purely local political and policy priorities (see
Brenner 1998).

Third, a number of authors have highlighted how the notion of
geographical scale can become politicized, in the sense that the act of
determining the geographical scale in and through which practices take
place can lead to various types of advantages accruing to certain
individuals and groups. Swyngedouw (1997a: 139), in particular, has

drawn attention to the need to think through 'scalar narratives' or, in other words, how 'places and spaces at different geographical scales are invoked in attempts to account for dramatic events that have major local, national, and international implications'. These scalar narratives, in effect, provide the scalar contexts through which explanations for particular events are positioned: this is a global issue; this is a local problem and so on. As an example of such a politics of scale, one can think about the way in which politicians throughout much of the contemporary world have sought to justify a series of neoliberal policies by arguing that any instances of unemployment or social deprivation emerging within their states or localities are the product of inherently global processes, which lie beyond their control (ibid). Positioning such problems as global ones, rather than national or local ones, effectively absolves politicians of any responsibility for either their creation or their amelioration.

The concern with explicating the contours of geographical scale within human geography has led to the propagation of many fruitful lines of research in recent years. Nonetheless, it is apparent that the work on geographical scale has only been explored in a limited range of thematic contexts. Marston (2000), in particular, has noted the tendency for studies of the production of scale to focus on processes relating to capitalist production and to the state. Few contributions have sought to extend our understanding of the social construction of scale into other areas of research (though see Smith 1992b; 1993; 1996; Taylor 1999). Marston (2000), however, has attempted to argue that the theoretical concerns of the current literature on geographical scale are of considerable value to studies of personal and group identity. Her research has focused on the association between the scale of the household and the national scale in the US during the nineteenth century. She has showed how large-scale changes in the status of women within the political nation of the US were the product and producer of equally fundamental changes to the roles played by women in the home. In this way, Marston (2000: 235) maintains that 'a discourse about women as "female citizens" operated among and between scales from the household out to the globe'. Marston's work, therefore, seeks to demonstrate the value in expanding our conception of the usefulness of ideas concerning the construction and the politics of scale into other areas of research (see also Marston and Smith 2001). Our argument, in this respect, is that geographical studies of the reproduction of nationalism and nationalist discourse would also benefit immeasurably as a result of incorporating the key tenets of theories of geographical scale into their field of enquiry.

Two issues, in particular, would seem to us to be especially pertinent to a more sustained scalar enquiry into the geographical reproduction of the nation. First, conceiving of geographical scale as something that does not pre-exist the given social and spatial circumstances within which it is produced – being something that is constituted as a result of active political and social struggle (see Delaney and Leitner 1997; Herod 1997; Jonas 1994) – reaffirms social constructivist accounts about the group-making project of nation, which is viewed as something that is actively produced and contested by a variety of different individuals, groups and institutions. These individuals, groups and institutions can be internal to the national project itself but can also be associated with a variety of other territorial identities, ranging from the local through to the trans-national (see the discussion in Kaplan 1999). Second, if geographical scale is something that should be considered in a plural sense, then we need to think about the way in which a putative national group, place and scale is both the product and producer of processes and institutions that exist at other geographical scales. In the context of this book, therefore, it is impossible to study the production of the discursive and material aspects of a national grouping, which exist at a national scale, without also considering the way in which other processes and institu-tions – existing at other geographical scales – are dialectically inter-twined with it.

Some work in the social sciences has already begun to apply concepts of scale to our conceptual and empirical understanding of nationalism. Some of this work has not always heeded the more theoretical insights of recent approaches to geographical scale. Herb and Kaplan's (1999a) recent edited collection on *Nested Identities* is a good case in point. Its aim, stated in a promising enough manner, is to examine how 'national identity is negotiated within a hierarchy of geographical scales' (Herb and Kaplan 1999b: 4). While such an aim could potentially provide scope to examine the way in which a national identity is produced through a range of processes taking place at a variety of scales, it is clear that the authors have a far more static and nested vision of individual and group identities in mind. In this regard, there is almost a reification of nation-alism as something that solely occupies the national scale and which must struggle against other, equally distinct, identities that exist at other geographical scales. National identity, in this sense, 'is situated within a hierarchy of geographically based identities that coexist and sometimes compete against it' (Kaplan 1999: 31). The thematic structure of the book reinforces this hierarchical and nested vision of geographical scales as various contributors discuss the various territorial identities that exist at the macro, meso and micro scale, which may either support or subvert nationalist discourse. While such a project is worthwhile, it can be criticized for viewing group identities in a rather static and pre-given way. A variety of group identities are almost necessarily linked to specific geographical scales. Needless to say, we think that an alternative approach is possible, in which the discursive and more material aspects of national groups are viewed as the products of processes occurring at a variety of different geographical scales.

Confino and Skaria's (2002a) work on the active production of German nationalism in the post-war period, in this respect, is more attuned to the approach that we advocate in this book. An important, if largely implicit, aspect of their work is their focus on how the production of an imagined German nation came about as a result of the intermeshing of processes and ideologies at different scales within Germany. As they put it, 'the *Heimat* idea represented interchangeably the locality, the region, and the nation through an interlocking network of symbols and representations in which the nation appeared local and the locality national' (Confino and Skaria 2002a: 11). The geographical imaginations contained within the notion of *Heimat*, therefore, were equally local, regional and national visions. Agnew's (see especially 1997) work on Italy, too, also alludes to an interesting interplay between different geographical scales with regard to the reproduction of an Italian national group. He has, among other things, examined the influence of political parties – most notably the Northern League or *La Lega Norda* – during the 1990s in actively producing particular images of Italy and the Italian nation within their nationalist discourse. Significantly, these national imaginations are predicated upon considerations of local and regional politics and identities. In this sense, the active production of an imagined Italian nation, existing at a national scale, and of the place of particular localities and regions within it, have been intimately intertwined.

We maintain, in this regard, that we need to focus on the role of political, social and cultural processes in producing the national scale, along with the embeddness of different scales one within another, with regard to nationalism. One obvious way of conceptualizing how this 'scalar scaffolding' (Brenner 2001) helps to produce nations as groups is to adapt Massey's (1994) notion of place as a meeting point that exists within a network of associations that are stretched out over a number of different scales (see also Appleton 2002). By adapting her object of enquiry somewhat, it is possible for us to think of the group of the nation as something that is actively produced out of its connections with the local, the regional, the international and the global. Similarly, the project of 'framing' or group-making that is associated with the discursive and more material aspects of nationalism has the potential to condition the ways in which people, individuals and institutions existing at other geographical scales interact with nationalist discourse. In this way, for instance, the important sociological work on Wales, discussed above, begins to show how processes occurring at the local scale reproduce a group sense of Welshness, existing at the national scale. Discussions and debates taking place within pubs (Thompson and Day 1999) and with regard to the local housing market (Fevre et al. 1999) in north-west Wales, as well as being positioned within the context of broader debates concerning Welsh nationalism, may also be generative of broader nationalist discourses. Similarly, Boyle (2002), Mulligan (2001) and Nash (1999) have shown how the transnational scale has been associated with the reproduction of an Irish nation in discursive contexts. The Irish diaspora, in this respect, has provided a focal point for geographical imaginations of the Irish nation. This has been especially significant for the reproduction of Irish national history, given the Irish nation's sense of communal loss, as a result of the famine and the large-scale migration of Irish people to other countries (see also Wiebe 2002).

An emphasis on the relational quality of scales, although laudable in ontological and epistemological contexts, can lead to methodological and representational difficulties. Methodological difficulties can arise when one attempts to consider one scale as something that manifests a range of processes and practices taking place at other geographical scales. It is not difficult, in this respect, to imagine a nightmarish vision in which all spatial scales ultimately collapse, one into the other. This 'scalar mush' is especially worrying when studying the empirical connections and interlinkages between different scales. Despite the conceptual benefits of seeing all scales as being mutually constituted, it is inevitable that empirical research will rely on the foregrounding of one scale above others but, nonetheless, with the specific aim of explicating the complex 'mosaic' of connections between the chosen, and other, scales (Brenner 2001: 606). In this way, it is possible to address the 'kaleidoscope effect' (Smith 1987: 64), in which the character of scalar connections varies with regard to the particular scale being studied. Difficulties can also arise with regard to the representation of geographical scale in academic discourse. Human geographers and others have been less than successful in articulating the fluidity and relational characteristics of geographical scale in their academic writings. Collinge (2005), in a recent contribution, for instance, has deconstructed the language used within Swyngedouw's (1992; 1996; 1997a; 1997b; 2000;

2003) numerous writings on the politics of scale. Following this work, Collinge (2005: 200) lists a number of seeming deficiencies or inconsistencies in Swyngedouw's work. Although Collinge's critique is wide-ranging, it centres on Swyngedouw's tendency to conflate two distinct aspects of the characteristics of geographical scales, namely a more traditional view of their existence as physical areas with a more contemporary understanding of scale as the product of various social institutions and processes. More damning still, Collinge suggests that Swyngedouw's work gives epistemological and ontological precedence to the notion of scale as physical area. In other words, Swyngedouw, through his use of language, is accused by Collinge (ibid) of reinforcing the more traditional takes on scale by inadvertently referring to them as 'standard areal size categories or as areas of the state whose existence need not be demonstrated'. To a certain extent, such a regression is almost inevitable. A grammar of pre-existing areal units of scale has entered the popular and academic lexicon to such an extent that it is difficult to avoid using them as convenient labels to describe various socio-spatial processes. Indeed, the difficulty inherent in devising a means of escaping a latent spatial fetishism of scale has led certain authors to call for a total jettisoning of the language of scale from the social sciences (Marston, Jones and Woodward 2005). While we have some sympathy with this critique of the scale literature, we do not believe that the deficiencies associated with contemporary efforts to study and represent fluid and relational scales warrant a rejection of the language of scale per se. In studying and referring to particular scales within this book – most notably the local and the national – we seek to emphasize the multitude of connections between them and other geographical scales.

Taken as a whole, we believe that the above discussion illustrates a potentially useful theoretical framework for understanding the mechanisms through which nationalist discourse, nations as groups and, by implication, national territories are reproduced. While social constructivist accounts of nationalism have correctly drawn attention to the way in which social categories may complicate dominant nationalist discourses, we believe that a focus on the places within which nationalist discourse are produced, circulated and consumed can provide a powerful way of examining the politics inherent within the reproduction of nationalist discourse and the related group-making project of nationalism. An exploration of place-based politics has the potential to show us how a dominant nationalist discourse is inherently fractured and contested from within. At the same time, a geographically sensitive reading of the reproduction of nationalist discourse also, inevitably, turns into a story about scale; the relationship between localized places and the national place, as expressed through discursive and more material social and spatial formations. The group of the nation, as such, always displays a spatial and scalar tension that is a product of multiple politics of place and scale taking place within and outside its boundaries. In order to understand the complex and contested reproduction of nations, we maintain that we need to explore how active and productive places connect to the continually emerging territories, politics and cultures of the nation – in particular places and times.

As well as providing a more refined theoretical framework for understanding some of the key geographical aspects of the reproduction of the nation, our contention is that such an approach also enables us to cast different light on some broader debates about the social construction of the nation. It is the added value that a geographical approach may bring to constructivist accounts of nationalism that is discussed in the following section.

GEOGRAPHY AND THE REPRODUCTION OF NATIONALIST DISCOURSE

The previous section has centred mainly on the benefits accruing to human geography through extending its sphere of interest with regard to studies of nationalism and nationalist discourse; most notably from an extension of research interest solely in issues relating to representation to a broader focus on the reproduction of nationalist discourse. At the same time, the above discussion has also hinted at how advocating a more geographical approach – and specifically an interrogation of the key concepts of place and scale – could actually enhance social constructivist interpretations of nationalism. As a way of further highlighting the saliency of these latter claims, we want to explicate systematically in the final substantive section of this chapter the numerous ways in which a more geographically sensitive approach can help contribute to the revitalization of a social constructivist agenda that has, according to Brubaker (2004: 3), become rather stale.

We focus in particular on Brubaker's (2004: 11–18) eight basic parameters of a social constructivist account of non-groupist ways of thinking about nations and nationalism and seek to demonstrate how each, in turn, can be augmented by fusing them with contemporary understandings of place and scale:

1   *Viewing groups as dynamic social products, rather than pre-given social entities.*
    Brubaker (2004: 11) argues that we should think of nations and other groups
    in 'relational, processual, dynamic, eventful, and disaggregated terms'. If we
    agree with such a statement, as surely we must, then one particularly useful
    way of demonstrating the processes through which nations 'become' rather
    than exist is through highlighting their variegated geographies. Particular
    localized places within – and, indeed, without – the national territory may
    contribute in different ways to the processes through which a national
    discourse is produced, circulated and consumed by different people. The
    process of reproducing a national discourse is also shaped by numerous
    scalar connections ranging from the body through to the global. These
    place-based and scalar processes and connections are all politicized and
    highly contingent in character.

2   *The reality of the nation as group comes about as a result of the promotion of
    national discourses.* Despite the processual aspects of nations, it is clear that a
    key aim of nationalist discourse is to sediment a common sense and
    homogeneous understanding of the nation in cultural, historic and territo-
    rial terms. Geographers occupy an excellent position from which to high-
    light this process of embedding the nation as group within popular
    imagination and more formal organizations and institutions by showing
    how national places are brought into existence through a combination of
    nationalist discourses, practices and organizations. At the same time, a more
    geographically sensitive approach can illustrate the way in which particular
    places and scales assume critical roles in defining the different aspects of a
    national culture, history or space within the imaginations of the nation's
    population, as well as within the more formal organizations created in order
    to reflect the existence, and shape the future, of the nation.

3   *Groupness is a contingent event, which may or may not happen.* As well as being
    something that occurs at certain times, we need to think about the group-
    ness of the nation as something that happens in particular places. A
    concatenation of circumstances within particular localities may be needed in
    order to forge a sense of groupness within that place and further afield. By
    the same token, a particular cultural, economic and social mix – to name but
    a few variables – within certain places may well mitigate against a success-
    ful definition of a nation as a group. In a similar way, geographic scale is
    scripted into the events, which may or may not define the nation as a group.
    The successful definition of a nation as a group depends, ultimately, upon a
    meaningful ascription of culture and history to the national scale; turning a
    national space into a national place.

4   *Distinguishing between nation as group and nation as category.* A nation as
    group implies 'a mutually interacting, mutually recognizing, mutually
    oriented, effectively communicating, bounded collectivity' (Brubaker 2004:
    12), whereas a nation as category represents merely the idea of the nation as
    a group, and the way in which this idea is scripted into national discourse
    and 'become[s] institutionalized and entrenched in administrative routines'

(ibid: 13). The key geographical focus, in this respect, must be on how people, groups and institutions within particular places play an important role in defining the nation as category, as well as the ways in which certain places and scales become important elements within the broader narrative of the nation. It is in this way that we able to show how a nation as a category becomes part of a broader geographical imagination (Gregory 1994; Paasi 1996).

5   *Nations are formed through a group-making project.* Thinking about nations as groups that come about through contingent events, of necessity, focuses our attention on the practices through which a nation-building project is attempted. The key, but contingent, role played by a national elite is important here as they seek to promote or rework particular national discourses and practices. An explicitly geographical focus on the activities of a national elite can enable us to demonstrate how particular place-based cultures, events and so on are enrolled as ideas and themes within the group-making project of the nation while others are excluded from the national story. At the same time, adopting such a perspective allows us to show how different kinds of actors – operating in different places and across different scales – are connected through their role as narrators or promoters of the national discourse.

6   *Nations as groups are not necessarily the same as national organizations.* In broad terms, we need to distinguish between nations as groups and the various types of organization and movements that seek to represent a nation or promote a particular national discourse. It is possible, in this way, to show how different individuals, organizations and movements nominally associated with a particular nation promote different group-making projects. A useful way of illustrating these conflicting national discourses is through focusing on the different places and scales that are enrolled by different organizations within their national discourse. Doing so would allow us to complicate our understanding of the nation as a group by showing the differing, and sometimes contradictory, geographical imaginations of various types of nationalist organization.

7   *Nations and national conflict are defined as such through a process of framing or coding.* Nations as groups, and the nationalist agitation that they are linked to, are not, in essence, instances of nations or nationalist agitation. Rather they are defined as such through a particular national discourse or script. In this way, particular social or cultural ills, or particular forms of conflict, may be defined by a nationalist elite as instances of national ills or national conflict. We must be aware, nonetheless, of the possibility that other people might well define the same ills or conflicts in totally different ways; for instance, through recourse to ethnic, racial or even socio-economic discourses. One potentially important contributor to this differential definition of particular events is the locality within which people are socialized. Particular place-based cultures encourage individuals to frame events and practices in certain ways – either as instances of nationalist conflict or

otherwise – and this is what a geographically sensitive approach to the group-making project of the nation can demonstrate.

8   *The groupness of nations is related to issues of cognition.* If, as Brubaker (2004: 17) argues, 'ethnicity, race, and nationhood are fundamentally ways of perceiving, interpreting and representing the social world', which are based in large part on the 'tacit, taken-for-granted background knowledge' that people possess, then we need to grapple with the way in which such knowledges are learnt within particular localities and across different scales. What encourages certain people to 'read' particular events or practices as instances of nationalism or national conflict while deeming others to be examples of other types of event or practice? What types of geographical imaginations are enrolled by individuals in order to make sense of these differing events and practices? Which geographical scales, and what types of relationship between them, are more important within this process of cognitive framing?

It is by examining these different issues, we argue, that we can begin to grapple in different ways with the social construction of the nation. We can begin to show the dynamic process through which nations are constructed as groups, not merely as a result of social interaction – whether in terms of domination, resistance or conflict – but also through critical spatial interactions; within and between places and over different scales.

CONCLUSIONS

In this chapter, we have sought to set out a manifesto for a more geographically sensitive approach to social constructivist accounts of the nation. While geographers have increasingly attempted to promote a more geographical take on nationalism, their efforts, to date, have centred on comprehending spatial representations that exist within nationalist discourse. It is possible to extend this sphere of research to begin to study how different geographical concepts or processes are implicated in the reproduction of nationalist discourse; how it is pro-duced, circulated and consumed. Two geographical concepts would seem to us to offer especially propitious avenues of enquiry: place and scale. There is a dire need to take more recent work on these concepts within human geography and to apply it to the study of nationalism. As well as broadening the type of work that may be conducted on the geography of nationalism, following such a research agenda may also benefit constructivist understandings of the nation in disciplines other than geography. Taken together, we believe the approach advocated in this book will lead both to an energizing of geographical approaches to nationalism and an increased awareness amongst other social scientists of the added value of an increased cognisance of the manifold geographies of national group-making projects. Our aim in this chapter has been to show the validity of such claims in largely theoretic contexts. The following chapters in this book demonstrate the empirical worth of such undertakings.

NOTES

1   Another area of research has focused on the 'why' of nationalism. Work in this area has examined the use made of nationalism by polities and political movements, specifically as a way of supporting or subverting state forms (Mann 1995; Tilly 1975; Hutchinson 1987). In another context, authors such as Kedourie (1960; 1971) have sought to evaluate the psychological value of nationalism, viewing it as something akin to a secular religion.

2   In addition, there is an important literature that seeks to distinguish between terms such as place, locality and the local scale (see Agnew 1987). We acknowledge the importance of such distinctions but draw on a variety of literatures that tend not to distinguish between these three concepts. The main emphasis in this chapter, however, is on the two concepts of place and the local scale.

3   It may well be possible to develop a synthesis of the role of metonymic and concrete places within the reproduction of nations. For instance, particular processes occurring within an actual place may also take on symbolic qualities as it is reworked as part of the national imagination.

3

Timing and spacing Welsh nationalism

INTRODUCTION

Our aim in this chapter is to provide an empirical grounding for the more specific themes discussed in the remaining chapters by elaborating upon the temporal and spatial trajectories that have affected Welsh nationalism over the past 150 years. We begin the chapter by seeking to show, in general terms, the fundamental developments that have taken place within Welsh nationalism over time. Similarly, and again in a relatively broad brush way, we try to illustrate the way in which particular places have played a significant role within this nationalist discourse; as symbolic elements within that discourse and as key sites that have helped to produce that discourse. We then proceed to discuss in more detail the organizational basis for the reproduction of Welsh nationalist discourse over the past 150 years, focusing in turn on the Liberal Party, Plaid Cymru, the Welsh Language Society and Cymuned. Our goal, in this respect, is to show how different nationalist organizations have promoted a range of alternative nationalist discourses within Wales. Finally, we seek to outline one key geographical facet of the production of Welsh nationalist discourse for much of this period, namely the important role played by the town of Aberystwyth within this process. The chapter draws attention to the numerous formal and informal locations that have been part and parcel of the reproduction of Welsh nationalism within the town. Taken together, therefore, the material discussed in this chapter acts as an important empirical springboard for the more thematic discussions contained in the following chapters.

THE HISTORICAL GEOGRAPHIES OF WELSH NATIONALISM

Issues of time and space have been crucial to the emergence of Welsh nationalist discourse during the modern period. The twin motors of modernity – industrialization and urbanization – have been particularly important drivers behind the emergence of a Welsh nationalism. During the nineteenth century, Wales was transformed from an essentially peasant society into one of the most economically advanced regions in the world, with industrial growth spearheaded by coal mining (John Davies 1993: 398). The geographic nucleus of these developments was the valleys region of south Wales – Glamorgan and Monmouthshire (latterly Gwent) (ibid: 402; for accounts of industrialization elsewhere in Wales, see Pryce 1975). Industrial growth also induced huge demographic changes across Wales. In the period between 1851 and 1914, Wales' population doubled to over 1,000,000. What is of even more significance, however, was the geographical redistribution of the population of Wales that took place through the process of urbanization. As a percentage of the Welsh total, rural counties incurred dramatic losses to the coalfield counties of Glamorgan, Gwent and Flintshire. The coalfield counties witnessed a further source of heavy in-migration, principally from south-western counties of England. As Morgan (1980 [1963]: 55) states:

> in the period 1851–1911 a net loss of 388,000 out of rural Wales was counterbalanced by an inward migration of 366,000 into the Welsh coalfield. In this way, Wales was saved from the worst effects of rural depopulation and poverty that so seriously disrupted the social development of Ireland.

The significance of these large-scale societal changes, of course, was that they created the preconditions within which Welsh nationalism could emerge. The large-scale processes of modernization that were taking place in Wales and a broader Britain at this time were accompanied by the beginnings of a similarly large-scale cultural shift in political identity. Echoing the work of Gellner (1983), Morgan (1982) has argued that Welsh nationalism derived much of its impetus from the processes of industrialization and urbanization that were taking place at such unprecedented rates during the nineteenth and early twentieth centuries. The location of these twin motors of modernization within Wales – rather than outside its borders – was also significant, as the Welsh economist, Thomas (1959), has shown. In his work, a connection was made between industrialization and urbanization and the Welsh language, but his ideas are also significant for broader questions relating to Welsh political identity. Thomas (ibid) argued that the development of the south Wales coalfield in particular served as a mechanism for population retention for the whole of Wales. A stable population provided for the retention of a living Welsh language within the territory of

Wales. By extension, we can argue that the impact was similar upon Welsh identity in more general terms.

Thomas' (1959) and Morgan's (1982) work also begins to draw our attention to the spatial specificity of the reproduction of Welsh nationalist discourses, practices and institutions at this time. Thomas (1959), for instance, showed how the processes of urbanization and industrialization within the south Wales coalfield contributed to the reproduction of a Welsh linguistic culture within these particular areas during the nineteenth and twentieth centuries. Similarly, Morgan (1982: 8–9) has convincingly argued that

> the growth of new towns, the new bourgeoisie that they produced made a modern Welsh national movement possible. It was here in the major towns that the chapels, the newspapers, the eisteddfodau, and the choral festivals flourished above all. If there was an outstanding cradle of the national revival in modern Wales, it may not be found in the sparsely populated countryside . . . but in the grimy iron-works and winding-shafts of the working class metropolis of Merthyr Tydfil.

Such ideas challenge much of the geographical discourse that has been prevalent within Welsh nationalism, in which urbanization and industrialization is often viewed as a threat to an allegedly pure Welsh national culture. This is an argument that has re-emerged at different points in time throughout the twentieth century. While different groups of Welsh nationalists – e.g. Plaid Cymru during the interwar period (Gruffudd 1994), Adfer (Llewelyn 1972a) during the early 1970s and mid-1980s and Cymuned (2001) in the 2000s – have advocated the need to protect rural Wales from the cultural threats posed to it by an Anglicized and urbanized society, others (e.g. Smith 1984; 2001) have emphasized the role played by an urbanized south Wales in fostering a (different kind of) Welsh identity. The debate concerning the geographies of the reproduction of Welshness seems set to continue unabated and unresolved. Their continued salience testifies to the different geographical imaginations that are incorporated into the group-building project of the nation. This is a theme that we take up at further length in Chapter 7.

But if the nineteenth and early twentieth centuries was a period during which the large-scale processes of modernity provided the conditions for the reproduction of Welsh nationalist discourse, it is clear that the twentieth century has posed numerous other socio-economic challenges, within which Welsh nationalist discourse has been positioned.

Wales, as with the majority of so-called 'developed' countries, has experienced problems of social dislocation and decline during the twentieth century:

> For most of this century, Wales has experienced rapid social and economic change: an accelerating process of rural depopulation, only halted in the last decade; a high level of migration, both inward and outward . . . a steepening decline of basic industries such as coal and steel; the 'greening' of industrial valleys; the progressive weakening of nonconformity, historically the most potent element in the Welsh political culture; and last, but obviously not least, the continuing fall in the proportion of the population speaking Welsh (Jones 1988: 50–1).

These fundamental changes to the character of the Welsh economy, society and culture have had far-reaching effects on the production of nationalist discourse within Wales. The economic success experienced by an industrialized and urbanized Wales during the nineteenth and early twentieth centuries has given way to a process of socio-economic stagnation and decline. It is significant that these far-reaching changes have provided fertile ground for the propagation of nationalist discourse. Welsh nationalists, specifically, have described the socio-economic and cultural challenges facing Wales as factors that are symptomatic of Wales' unequal relationship with England/Britain. In broad terms, the act of defining one nation in opposition to another is, obviously, one of the most common rhetorical devices used within nationalist discourse (Conversi 1995; see also Said 1978). Another more specific, if problematic, explanation of this unequal relationship between Wales and England revolves around Hechter's (1975) concept of internal colonialism. According to Hechter, political, military, economic and cultural power becomes centralized in certain regions of all states. The unequal distribution of power between the centre and the periphery leads to efforts by the core both to exploit the periphery economically within the capitalist process, and to impose its own cultural norms on it. Hechter argues that this process operated throughout the whole of the United Kingdom during the modern period. For instance, he maintains that

> the Union with Wales imposed English land law, English courts and judges, and the Church of England upon Wales. All Welsh affairs were to be settled in London by the King and Parliament. Only English-speaking Welshmen were permitted to hold administrative office in Wales (Hechter 1975: 67).

The characteristic feature of the British and Irish Isles during the modern period, according to Hechter, was one of an internal colonial exploitation of a Celtic periphery by an English core region. What is significant, of course, is that Hechter argues that this internal colonialism explains the emergence of nationalist politics within places such as Wales as the current and past inequities visited upon the country by England are used as motivating factors for the generation of nationalist discourse.

It is fair to say that Hechter's ideas have been the subject of much criticism, most notably with regard to their use as an explanation for the development of nationalist politics (see Smith 1982; 1998: 57–69; Page 1977). And yet his ideas, either implicitly or explicitly, have provided an intellectual justification for the ideological stances exhibited by many nationalist organizations within Wales (e.g. Cymuned 2001a; Llewelyn 1972a; 1972b; Miles 1972). In more popular contexts, it is clear that Welsh nationalists of many hues have used the perceived unequal relationship between Wales and England as a means of furthering a more energized, exclusive and radical nationalist discourse. The use of Welsh water by English municipalities, for instance, has acted as a raw nerve within mainstream Welsh nationalism, since it illustrates the exploitation of Welsh resources by external bodies (see Roberts 2001; Whitehead et al. 2007). The English state's domination of a Welsh culture has also provided another context for the emergence of a Welsh nationalist politics. Many nationalist organizations, for instance, maintain that the English state has played an important role in seeking to undermine the Welsh language, most notably in the context of the Acts of Union during the sixteenth century and during the mid-nineteenth century, when the British state's education inspectors denounced the Welsh language as a barrier to the moral and economic progress of the Welsh people (see Jones 1997: 132–9, 142–8, 266–74, 275–80). As is well known, the report provoked a series of sustained rebuttals by a range of individuals and organizations within Wales. While the majority of the responses centred on the need to demonstrate the inherent morality of the Welsh people – and of the nonconformist religion practised in Wales – some also took aim at the various linguistic claims made within the report. The linguistic rebuttals outlined the more positive connections between the Welsh language and the Welsh people. Admittedly, the arguments put forward by some commentators during this period have been criticized in recent years as ones that betray an almost apologetic and sentimental attitude towards the role of the Welsh language within a Welsh national culture (e.g. Edwards 1987: 138; Jones 1997: 276–7). At the same time, other more radical individuals, such as Michael D. Jones, propounded a more confident and far-reaching vision of the role of the Welsh language. Instead of being a quaint relic of Wales' past distinctiveness, the 'linguistic nationalism' (Janet Davies 1993: 44) promoted by Michael D. Jones was predicated on a far more proactive and self-confident vision of a Welsh-speaking future for Wales, in all linguistic domains. We discuss this issue at further length in Chapters 4 and 5.

But of course, another way in which we can consider the relationship between Welsh nationalist politics and the broader British state is by examining the degree to which the latter has recognized the distinctiveness, if not the separatedness, of Wales and Welshness. A number of organizational developments over the twentieth century, in particular, testify to an increased awareness on behalf of the British state of Welsh affairs (with regard to education, see Evans 2000). Most significant, in this respect, was the administrative devolution of power, reflected in the creation of a Welsh Office in 1964, and the subsequent executive devolution of power, as evidenced in the establishment of the National Assembly for Wales (NAfW) in 1999. The impetus for the creation of the NAfW has been viewed as something that derives from a variety of factors. In large measure, it is seen as a way of securing economic prosperity and competitive advantage under globalization (see Labour Party 1997; 2001; NAfW 2002a). But it also it has been seen to reflect long-term demands for political representation and democracy by nationalists within Wales (e.g. Chaney et al. 2001; Jones and Osmond 2002; Morgan and Mungham 2000; Taylor and Thomson 1999). While the formation of the NAfW has provided new opportunities for nationalist organizations in Wales, it is clear that it has also posed considerable challenges for them as they seek to negotiate new policies, strategies and compromises within a new devolved landscape.

This necessarily brief outline of the history and historical geography of Welsh nationalism has only provided a brief overview of some of the key events and processes that have underpinned the reproduction of Welsh nationalist discourse. But of course, one can only excavate a certain amount when considering Welsh nationalist discourse in such broad generic terms. As Brubaker (2004: 14–16) has shown, we must focus on particular nationalist organizations if we are fully to appreciate the production of nationalist discourse. With this in mind, we move on in the following section to chart the main organizations that have acted as the vehicles for the reproduction of nationalist discourse in modern Wales.

THE ORGANIZATIONAL BASIS OF WELSH NATIONALISM

Welsh nationalism, since the outset, has been reproduced through a variety of different organizations. Some organizations' sole reason for existence has centred on promoting a Welsh nation-defining and nation-building project. Other organizations possess a range of different remits, within which the promotion of an ostensibly nationalist discourse is but one element, while others have addresses nationalist concerns merely in tangential ways. The range of different organizations that can legitimately lay claim to be associated with a broader nation-building project within Wales precludes a detailed discussion of each in turn. We focus here on the main organizations that have contributed to the production of Welsh nationalist discourse from the mid-nineteenth century onwards. In some measure, the different organizations reflect a range of different time periods with regard to the production of Welsh nationalist discourse. To a lesser extent, the various organizations that we focus on also reflect different political and cultural emphases within the broader sweep of Welsh nationalist discourse.

The Liberal Party and Welsh nationalism, 1868–1922

The Liberal Party was the main organizational vehicle for Welsh nationalism during the late nineteenth and early twentieth centuries. Nationalism, in the Liberal sense, did not revolve around the need to designate Wales as a separate nation-state. Nonetheless, the nationalist discourse promoted by the Liberal Party sought to promote and consolidate Wales as a territorial political entity, possessing a certain distinctiveness and a degree of separatedness. In this sense, the Liberal Party came to represent and symbolize a set of political and cultural norms and values that would persist in the popular memory and myth of Wales. Significantly, the Welsh language did not feature much in Liberal campaigns for Welsh national institutions during this period. This outlook may be attributed to a widespread sense of optimism, or indeed complacency, about the future of all things Welsh under the wing of the British Empire (Morgan 1980 [1963]: 300). Moreover, the Liberals came into ascendancy in Welsh politics at a time when the Welsh language was still a majority language in Wales. The principal catalyst for Liberal political agitation at this time, rather, was Welsh nonconformist religion. Nonconformist religion informed the Liberal policy platform in Wales during the late nineteenth and early twentieth centuries in the context of three interrelated policy areas: education, land reform and church disestablishment. Moreover, each of these different policy areas was tied into the Liberal Party's conception of the need to consider Wales as a distinctive and separate political territory (Morgan 1980 [1963]; John Davies 1993; Nelmes 1979).

In terms of education, much was made by the leaders of the Welsh Liberal Party of the denominational nature of schooling in Wales, which reinforced a perceived 'alien' set of cultural norms on the Welsh population (Morgan 1980 [1963]: 44–6). In this way, the administrative dominance of a minority religion, the Church of England, within the context of Welsh education was considered to be an affront to the largely nonconformist Welsh population. The upshot of this nationalist-informed educational debate was the 1889 Intermediate Act, which enabled local government to invoke local taxes to support secular-based intermediate level schools in Wales (Combs 1977: 73). In supporting such an Act, the Liberal Party sought to enable a form of intermediate education that was more attuned to the cultural and religious specificities of the Welsh people. Land reform was another means through which the Liberal Party sought to articulate and promote a Welsh nation-building project. Land reform was an issue ripe for political mobilization in Liberal Wales (Evans 1989: 200–201). The distinctively Welsh component to the land crisis derived from the religious complexion of Wales. The most fundamental grievance was the mandatory payment of a tithe to the Church of England parish, which was a religious irrelevance to the majority of the Welsh population. Furthermore, the issue of land reform became a marker of nationalist attitudes towards the end of the nineteenth century as a reformist and Welsh nationalist group, led by the Liberal Party, was pitted against a coalition of more conservative and Anglicized groups. The Liberal Party sponsored the establishment of a Land Commission in May 1893, which settled the issue of land reform in the period between 1893 and 1896 (Morgan 1980 [1963]: 126). The Liberal Party, in this sense, became the flag bearer of a distinctive Welsh nationalist discourse that was based upon broader debates concerning the control of agricultural land within Wales.

In the two instances, discussed above, we witness how the Liberal Party furthered what we may term a Welsh nationalist politics through its efforts to promote an educational and landholding system that was less Anglicized in outlook and more attuned to the needs of the Welsh people. It is clear, also, that issues relating to the dominance of the established religion of England within Wales lay at the heart of these debates. It should come as no surprise to the reader, therefore, that the disestablishment of the Church of England became the third key area of nationalist agitation in Wales and one, once again, in which the Liberal Party was directly involved. The Liberation Society had been established as far back as 1844, and had campaigned for the disestablishment of Church from state across England and Wales (Morgan 1995 [1966]: 147–8). In Wales, the discourses promoted by the Liberation Society coincided with the report of the Anglican-dominated education commissioners' report into education in Wales, in what became known as the 'Treachery of the Blue Books'. The report's broadsides against nonconformist religion had the political effect of galvanizing nonconformist unity, which crystallized into separate demands for disestablishment in Wales (Morgan 1995 [1966]: 148). The Church of England came to be regarded in Wales as an alien Church and, as such, Welsh disestablishment became an issue of national significance within British politics (Morgan 1980 [1963]: 68). Despite efforts to promote a disestablishment bill in 1895 (Morgan 1995 [1966]: 160), the actual disestablishment of the Church in Wales did not became law until 1914 under the Asquith government. However, it has been argued that its nationalist significance was mitigated by the fact that the social and economic climate of the day had changed beyond recognition since the demand originally surfaced (Morgan 1995 [1966]: 162–3).

To what extent, therefore, can we describe the Liberal Party during this period as advocators of a Welsh nationalist discourse? Their support of policies that would testify to the distinctiveness of Wales, the Welsh people and the Welsh nation would seem to suggest that they were nationalist in outlook, at least in relatively loose terms. At the same time:

> Welsh Liberals did not advocate separation from Great Britain. Welsh Liberals were radicals in the sense that they sought equality of status for Welshmen and for Wales within the British system . . . Wales identified as a distinct entity which deserved separate treatment from the British parliament . . . by dovetailing Welsh programs [sic] with the broader aims of Liberalism . . . Succeeding Welsh nationalists did not hesitate to refer to that precedent to bolster their arguments that Wales had special needs in regard to education and disestablishment which demanded parliamentary attention or even the devolution of administrative and legislative power (Combes 1977: 68–71).

It is important to bear in mind that UK territorial politics was dominated by the question of home-rule for Ireland at this point in time. Indeed, it can be said at this time that the national questions of Wales and Ireland were more closely linked than the Wales/Scotland comparisons, which would only become apparent a century later. During the late nineteenth century, Ireland offered for Wales the template of a set of social, cultural and economic demands resembling a coherent national 'programme' (Morgan 1980 [1963]: 68). The Welsh Parliamentary Party had been influenced by the existence of Parnell's Irish Home-Rule party and the Cymru Fydd group of Liberal MPs sought unsuccessfully to graft the Irish-originated demand of political home-rule onto the Welsh Liberal Party agenda. In this regard, the most fundamental contribution of Liberal political tradition in Wales was the promotion within Welsh national discourse of the idea that Wales was a political territory, which possessed an incomplete set of modern institutions. In addition, and more subtly, the Liberal era also led to the affirmation within Welsh nationalist discourse of certain popular definitions and perceptions concerning the character of Welsh nationalism and their purported political significance. Formally, Welsh Liberal policies were applicable to the whole population of Wales. However, the informal assumptions deployed in order to attain these policies were of a more exclusive character, borrowing heavily on nonconformist or even anti-Anglican religious sentiment. It has been argued that the broader legacy of this tendency is the persistence, at the end of the twentieth century, of 'ethnic' factors such as birthplace and language as common indicators of national identity in Wales (Jones and Trystan 1999). In more spatial terms, the legacy of the Liberal Party's nationalist discourse is also reflected in particular geographical imaginations concerning the territories and border of the Welsh nation.

Plaid Cymru: the national party of Wales

Plaid Cymru was a by-product of nationalist disaffection with the Liberal Party in Wales. The source of this discontent lay in the Liberals' failure to legislate for Welsh political home-rule. Whilst the Cymru Fydd lobby group of Welsh Liberal MPs had made this an explicit aim, it became clear that the most pressing Welsh nationalist demands had been successfully accommodated by the raft of Welsh Liberal policies described above. Home-rule only served as a divisive issue within the group of Welsh Liberals, and foundered on the vehement opposition of influential south Wales industrialists. It was as a result of this tension that a group of Welsh intellectuals concluded that a new party, independent of the main British parties, should begin to campaign for 'Dominion Status' for Wales within the British Commonwealth (John Davies 2000: 3; Davies 1983). On the constitutional issue alone, it can be said that Plaid Cymru has promoted a fairly consistent nationalist

discourse to the present day, with self-government seemingly condi-
tional upon the existence of membership of an external organization
such as the British Commonwealth or, subsequently, the European
Union. At the same time, Plaid Cymru has been willing to campaign for
and co-operate with Welsh institutions within the UK state, whose aims
have fallen short of demanding Welsh national sovereignty or independence. As such, Plaid Cymru's approach has important theoretical ramifications. It has been stated that 'Wales must be the only place where one
regularly hears nationalists denouncing nationalism' (Nairn 1977: 214).
In this light, Plaid Cymru should be regarded as an integral and
component part of a broader-based form of nationalism that encom-
passes the role of other political parties and a wider civic society in
Wales.

The party has campaigned since 1925 on a platform of national
self-government and a commitment to safeguard the language and
culture of Wales (McAllister 2001). For much of its period in existence,
the party was somewhat of an irrelevance within British parliamentary
politics. Although some electoral support was gained, most notably for
Saunders Lewis' candidature in the University of Wales seat in 1931
(where he gained 17.9 per cent of the votes), and although the number of
seats that the party fought had doubled by 1945, Plaid Cymru struggled
to make a meaningful electoral breakthrough (McAllister 2001: 97). The
immediate post-war period witnessed more heartening electoral results
for the party, particularly in the Ogmore and Aberdare by-elections, and
this was followed by the 1959 general election in which Plaid Cymru
succeeded in enhancing its political profile and support substantially.
Twenty candidates managed to poll 77,571 votes (Williams 1982: 161)
and this result was viewed by many prominent figures in Plaid Cymru
as a 'turning point' in the party's electoral fortunes (e.g. Phil Williams,
quoted in McAllister 2001: 112). Further impetus was provided in the
1960s by a series of events. First, Plaid Cymru's organization consoli-
dated, albeit slowly, under the auspices of Gwynfor Evans during this
period (McAllister 2001: 62–72). Second, the party's political demands
were energized by a number of milestone events during the course of the
1960s. The first of these was the Tryweryn Valley incident. The damming
and flooding of this north Wales valley provoked feelings of democratic
deficit in Wales, as most of the territory's MPs had voted against the plan
in parliament. The fact that the valley was an indigenous Welsh-
speaking area strengthened connections between the self-government
and Welsh language campaigns. The second key event was the important intellectual statement made by Saunders Lewis in 1962, in his

Tynged yr Iaith (fate of the language) BBC Radio lecture (Lewis 1962). It was argued by Lewis that the decline of the Welsh language was such that 'revolutionary methods' were now required in order to stem the decline and that 'the language is more important than self-government' (Lewis 1962: 32). The Welsh language came to represent the overriding political priority for many Plaid Cymru activists, thus adding another dimension to the relationship between the campaigns for the Welsh language and for political self-government for the territory of Wales (McAllister 2001: 104–6). Third and, perhaps most important, was the political success experienced by Plaid Cymru in winning the Carmarthen seat in a by-election in 1966. McAllister (2001: 114–15) has rightly noted that this victory led to a 'substantial transformation of both Plaid's self-image, and the way in which the other parties perceived it'. Williams (1982: 164), too, has argued that the 1966 result represented the beginning of a period of 'political maturity' for the party since it 'was no longer a cultural-political pressure group outside the established political system' (see also Combs 1977: 246–7).

After 1966, Plaid Cymru can be said to have adopted aspects of both a political party and a pressure group in terms of demand formation and articulation (Mitchell 1996; McAllister 2001: 93–111). In the two General Elections of 1974, Dafydd Wigley and Dafydd Ellis-Thomas established electoral strongholds for Plaid Cymru in the north-western constituencies of Caernarfon and Merionnydd respectively. During the 1974–9 parliament, Plaid Cymru's three MPs occupied a pivotal bargaining position at a time of minority Labour government. We might even go as far as to describe Plaid Cymru in this period as the most successful parliamentary grouping from Wales since the Welsh Liberal era, at least in terms of gaining a series of tangible policy outputs targeted specifically at Wales (Wigley 1992). The development of the Welsh Office and its affiliated agencies between 1966 and 1979 can be said to have been, at least in part, a direct response to the electoral threat posed by Plaid Cymru. Specific examples of this threat occurred during the final weeks of the minority Callaghan Labour administration, after the failed devolution referendums in 1979. Plaid Cymru secured a number of specific policy pledges from Labour in return for Plaid support on the government's impending vote of confidence (John Davies 2000: 11). The most symbolic policy concession was the promise of a Welsh language television station, which both main British parties had adopted in their manifestos for the 1979 General Election. The Thatcher government's subsequent refusal to implement the promised policy led to an emotive and successful campaign by Plaid Cymru and Cymdeithas yr Iaith

Gymraeg, including the threat of a hunger strike by Gwynfor Evans (John Davies 2000: 12).

For the most part, however, Plaid Cymru can be described as a fringe player in Welsh politics during the period 1979–99 (J. B. Jones 1997). The heavy defeat for Labour's devolution proposals in the 1979 referendum was widely understood as a defeat for Welsh nationalism per se. For much of this period, Plaid Cymru never posed a serious threat outside their five 'heartland' constituencies in Welsh speaking Wales (J. B. Jones 1997; R. Davies 1999). And yet, Plaid Cymru has emerged in recent years as a genuine electoral force in Wales after the formation of the National Assembly for Wales. Most significantly, Plaid Cymru won three seats from Labour in the former south Wales coalfield. The key to Plaid Cymru's success resided in a popular perception that, in the new Welsh electoral context, it most appropriately represented the new Welsh interest, regardless of how ill-defined that Welsh interest actually was. No doubt, Plaid Cymru did benefit from internal discord within the Labour Party, and from public discontent within certain Labour-led local government administrations. However, the nature of Plaid Cymru's new appeal seemed to reflect, in some ways, that of the old Liberal Party in Wales. Namely, a broad appeal to various interests across a swathe of rural Wales and the south Wales coalfield. On this basis, Plaid Cymru could appeal effectively to former coalmining constituencies as it had previously done in rural seats. In 1999 Plaid Cymru gained seventeen seats in the new sixty-seat National Assembly and thus became the largest opposition party.

And yet, the narrative that we have provided above can give the impression of far-too-simple rise to political prominence for Plaid Cymru. We want to refer briefly to one particular challenge that faces Plaid Cymru as the main promoters of nationalist discourse within contemporary Wales. Significantly, the challenge is based upon the geographical disparities that exist in Wales and the way in which these are manifest in the internal tensions within the Party. Viewed in isolation, there is no reason why the demand for political self-government, and electoral or emotional support for Plaid Cymru, should be more popular in some parts of Wales than in others. However, the process of self-government for Wales is not an isolated issue. Welsh self-government has been bound up with wider considerations of culture, language and locality, making it a contentious and 'value-laden' issue in all parts of Wales. Moreover, the priorities and political campaigns of Plaid Cymru have added further sets of ideas and connotations to popular perceptions of the meaning of self-government in Wales. The most important aspect to be considered in this respect is the relationship between political self-government and the future of the Welsh language (John Davies 2000: 4). Moreover, the party's leaders and activists have viewed the language, more often than not, as an urgent policy priority. It is for this reason that contemporary political commentators continue to refer to Plaid Cymru electoral 'heartlands' of the west and north-western Wales, thus suggesting an implicit political boundary that runs largely co-terminus with the limits of those areas where Welsh is regarded as the first language. The existence of the internal tension within Plaid Cymru is also reflected in the Party's continual efforts to rebrand itself in recent years as it has changed its title from 'Plaid Cymru' to 'Plaid Cymru: the Party of Wales' to merely 'Plaid'. Many of these changes allude to the Party's perceived need to reach out to an English-speaking electorate living outside the Welsh heartland but there is a danger that such changes may well serve to alienate the party's traditional core vote. In this regard, there is some tentative evidence that the Party has not been altogether successful in marketing its new-found identity. The Party's heavy losses at the 2003 National Assembly elections heralded a new period of crisis for the party. Its losses to Labour in the south Wales valleys were politically poignant and it remains to be seen whether Plaid Cymru will be able to refloat itself, again, as a credible prospective government of Wales.

Cymdeithas yr Iaith Gymraeg

We noted above that one key incident that helped to energize the Welsh nationalist movement during the 1960s was the broadcast of Saunders Lewis' lecture on the 'Fate of the Language'. The meaning of Saunders' Lewis demand for 'revolutionary methods' that would save the Welsh language from extinction was interpreted in different ways (Phillips 1998: 305–6). The immediate response was the formation, in 1963, of Cymdeithas yr Iaith Gymraeg (the Welsh Language Society), who advocated a strictly non-violent repertoire of direct political action in order to gain bilingualism within public sector agencies in Wales (ibid: 236–41). We do not want to describe in detail the processes and events that facilitated the formation of Cymdeithas yr Iaith since these issues form the basis for much of the discussion in the following chapter. Rather, we want to discuss briefly the contribution that Cymdeithas yr Iaith has made to the production of Welsh nationalist discourse since its establishment during the 1960s. In this respect, our account is dependent upon

Phillips' (1998) thorough history of the organization, as well as the semi-autobiographical descriptions of the Society's history written by Cynog Dafis (Davies 1973) and John Davies (1976).

For much of its early period in existence, it is clear that nationalist politics – thought of in terms of a political desire for self-government – were of little concern to Cymdeithas yr Iaith. During this early period, the Society was, in effect, a single-issue campaign movement that sought to increase the status of the Welsh language within the public administration and the legal system within Wales. As we show in the following chapter, it was such sentiments that underpinned the Society's first campaigns to increase the use of the Welsh language in court summonses, in road signs and in other forms of governmental correspondence and documentation. During this early period, Cymdeithas yr Iaith could be considered as a nationalist organization only in implicit terms. It was far more concerned with the fate of the Welsh language than it was with the broader sweep of nationalist politics. Phillips (1998: 145–55) has elaborated, however, on the way in which Cymdeithas yr Iaith's policy agenda evolved during the late 1960s and early 1970s as it gradually transformed into an organization possessing a viewpoint on a range of different issues pertaining to Wales and the Welsh language. It is through this realignment and broadening of its policy interests that Cymdeithas yr Iaith emerged as an organization that was explicitly concerned with nationalist issues. The most potent symbol of this shift came with the publication of the Society's Manifesto during the early 1970s (Cymdeithas yr Iaith 1972). Although the Manifesto's main aim was to chart a way of preserving the Welsh language, its various policies were predicated on an alternative nationalist vision of Wales. In this way, the Society advocated the need to promote the official use of the Welsh language in: courts of law, central and local government; trade, business and advertisements; in education and media in Wales. In addition, it argued for the need to protect those communities in which Welsh was spoken habitually (Phillips 1998: 145).

Importantly, many of the Society's manifesto pledges and policies – not least the final one referred to above – reflected a geographical tension that we have already referred to in this chapter. Specifically, the Society's policies sought to protect a Welsh-speaking heartland from further social and cultural erosion as well as reaching out to secure the linguistic future of a broader Wales. The Society, at one level, believed that there was a dire need to focus attention on the needs of a Welsh-speaking heartland. The clearest reflection of this type of attitude is to be found in the Society's Manifesto, published in 1972 (Cymdeithas yr Iaith

1972: 18). It is stated here that *'cefn gwlad Gymraeg yn ganolog bwysig yn awr i sicrhau goroesiad yr iaith*/a Welsh countryside is now of a central importance for the survival of the language'. Similar thoughts appeared in the more unofficial literatures produced by the Society and its members. Owain Owain, leader of the Bangor cell of Cymdeithas yr Iaith and founder of *Tafod y Ddraig* (which would later become the Society's newsletter at the national scale), for instance, highlighted the importance of *y Fro Gymraeg*, stating that 'the language's revival must be based on its continuance there as the main normal daily medium of communication' (Davies 1973: 252). Dafydd Iwan (*Y Faner* 1969), too, could state unequivocally as follows:

> *Ni ellir ysgaru iaith oddi wrth y gymdeithas y mae'n gyfrwng iddi. Nid rhywbeth i'w hystyried ar ei phen ei hun yw iaith, ond rhan annatod o wead cymdeithas gyflawn. Nid brwydro dros yr iaith Gymraeg er ei mwyn ei hun yr ydym ni . . . eithr brwydro dros hanfod y bywyd Cymraeg.*

> [A language cannot be divorced from the society that acts as its medium. A language is not something to consider in and of itself, but rather as an integral part of the fabric of the whole society. We are not fighting for the Welsh language for her own sake . . . rather fighting for the essence of the Welsh way of life.]

As Davies and Phillips rightly note, such a position found intellectual justification in the writings, among others, of J. R. Jones. His account of *Prydeindod* (Britishness), for instance, drew attention to the strong normative and moral connections between the Welsh language, the land of Wales and its people (Jones 1966). The rural communities of Wales were seen to occupy an immensely significant position within this broader emphasis on the 'inter-penetration of land and language' (Davies 1973: 255). What helped to illustrate the significance of these rural communities for the Welsh nation for many Welsh nationalists was the sustained period of linguistic decline that had been experienced by them over the twentieth century, and which had drawn the lifeblood out of the Welsh nation. The philosopher J. R. Jones (1970: 81–2, quoted in Jenkins and Williams 2000: 15) described the process as

> the experience of knowing, not that you are leaving your country, but that your country is leaving you, is ceasing to exist under your very feet, being sucked away from you, as it were by a rapacious swallowing wind, into the hands and possession of another country and civilization.

At the same time, the Society was well aware of the need to demonstrate the significance and importance of the Welsh language for the whole of the territory of Wales and not just a proportion of it. The

Society, from the early 1960s onwards, had already been engaged in a series of protests and campaigns dotted throughout the whole of the territory of Wales. These practices reflected a deeper commitment to ensuring the re-integration of the Welsh language into the social and cultural fabric of the whole of Wales. The Society's manifesto in the early 1970s (Cymdeithas yr Iaith 1972: 25), for instance, boldly asserted that

Na foed i neb ... gredu mai â'r 'ardaloedd Cymraeg' yn unig y mae a wnelo Cymdeithas yr Iaith. Priod iaith Cymru gyfan yw'r Gymraeg.

[Let no one believe that Cymdeithas yr Iaith is only concerned with the 'Welsh areas'. Welsh is the appropriate language of the whole of Wales.]

Individual members claimed a similar need for the Society to engage with the linguistic politics of the whole of Wales. Dafydd Iwan, for instance, whose earlier quote illustrated his commitment to securing the linguistic future of Welsh-speaking communities, could also maintain that he did not want to see a situation in which the boundary of Wales was re-drawn at the Pumlumon range of mountains (quoted in Phillips 1998: 151). The Society, therefore, viewed the whole of the Welsh territory as one that was relevant to the linguistic integrity of Wales.

In more recent years, the Society has sought to formalize a range of different policies with regard to the Welsh language. Its two main policy planks for much of this period have focused on the need for a Welsh Property Act and a new Welsh Language Act. The Society's demands for a Welsh Property Act is based on Saunders Lewis' premise that the Welsh language must be protected in those communities where it is spoken on a habitual basis (see Cymdeithas yr Iaith Gymraeg 1999; Cymdeithas yr Iaith Gymraeg Planning-Economic Group 1989). The Society states that its key aims within the most recent proposed Property Act are to apply 'an element of control over the housing and property market in order to meet the housing needs of the people of Wales', to safeguard the 'sustainability of Welsh communities and the Welsh language' and to 'safeguard the environment' (Cymdeithas yr Iaith Gymraeg 2005a: 7). The proposed Property Act, therefore, seeks to establish formal means through which Welsh-speaking communities can be protected from further erosion through insensitive housing developments and, presumably, additional in-migration into rural Wales. In many ways, such statements echo broader arguments that have been made concerning the symbolic significance of a national territory, along with national landscapes, within nationalist discourse (e.g. Anderson 1988; Williams and Smith 1983).

The Society's calls for a new Welsh Language Act were made in response to the perceived weaknesses of the Welsh Language Act of 1993 (see Welsh Language Board 2000). The 1993 Act was deemed to be insufficient by the Society in that the Welsh Language Board that implements the terms of the Act is merely an advisory body and does not possess the capacity to be able to force public bodies to comply with the requirements of the Act. In the second place, the Board and the Act does not apply to private institutions operating in Wales. More generally, even though the Act seeks to promote the equality of Welsh and English in Wales in principle, the application of this principle was only to occur in appropriate circumstances that were 'reasonably practical' (Williams and Morris 2000: 172). As a result of these perceived weaknesses, the Society has called for a new Welsh Language Act (Cymdeithas yr Iaith Gymraeg 2005b), which would:

> recognize the unique position of Welsh as the indigenous language of Wales; provide Welsh with official status; establish the Welsh language's right to survive as a living community language and define basic language rights that will enable the people of Wales to use Welsh in all aspects of life; make it illegal to discriminate against the use of Welsh; confer a responsibility to provide commodities, facilities, information and services in Welsh on the provider(s) – in accordance with the rights of the recipient – regardless of the status of the provider(s); establish the role and office of Comisiynydd y Gymraeg (Welsh Language Commissioner); establish Cyngor i'r Gymraeg (National Council for the Welsh language) as a democratic and inclusive consultation body.

Once again, there seems to be somewhat of a geographical tension within the Society's recent policies, which reflect long-standing themes within Welsh nationalist discourse concerning the place of the Welsh nation. While the proposed New Language Act alludes to the need to support the Welsh language throughout the whole of Wales, the proposed Property Act is predominantly geared more towards securing the future of the Welsh language and culture in certain parts of Wales only. These important themes concerning the sometimes contradictory geographical imaginations that are contained within Welsh nationalist discourse are taken up at greater length in Chapter 7. Significantly, debates concerning the appropriate location of a Welsh culture and nation have contributed in recent years to the establishment of new organization, which has promoted a far more exclusively ethnic version of Welsh nationalism. The establishment of Cymuned, along with its distinctive Welsh nationalist discourse, is discussed next.

Cymuned and the re-emergence of a Welsh ethnic nationalism

The Cymuned pressure group is a very recent development in Welsh nationalism. Formed as recently as 2001, Cymuned can already boast a quote from the *Rough Guide to Wales*: 'Cymuned is slick, modern and thoughtful, and could well prove to be the intellectual driving force for modern Welsh nationalism' (Rough Guides 2003: 524–5). Cymuned was formed out of a melange of debates during the spring and summer of 2001 and we discuss these themes at length in Chapter 7. The circumstances that led to the establishment of Cymuned, to be brief, ranged from a radio interview conducted with Seimon Glyn in January 2001, Ieuan Wyn Jones' indecisive response to the questioning of Jonathan Dimbleby and Glenys Kinnock on the BBC's Question Time programme, a series of informal meetings held in various pubs in Aberystwyth and Tal-y-bont, Ceredigion between February and May 2001, and a range of statements and incidents centred around the National Eisteddfod of that year. Although Cymuned is a pressure group, it is clear that it has been successful in engaging effectively with the political process in post-devolution Wales. So, despite deciding in one of its early meetings that it should *not* aim to become a political party (Cymuned 2001: para 2.1), Cymuned's outspoken stance on in-migration threatened to severely destabilize Plaid Cymru. The 'Seimon Glyn' episode precipitated a series of internal problems for the leadership of Plaid Cymru, as well as electoral losses at local, National Assembly and Westminster levels. By 2004, Cymuned members formed the vanguard of the Llais Ceredigion (Voice of Ceredigion) party, formed specifically to fight the local elections in that county. Llais Ceredigion failed to make any electoral inroads and appears to have disappeared as an entity. The failure of Llais Ceredigion also destabilized Cymuned. At the time of writing, Cymuned has regrouped under new leadership and is maintaining a stable, if somewhat tangential presence on the Welsh nationalist scene.

We do not provide too much detail on Cymuned's ideological stance in this chapter since this theme is taken up at length in Chapter 7. Rather we offer a brief appraisal of those nationalist discourses that have emanated from both Cymuned in recent years. In this regard, we would argue that the emergence of Cymuned as a lobby group for Welsh-speaking areas of Wales has been one of the most remarkable developments of post-devolution Welsh politics. And yet, it is clear that Cymuned is still seeking to formulate a consistent approach within its nationalist discourse. In fact, there appear to be a number of co-existing strands of theory within Cymuned's early ideological composition.

Jones (2001a: 10) described the unorthodox ideological composition of the language movement, as it was emerging in 2001:

> The new language movement which, in three short months, has developed into such a prominent part of our public life, is something of a mixed bag. It contains fairly disparate elements ranging from the post-modern to the pre-Cambrian, and from the sophisticated to the less than enlightened.

This mixed ideological make-up was also acknowledged up by Cymuned's most prominent spokesperson, Simon Brooks (2002: 10), when he stated that 'its politics are a peculiar hybrid of the anticolonial logic of the radical nationalist left, and community conservatism'. Furthermore, Brooks (ibid: 11) observed other geographical and social differences between Cymuned and their predecessors:

> Despite its hinterland in the world of academia, Cymuned is not merely an exercise in language ideology. It also has deep roots in real communities. Where Cymdeithas yr Iaith has tended to be a movement of student radicals based on the university towns, Cymuned has its real support in the countryside and small urban centres.

Thus far, therefore, Cymuned have not espoused a specific and formalized ideology. For example, there is nothing in Cymuned's formal documents to compare with Plaid Cymru's constitutional aim of decentralist socialism. In order to uncover Cymuned's variegated nationalist discourse, we must turn instead to a series of informal discussion papers and journal articles produced in the period 2001–4. These contributions demonstrate that Cymuned is a pressure group based primarily on the defence of a self-ascribed ethnic identity (Welsh speaking), rather than a national identity (Welsh). This observation is based on an interesting series of dichotomies. Brooks (2001), for instance, promotes an explicit dichotomy between two 'ethno-linguistic' groups in Wales: Welsh-speakers, and English-speakers. At first glance, this seems an unremarkable, empirical observation. However, the statement gains extra significance when viewed through the lens of the wider context of Welsh nationalist discourse. It is unlikely that any mainstream political leader in Wales has made this dichotomy explicit, and brought it to the fore of political debate. A subsequent dichotomy focused upon the future complexion of Welsh nationalism and this is where we witness Cymuned's effort to distinguish its more exclusive nationalist discourse from the more inclusive and civic version of nationalism espoused by Plaid Cymru. Plaid Cymru is criticized for adhering to a 'civic' model of nationalism which has, allegedly, systematically underplayed the importance of Welsh language issues since 1997. Brooks (2001: 6) argues for

instance, that 'in my opinion, the exclusive promotion of civic nationalism is wrong, immoral and damning to the continuation of a national
minority such as the Welsh-speakers'. He reinforced such an opinion
when he stated that 'we will have to argue that the idea of civil society,
in its current guise, militates against our existence as Welsh speakers'
(ibid: 8).

In summary, Cymuned's nationalist discourse is predicated on an
ethnic vision of Welshness, which is something that is totally at odds
with the pragmatic, civic nationalism presented over the years by Plaid
Cymru (and, nominally, Cymdeithas yr Iaith). The position was summed
up clearly by the renowned writer Jan Morris (2003: 4) in the first edition
of Cymuned's newsletter, *Gwreiddiau*:

> Politically ... 'nationalism' will be stone dead before too long ... But
> culturally, it is a different story. In Wales ... is it not the case that by now
> the only point of belonging to a nation is to safeguard a way of life, a way
> of thinking, a tradition and a language? ... And in this regard, there will
> be room for a kind of nationalism. Cultural nationalism ... This is how I
> view Cymuned: it is not exactly nationalistic.

One key way in which this exclusive and ethnic nationalist discourse
is articulated is through reference to ideas of colonization and colonialism. Webb (2001), for instance, describes colonization as a force which
'... destroys and replaces languages, cultures, communities and
nations'. Colonization, in this way, can occur in three different forms,
through: the 'negative attitude' of incomers; an influx of 'greater numbers than can be absorbed' into the community; the 'forced' removal of
natives from their land. Each of these different processes ultimately has
the same effect on a given community. Webb (2001) cites two reasons
why 'colonization' should be opposed in Welsh-speaking communities.
First, he argues the Welsh language 'heartlands' are the only places in
which Welsh remains a majority language and, as such, they should be
preserved. Second, and more subjectively, he argues that colonization is
'immoral' since it is a form of 'theft' whose end result is 'ethnocide',
which is a 'crime' against humanity. These ideas are important since they
reflect the underlying currents of the more exclusive form of nationalist
discourse promoted by Cymuned in recent years, namely the need to
construct the Welsh nation as a Welsh-speaking one, which must be
protected at all costs. The debates generated by such assertions form the
substance of the discussion in Chapter 7.

In this section we have sought to chart the different discourses that
have existed within Welsh the nationalist movement over the past 150

years. It becomes apparent, in this regard, that Welsh nationalist discourse has been very varied in character, as one might expect. The themes emphasized within Welsh nationalist discourse have varied over time with the importance of nonconformity during the late nineteenth century, for instance, giving way to linguistic concerns during the twentieth century. Even during the same time period, it is clear that the exact contours of Welsh nationalist discourse have varied between different kinds of nationalist organization. As we shall see in the following chapters of this book, there is even a case to argue that Welsh nationalist discourse has varied from one individual to the next. Finally, it is evident that issues relating to geography have helped to contribute to the variegated character exhibited by Welsh nationalist discourse. Certain places more than others, for instance, have informed the geographical imagination that helps to structure Welsh nationalist discourse. At the same time, we have also seen how different places have played various roles in the reproduction of Welsh nationalist discourse and practice. Such a theme is explored at length in the following section, in which we begin to elaborate both on the significance of Aberystwyth for the reproduction of Welsh nationalism and on the important role played by particular locations in the town within this process.

SPACES OF NATIONALISM IN ABERYSTWYTH

Aberystwyth is located on the west coast of Wales and is a town with a population of approximately 15,000 people (see Plates 3.1 and 3.2). It was originally a relatively small port and market town and, with its connection to a rail network during the nineteenth century, subsequently became a fashionable Victorian resort town. Although tourism remains important within the town, its economy is now largely based on public sector employment. The relatively small size of the town, however, belies its significance in the political, cultural and social life of Wales. This elevated status is due, in part, to the location of two important institutions within the town, namely the University of Wales, Aberystwyth and the National Library of Wales. Indeed, the town is dominated by the University in particular: over 8,000 students study in Aberystwyth and the institution employs over 1,000 people locally. The mixing of people facilitated by the University and the National Library has given the town and the surrounding county somewhat of cosmopolitan feel leading it to be described commonly as a 'microcosm' of the whole of Wales. The town has served too as an important location for the development of various nationalist organizations, such as Plaid Cymru, Cymdeithas yr Iaith Gymraeg and Cymuned. In addition, it has been the location of the headquarters of a large number of other organizations, whose existence testifies to the distinctiveness of Wales as a political and cultural territory, including: the Welsh Books Council; the Urdd (the Welsh Youth League); the Farmer's Union of Wales; Merched y Wawr (the Welsh equivalent of the Women's Institute); Mudiad Ysgolion Meithrin (the charity established to promote Welsh-medium pre-school education in Wales; the Welsh Learner's Council; UCAC (the Union of Welsh Schoolteachers). As such, Aberystwyth can lay claim to being a key site for nationalist organizations of different hues – and, relatedly, of the generation of nationalist discourse, broadly conceived – in Wales since the 1960s. These various organizations have provided official spaces in Aberystwyth within which Welsh nationalist discourse of different kinds has been produced and circulated. But in addition to these more formal spaces, we may also note the existence of alternative and more informal 'spaces of nationalism' within the town and its environs, from small business enterprizes to rooms in the houses of individual protagonists. For the remainder of this section, we hand over the bulk of the commentary to the interviewees of our project. We feel that the interviewees' experiences during the past few decades convey in a more lucid and colourful manner the significance of particular places, organizations and networks of people for the reproduction of Welsh nationalist discourse within.

Many of our interviewees drew attention to the importance of the University as a space within which nationalist discourse could foment. Gwilym ab Ioan, who defected from Plaid Cymru to set up Llais Ceredigion in 2004, argued that the University and the National Library had given a cultural 'balance' to the town. He maintained further that had it not been for the two institutions 'Aberystwyth would have been a completely English town in character'. Ellen ap Gwynn, a Plaid Cymru councillor who has lived in the Aberystwyth area since her student days in the 1960s, concurred that the University 'ensured that a strong nucleus of Welsh speaking nationalists has been present . . . it's as if the town attracts them back . . . it's like a spiritual home'. In many ways, such sentiments echo the broader work that has been conducted on the significance of education systems for the reproduction of both a national elite and the nationalist discourses that they purvey (Gellner 1983; Burgess and Hyvik 2004). But the University has a further significance in that it also creates new generations of nationalist activists who are, over time, able to cross over into the non-academic nationalist politics of the town proper. One long-standing language campaigner, 'Rocet' Arwel Jones, suggests that the tendency has been for students to slowly emerge from their undergraduate and postgraduate studies and emerge into the social circles of the town. As well as impacting on the politics of place within the town, the University was also said to have contributed, in direct ways, to the emergence of nationalist sentiment throughout Wales. The historian John Davies told us that the development of education was the 'second main story' of modern Wales, second only to the development of the south Wales coalfield. He added that 'there would not have been a national revival in Wales had it not been for Aberystwyth College' and that as home to the first college of the University of Wales, Aberystwyth possessed the main symbol of educational renewal in Wales.

The other key national, if not nationalist, organization located within the town, the National Library of Wales, was also discussed at length by our interviewees. Jane Aaron, a professor at the University of Glamorgan who had also been on the fringes of Cymdeithas yr Iaith Gymraeg in Aberystwyth, highlighted the fact that around 250 high quality jobs were located in the National Library. She argued that 'many of these jobs will be associated with the Welsh language or culture. These people live in the town. Of course, this adds a lot to the town's Welshness, and to cultural awareness in the town'. Enid Gruffudd, who has been involved in Welsh nationalist politics within Aberystwyth and Ceredigion over the long term, argued that 'the National Library of Wales has not been important to me personally' but that 'many of the Welsh middle and upper classes' live in Aberystwyth because of the Library's existence and, as a result, were said to 'enrich' the local society. In a similar way to the University, therefore, the National Library of Wales was described as an organization that was able to reach out and enrich social, cultural and political life within the town.

Hitherto, we have concentrated our attention on the dynamic of two elite institutions in Aberystwyth: the University of Wales and the National Library of Wales. But, as we have already noted, other organizations have made Aberystwyth their institutional home. These smaller institutions tell us as much about the complexion of Welsh nationalism as the grander institutions already discussed. Most of the smaller institutions have been concerned with Welsh nationalism in the 'small-n' sense (Calhoun 1997; Smith 1998) or, in other words, nationalism as a means of enhancing the culture, values and traditions of the Welsh nation. Most of these organizations have an educational dimension, and all of them embody Welsh as their official internal language of communication. In our interviews, various respondents emphasized the importance of the following institutions having their official headquarters in Aberystwyth: Merched y Wawr, a Welsh-speaking counterpoint to the Women's Institute; the Farmers' Union of Wales, which was set up in response to the perception that the National Farmers' Union was in hoc to the interests of south-east England; UCAC, which was formed as a union for Welsh speaking teachers (Williams 1991), and shares a building with Cymdeithas yr Iaith Gymraeg on the Aberystwyth promenade; the Welsh learners' society, Cymdeithas y Dysgwyr, which was initially formed in Aberystwyth and now has a branch structure covering the whole of Wales; the Welsh language playgroup movement, Mudiad Ysgol Meithrin, which also has its headquarters in the town.

Perhaps the most intriguing of these 'quasi-nationalist' organizations is Urdd Gobaith Cymru (Welsh Guild of Youth) (see Griffith 1971–3) . The Urdd was formed in 1922 and its motto still pledges its allegiance in 'Wales, mankind and Christ'. In the context of devolution, Urdd Gobaith Cymru is distant from political parties of all shades. However, some of our respondents recalled a previous era when the Urdd was, informally, part and parcel of the networks of people and organizations that would reproduce nationalist discourse in the town. Lili Thomas was our oldest interviewee and perhaps the individual with the longest association with Plaid Cymru in Aberystwyth. She outlined her view of the link between educational groups, such as the Urdd, and the political nationalist 'movement':

> Rownd i bob mudiad mae gynnoch chi grwp o bobl ond oes e. A rheini'n ddylanwadol ... Grwpiau addysg Gymraeg. Wedi'r cwbl, yn Aberystwyth ffurfiwyd yr Ysgol Gymraeg gyntaf, yma yn Lluest. A'r cysylltiad rhwng hynny a'r Urdd, ac mae'r Urdd wedi dylanwadu'n fawr iawn ar Aberystwyth dwi'n meddwl. Nid dim ond y staff, ond y ffaith bod pobl ifanc yn arfer mynd yno ... fan ni oedd yr Ysgol Feithrin yn cwrdd. A mae pobl yn cysylltu'r Urdd wedyn a'r haenen 'ma o addysg ac yn y blaen.

[Around every movement, you have a group of influential people... In Aberystwyth the first Welsh School was founded, in Lluest. And so there is the connection between that, and the Urdd. I think that the Urdd has influenced a lot on Aberystwyth. Not just the staff, but the fact that the young people would attend [the Welsh school] ... and that's where the Ysgol Meithrin would meet, too. So people connect the Urdd with this layer of education.]

Other interviewees were less subtle. Plaid activist Iolo ap Gwynn remembers the Urdd as a means of 'organising' young Welsh people to socialize together. As well as enabling young people to socialize together, he maintained that the organization's other aim was to socialize these young people into the Welsh nationalist project:

> *Achos dwi'n cofio lot o'r ganeuon o'n ni'n canu, cofio'r caneuon 'Pan ddaw Cymru'n rhydd' a bob math o bethau. Hynny ydy, oedd y peth yn, cenedlaetholdeb Cymreig yn drwch drwy'r peth, ond oedd na ryw haenen barchus yn trio cuddio'r peth ond y gwir amdani oedd y pobl oedd yn gweithio yn yr Urdd oedd y pobl oedd hefyd yn gweithgar yn y Blaid ac yn y blaen. Oedd na gysylltiad agos iawn.*

> [I remember a lot of the songs we would sing – 'when Wales will be free', and all sorts of things. In other words, Welsh nationalism was present throughout the whole thing. A more respectable layer tried to hide it but the truth was that the people working in the Urdd were the people who were active in Plaid Cymru, etc. There was a very close relationship.]

In addition to these public and quasi-public agencies, we should not underestimate the important role that has been played by various private enterprizes within the town in promoting the Welsh language and a Welsh nationalist agenda (see Plate 3.3). Certain Welsh nationalists have argued for the need to revitalize the rural Welsh-speaking heartlands through the development of private enterprizes that would help to retain Welsh-speaking professionals within these areas (Davies 1973; Llewelyn 1972a; 1972b). Two private enterprizes in Aberystwyth and its environs are deserving of especial attention in this respect. Siop y Pethe is a Welsh language bookshop that has occupied a corner of the central square in the town for a number of years. Gwerfyl Pierce-Jones of the Welsh Books Council described the shop as 'more than just a shop. It was a crusade ... Welsh-language books as a focal point for Welsh language activities and that crusading spirit has continued'. The current Plaid Cymru Assembly Member for Ceredigion, Elin Jones, told us that it had become something of a 'tradition' for Plaid Cymru to set up their campaign stalls outside Siop y Pethe. She also suggested that it was a good thing for Plaid to be seen in spaces *other* than outside Siop y Pethe. This indicates that the physical space occupied by Siop y Pethe has also become invested with certain cultural and political values. The second small enterprize discussed in our interviews was the Lolfa publishers of Talybont. Although Talybont is a village several miles north of Aberystwyth, its family owners have played direct and indirect roles in the Welsh language movement in Aberystwyth and beyond. Lefi Gruffudd, son of the founder, Robat, emphasized that the employment of 'thirty people in a rural village in Ceredigion' was the fundamental economic role of Y Lolfa. He also suggested that 'by getting things to happen in the villages ... one thing can lead to another', thereby implying a more subtle cultural or political role outwith specific party political labels.

Finally, we would like to flag up the role of pubs and cafes of Aberystwyth as spaces within the town that have facilitated many significant meetings connected to Welsh nationalism. At various points in the book, mention will be made of various cafes and hostelries where meetings took place. Here, we may invest the cafes and pubs with some historical and social context. In chronological terms, it seems as if cafes acted as the first main locations that helped to ground networks of nationalists. Geraint 'Twm' Jones informed us that activists during the early 1960s 'didn't go to a pub ... but to a café, and to the upper floor of the Home Café ... We would sing and drink coffee very, very respectably. . . I'm sure that we were still in the tail end of the respectability of Welsh nonconformism'. Dafydd Iwan, President of Plaid Cymru, concurred that the Welsh-speaking society of the time was at a 'crossroads' between old (café) and new (pub) traditions. Only during the latter part of the 1960s was a 'fairly deliberate attempt made to drag the Welsh society into a new era, and new connections ... It could be seen now as an excuse to go and drink. But it was more than that.' And yet, cafes still retain a significance within the Welsh nationalist scene. According to Siôn Jobbins, a former Plaid Cymru mayor of the town and more recently a member of Cymuned, cafes are seen as a 'central' part of life in Aberystwyth. He suggested that the cafes have continued to help frame nationalist deliberations in the town:

> *Tasen i mewn cyfarfod yn Aberystwyth, boed e'n UCAC, neu Cymdeithas yr Iaith, neu Cymuned neu Plaid Cymru, Merched y Wawr ... a wedyn bydden nhw'n cwrdd yn Y Cabin am baned, wedyn neu cyn hynny, a mae rhywun yn trafod syniadau. Dyw hwnna ddim yn digwydd yn unrhywle arall yng Nghymru.*
>
> [If I was in a meeting in Aberystwyth, whether it be UCAC, Cymdeithas yr Iaith, Cymuned or Plaid Cymru, Merched y Wawr ... they would meet in The Cabin for a cuppa at some stage, and one discusses ideas. That doesn't happen anywhere else in Wales.]

Elin Jones AM also confessed to us that she had in the past used the Cabin cafe as a 'sounding board' for Plaid Cymru matters, including the question of the party's leadership. Simon Thomas, the former Plaid Cymru MP for Ceredigion, added that Aberystwyth had a 'continental' or 'cafe society' feel as a town and suggested that the Cabin cafe's location opposite the Plaid Cymru office in the town gave that establishment particular status amongst the town's cafes. Similarly, pubs and hotels in Aberystwyth have been accorded with almost mythical status in the eyes of our respondents. The Belle Vue was a popular venue for formal and informal meetings of Plaid Cymru and Cymdeithas yr Iaith Gymraeg. Latterly, the Cooper's Arms became a more informal meeting place amongst activists. The 'Cŵps', in particular, was the hub of nationalist protests against the Queen's visit to the town in 1996. In 2001, the pub was an informal centre for deliberations which led to the formation of Cymuned in 2001. Our interviews suggest that the 'Llew Du' (Black Lion) has been less of an academic/political forum and more of a meeting place for rural elements of Ceredigion's society. However, the uncertain future of the 'Cŵps' suggests that the 'Llew Du' on Bridge Street may yet become the pre-eminent pub of Welsh speaking activists.

CONCLUSIONS

In this chapter, we have attempted to chart the broad contours of Welsh nationalism over the long term. By emphasizing Calhoun's understanding of nationalism as a discourse, we acknowledge that different aspects of nationalism are subject to greater or lesser emphasis at different points in time. For example, the language was hardly a factor in the nationalism of Liberal Wales. After 1962, language became a *sine qua non* of Welsh nationalism (Phillips 1998). Conversely, religion, which was the bedrock of nationalist sentiment in the nineteenth century, had by 2000 become a negligible factor in Welsh nationalism. Differences have also been apparent when comparing the nationalist discourses of different organizations, even at the same point in time. Indeed, in many cases, it is likely that the nationalist discourse promoted by one organization has been positioned with respect to another nationalist organization. For instance, Plaid Cymru was formed as a reaction to the Liberals' perceived failure to bring political home rule to Wales. Cymdeithas yr Iaith was a reaction by student activists towards the perceived failure of electoral methods to address the decline of the Welsh language. Cymuned was formed as the result of a perceived failure by both Plaid Cymru and Cymdeithas yr Iaith to address the issue of language shift in the so-called language 'heartlands' of rural Wales. Finally, we have attempted to show how geography has been implicated in the long-term reproduction of Welsh nationalist discourse. At a general level, it is evident that particular places and areas have featured heavily within nationalist discourse, as well as being places and areas that have been crucial locations for the reproduction of nationalist discourse and practice. For much of the twentieth century, in particular, we would maintain that Aberystwyth has been one such key location for the reproduction of different kinds of nationalist discourse in Wales. The University of Wales and the National Library have been two key institutions that have helped to attract and embed a Welsh nationalist intelligentsia within the town. Other Welsh language institutions, which emerged from the 1960s onwards, had a natural home in Aberystwyth given the existing institutional framework, combined with the geographical centrality of Aberystwyth in the territory of Wales. In a more informal sense, too, we argued that Aberystwyth's heritage of cafes, hotels and pubs – part of its inheritance as a Victorian holiday destination – has provided the physical infrastructure that has enabled the town to act as a convenient 'melting pot' for ideas, deliberations and the discourse of nationalism. In this way, it may be possible argue that many of the developments that took place within the reproduction of Welsh nationalism could only have occurred as a result of the numerous contributions made by people living, working and socializing in Aberystwyth. In this respect, a large number of our respondents referred to the fact that Aberystwyth should be considered the 'unofficial capital of Wales', as a result of its 'output *deallusol*, output *gwleidyddol, a'r* stamp *[sydd] wedi ei adael ar hyd y wlad*/intellectual output, political output, and the stamp [that's] been left throughout the country'.

Our aim in this chapter has been to provide a sense of the general contours of Welsh nationalism over the long term, as well as begin to illustrate the significance of particular geographies for the reproduction of Welsh nationalist discourse over time. Our goal in the following chapters is to use this background information as a springboard from which we can proceed to show in more detail the geographies of the reproduction of Welsh nationalism in Aberystwyth.

4

Aberystwyth and a linguistic nation-making project

INTRODUCTION: THE WELSH LANGUAGE AND WELSH NATIONALISM

The preceding chapters have elaborated on the key conceptual themes that underpin the book and explored some fundamental issues relating to Welsh nationalism. It is time now to synthesize this material in a more systematic fashion through detailed empirical discussions of key facets of the group-making project of the Welsh nation and the role that the town of Aberystwyth has played within their reproduction. In this chapter, we begin by demonstrating the significant associations that have existed between the town of Aberystwyth and the linguistic nation-making project within Wales.

The Welsh language has, of course, occupied an important position within Welsh nationalist discourse over an extended time period. As far back as the Middle Ages, the Welsh language was being used as part of a group-making project in order to signal the distinctiveness of the Welsh people when compared with their English neighbours. There exist many sources of evidence for the appearance of this Welsh *ethnie*, none so stirring as the statement given by the client lords of Llywelyn ap Gruffudd, the Prince of Wales, to the Norman Crown in 1282 (Martin 1884: 470–1; Richter 1978: 40):

> even if the prince would hand over their seisin [lordship] to the king, they
> were not willing to pay homage to a foreigner whose language, laws and
> customs were altogether unknown to them.

This is not the time to enter into a debate about whether such sentiments should be viewed as an early instance of Welsh nationalist discourse or merely as an example of a looser kind of ethnic identity (on this broader note, see Reynolds 1984; Jones 1999). What it does show is that an elite during the thirteenth century was using the Welsh language as a way of defining a Welsh identity in opposition to that of England.

Subsequent centuries also witnessed other attempts to enrol the Welsh language within a group-building project (for a review, see Jones 1973). The sixteenth and seventeenth centuries, for instance, were a period during which the Welsh language came under a series of interrelated threats. The Acts of Union of 1536 and 1542 relegated the Welsh language to an official secondary status within Wales. Linked to this change in status was a gradual shift in the linguistic and cultural mindsets of a large proportion of the indigenous Welsh gentry as they began to engage increasingly with the English language and culture (see Jones 1992). Partly in response to such changes, others during the same period sought to reaffirm the distinctiveness and value of the Welsh language. Welsh humanist scholars based on the continent, such as Gruffydd Robert and Sion Dafydd Rhys, for instance, published books on Welsh grammar. For the latter, 'there [was] no better way or means in the world of preserving a language from loss than preparing a grammar for and of it' (quoted in Jones 1997: 146).[1] Closer to home, too, William Salesbury published a Welsh-English Dictionary in 1547. As Jones (1997: 142–8) has noted, the actions of these individuals should not be viewed as instances of purely linguistic interest. Rather, their actions must be viewed, at least in part, as efforts to promote the Welsh language as a symbol of the distinctiveness of Wales and the Welsh people. A further illustration of the significance of the Welsh language for Welsh nationalism project can be found in the context of the controversy surrounding the use of the Welsh language in the education system in Wales during the nineteenth century (see Chapter 3). Some nationalists during this period, with Michael D. Jones foremost amongst them, viewed the Welsh language as a pivot around which much of Welsh nationalism could revolve. In many respects, the particularities of these brief examples need not detain us. Our aim, in briefly alluding to them, is to show how language has been used as a theme within the group-building project within Wales over the long term. Linguistic issues have not been the sole determining factor within Welsh nationalist discourse during this period. It played second fiddle to more religious issues, for instance, during the nineteenth century. And yet, concern about the Welsh language has always been a feature, to a certain extent at least, of Welsh nationalist discourse.

What characterizes these efforts to define the relationship between the Welsh language and a sense of Welshness is the fact that they represent *ad hoc* responses to external influences; English invasions; constitutional changes; reports on the state of school education. But from the late nineteenth century onwards, we witness the emergence of formal organizations, which have sought to promote the wellbeing of the Welsh language in more concerted and sustained ways. The first Cymdeithas yr Iaith Gymraeg (The Society for Utilising the Welsh Language), for instance, was formed in the National Eisteddfod in Aberdâr in 1885. The Society's aim was to promote the use of the Welsh language within formal school education in Wales. In advocating a bilingual curriculum, the Society's goal, according to Dan Isaac Davies, one of its leaders, was to see 'Three Million Bilingual Welshmen [*sic*]' by 1984 (Williams 1973: 96; Phillips 1998: 135). A broad commitment to furthering the status of the Welsh language was also witnessed in the policies of other key organizations during the late nineteenth and early twentieth centuries: Urdd Gobaith Cymru (Welsh League of Youth); Undeb Cenedlaethol y Cymdeithasau Cymraeg (National Union of Welsh Societies); and Pwyllgor Diogelu Diwylliant Cymru (Committee for the Defence of the Culture of Wales) (see Jenkins and Williams 2000: 13).

But the main organizational impetus for enhancing the status of the Welsh language during this period came through the formation of Plaid Cymru. Many commentators have noted the importance of linguistic concerns for Plaid Cymru in the period immediately after its formation in 1925 (Davies 1983: 73; Williams 1982: 152; see also Gruffudd 1994). The Welsh language represented a, if not the, key feature within their nationalist discourse. Saunders Lewis (1926: 6), for instance, could confidently associate the Welsh language with a Welsh nationalist and civilizing project. Of course, what fuelled such sentiments was the fact that the Welsh language was undergoing a sustained period of decline, both in absolute and relative terms. By the 1921 census, the absolute and relative numbers of Welsh speakers were both in decline and there is no doubt that such a deterioration acted as a clarion call for many Welsh nationalists at the time. Ambrose Bebb, for instance, maintained that 'one fact faces [the Welshman] [*sic*], and stares him in the eyes'; namely that 'the number of those able to speak Welsh is decreasing' (quoted in Davies 1983: 73).

The decline continued apace during the middle of the twentieth century: 36.8 per cent of the Welsh population spoke Welsh in 1931; by 1951, this value had decreased to 28.9 per cent (Aitchison and Carter 2000). But as long-time language campaigner Cynog Dafis (Davies 1973) has made clear, the statistical decline of the Welsh language, whether measured in terms of absolute or relative numbers, was not the sole concern for Welsh nationalists. Rather, it was the erosion in the numbers and percentages of Welsh speakers in the predominantly rural 'heart-lands' of the language (see Bowen 1959; Bowie 1993; see also Aitchison and Carter 1994; 2000). As a result of this 'erosion of the core' (Davies 1973: 248), there was a widespread belief that Welsh would cease to exist as a living language by the twenty-first century (Lewis 1962). Implicit here was the belief in the important connections that should exist between a nation and its language. Moreover, this was a connection that many nationalists during the period sought to promote above all other considerations. Here, we witness most clearly the role of the Welsh language within the group-building project associated with Welsh nationalism. The Welsh language, in this respect, became a key driving force behind a culturally orientated nationalism.[2]

The sense of linguistic and cultural loss being experienced in Wales during the middle decades of the twentieth century, not surprisingly, led to a concerted effort to attempt to arrest the decline in the speakers of the Welsh language and, more broadly, to ensure a greater constitutional status for the Welsh language within Wales. The most obvious manifestation of this linguistic re-awakening came in the form of the creation of Cymdeithas yr Iaith Gymraeg (the Welsh Language Society) in 1962. Our aim in this chapter is to show the tangled politics of nationalism associated with this event. In particular we seek to show how people and processes within the town of Aberystwyth were crucial for this key development in the linguistic politics of Wales. Our broader goal is to show how the geographical concepts of place and scale have been implicated in the reproduction of a linguistic nationalist discourse and, in so doing, to illustrate the value of a geographical perspective for re-energising social constructivist accounts of nationalism.

NATION, PLACE AND LANGUAGE: CYMDEITHAS YR IAITH AND WELSH LINGUISTIC NATIONALISM

As we noted in Chapter 2, there is a need for academic enquiry to distinguish between organizations that espouse different kinds of nationalist discourse and nationalist movements or nations per se. While much academic and popular attention would seem to draw attention to the agency of nations in promoting particular forms of nationalist discourse, we need to realize that nationalist discourse and action is directed in large part by certain organizations and the individuals that lead them (Brubaker 2004). This point is worth emphasizing with regard to linguistic nationalism in Wales. Whereas some would ascribe a necessary link between a support of the Welsh language and an adherence to Welsh nationalist discourse, it is clear that the nature of the connection between these two elements is highly contingent. In this regard, Bowie (1993) has demonstrated that the link between the Welsh language and Welsh identity is complicated and something that needs to be problematized rather than being accepted as a given. More pertinently in this context of this book is the need to show how different types of organization, whose remit extends into linguistic and nationalistic issues, espouse different visions of the place of the Welsh language within Wales. This is a theme that we expand upon at length in Chapter 7. Suffice to say at this point that in focusing on Cymdeithas yr Iaith in this chapter, we do not seek to give the impression that they represent the only, nor even the main, expression of linguistic nationalism within Wales. The Society merely represents one important element within a broader, more variegated, panoply of different organizations that are concerned with the role of the Welsh language within Wales and Welsh identity.

In this respect, the role played by Cymdeithas yr Iaith within the linguistic politics of Wales has been a source of considerable debate over a number of years. The organization has benefited from the publication of a number of 'insider' accounts, which have sought to demonstrate the Society's aims and functions, as well as recounting some of its most famous campaigning activities. Key contributions, in this respect, include: Davies' (1976) colourful and perceptive account of the formation of Cymdeithas yr Iaith Gymraeg, its Secretary during its early years; Dafis' (Davies 1973) description of the ideological reasoning behind the formation of the Society, and; Tudur's (1987) biographical account of twenty-five years of linguistic campaigning conducted by the Society in Wales. The value of these contributions is the way in which they provide personalized descriptions of the activities of Cymdeithas yr Iaith and of the motivations behind their campaigns. They are, as such, quasi primary sources since they show how different authors – each with strong connections to the Society – ascribe a particular status to the Welsh language and to its role as a key aspect of the Welsh nation. These authors have been part and parcel of the process whereby the Welsh nation has been constructed through linguistic debates. More academic in tone, and useful for different reasons, is Phillips' (1998) extensive and systematic study of Cymdeithas yr Iaith's campaigning activities over a period of thirty years. As well as elaborating upon some of the campaigning activities conducted by the Society, Phillips, to his credit, also examines some of the more mundane – yet equally crucial – aspects of the Society as an organization; its membership and administrative structure, as well as the broader political and societal reactions to

Cymdeithas yr Iaith, for instance. These contributions provide important contextual material for the remaining discussion in this chapter.

We begin the empirical section of this chapter by discussing the context for the formation of Cymdeithas yr Iaith Gymraeg. This discussion highlights the numerous spatial and scalar processes that were implicated in the formation of the Society. Following this, we move on to elaborate on their first protest, held in February 1963, before examining in detail the impact that the protest had on the place of the Welsh language; within nationalist and policy circles. Once again, the processes and debates surrounding the protest, as well as the many consequences of the protest, illustrate how a particular politics of place within Aberystwyth contributed in no small measure to the reproduction of a nationalist discourse at a broader national scale.

Sowing the seeds of linguistic dissent

While the decline in the numbers and percentages of Welsh speakers throughout the twentieth century provided the broad impetus for the formation of Cymdeithas yr Iaith, it is clear that we need to delve a little deeper if we are fully to comprehend the processes that led to its designation as an organization concerned with the wellbeing of the Welsh language. Key scalar connections were extremely important in this respect. At one level, we need to be aware of the significance of the late 1950s and early 1960s for the emergence at a global scale of social movements concerned with civil rights, anticolonial struggle and the rights of minority groups, within which the immediate linguistic claims of Cymdeithas yr Iaith could be positioned. In this respect, Cymdeithas yr Iaith could be viewed as but one amongst many new social movements formed during the 1960s, which were concerned with a whole range of issues relating to the environment, religion, peace, sexuality and gender (see Habermas 1981; Melucci 1980; Buechler 1995; Miller 2000). It is clear that individuals, who later became members of Cymdeithas yr Iaith during this early period, were well aware of this broader global context for their actions. Dafydd Iwan, a long-time political and linguistic campaigner, for instance, maintained as follows:

> *Ac wrth gwrs, mi roedd hi'n gyfnod felly trwy rhan helaeth o'r byd. Mi roedd 'na rhywbeth yn yr awyr ... Kennedy yn America, yr ymgyrchoedd yn erbyn Vietnam ag ati ... yn erbyn Apartheid, dros hawliau'r pobl dduon ... wedyn, o'n ni'n clywed am bethau tebyg yn digwydd yng Ngwlad y Basg, a Catalunya a Chile, fel pe bai 'na rhywbeth yn y cyfnod.*

[And of course, it was a period like that throughout much of the world. There was something in the air ... Kennedy in America, the protests against Vietnam and so on ... against Apartheid, for black rights ... later, I heard about similar things in the Basque Country, Catalunya and Chile, as if there was something in the period.]

Ffred Ffransis, another long-time language campaigner, argued in a similar vein and also began to draw attention to another notable aspect of the make-up of Cymdeithas yr Iaith and other similar new social movements:

Yn y 60au mi oedd na adegau o frwydrau yn yr Unol Daleithiau, hawliau sifil, cyfnod Martin Luther King. Hefyd, cyfnod y Mudiad Heddwch, di-arfogi niwclear, pwyllgor 100 y CND a protestiadau Aldermaston ... Roedd pobl ifanc yn dechrau sylweddoli dydy o ddim jyst yn fater o fwrw pleidlais unwaith bob pedair blynedd ond mae grym potential yn ein dwylo ni ac oedd rhywun yn profi ryw rhyddid wrth weithredu.

[In the 1960s there was a time of battles in the US, civil rights, the time of Martin Luther King. Also, the time of the Peace Movement, nuclear disarmament, the 100 committee of CND and the Aldermaston protests ... Young people were beginning to realise that it's not just a case of casting a vote once every four years but that we have potential power in our hands and one experienced a certain freedom through action.]

What the above quote begins to show is the way in which many of these new social movements emerging on a global scale achieved their momentum as a result of a disaffected youth, which was beginning to question some of society's – or, specifically, the older generation's – more traditional norms and rules (Phillips 1998: 19). The politicization of a Welsh-speaking youth, as part of a broader global shift, was apparent within the ranks of the Welsh Language Society. As Dafis (Davies 1973: 257–8), makes clear the individuals who supported the campaigning activities of Cymdeithas yr Iaith during the 1960s, and especially those who had been imprisoned as a result of their actions, were young people. Cymdeithas yr Iaith, when viewed through a global lens, was part and parcel of a much broader emergence of a range of new social movements, led by a politicized youth.

Another significant aspect of Cymdeithas yr Iaith's discourse and practice, which tied it into a far broader set of global social movements, was its long-standing commitment to non-violence (Williams 1977). Non-violent direct action, as Phillips (1998: 236) has noted, has been an important weapon in the Society's campaigning armoury throughout its existence and, indeed, was an official policy of the Society in the period between 1962 and 1992. In this respect, the 'spiritual leaders' of the

Society's attitude towards non-violence were Mahatma Gandhi and Martin Luther King. Ghandi's belief in *ahimsa* (non-violent action) and *satyagraha* (the force of will) and, in particular, Martin Luther King's Christian belief in love and patience, chimed well with the long-standing associations between Welsh nationalism and pacifism and non-violence (ibid: 237).

But as we have already alluded to, the key changes that were taking place at the national scale within Wales also helped to shape the emerging linguistic movement at this time. Saunders Lewis' lecture, broadcast on the BBC in 1962, informed much of the debate concerning the precarious status of the Welsh language at this time and, indeed, acted as the call to arms for linguistic nationalists throughout Wales (Davies 1973: 249; Davies 1976; Phillips 1998 passim). Some of the interviewees within our research made it clear that the radio broadcast served to galvanize the linguistic movement at this time. Gareth Miles, who was later arrested as a result of refusing an English-medium court summons, argued '*odd rhaid gwneud [rhywbeth], ar ôl darlith Saunders Lewis*/I had to do [something], after Saunders Lewis' lecture'. Dafydd Iwan, too, stated as follows:

> *Dwi'n meddwl y byddai Cymdeithas yr Iaith wedi cael ei sefydlu beth bynnag. Ond mi roedd [y ddarlith radio yn] ryw fath o gatalyst ac yn rhoi rhyw fath o barchusrwydd deallusol i ni.*

> [I think that Cymdeithas yr Iaith would have been formed in any case. But the [radio lecture] was some sort of catalyst and it gave us some kind of intellectual respectability.]

More interesting, in our opinion, is the way in which the national radio broadcast made by Saunders Lewis connected with individual language activists living and working in particular parts of Wales. In focusing on such connections, we are able to see how a particular national politics of the nation – productive of national discourses and embedded in national organizations – is 'read' and reworked by different kinds of organizations and particular people within certain localities. One significant example of this type of connection emerges in Davies' (1976) personalized account of the early years of Cymdeithas yr Iaith. What is significant within his narrative is his discussion of the impact of Saunders Lewis' lecture on his own beliefs and commitments. As well as showing the impact that the lecture had on Welsh linguistic politics at the national scale at this time, it is significant that Davies also felt it necessary to localize its effect by discussing his personal consumption of the broadcast in his family home in the small hamlet of Bwlchllan in rural Ceredigion. His reception of these ideas in rural Ceredigion was especially pertinent, according to Davies, given the fact that this area was losing its monolingual Welsh status for the first time, thus illustrating the themes that lay at the heart of Lewis' broadcast and broader call to arms (ibid: 6). Here, we witness important connections being made between Saunders Lewis' lecture and a more localized linguistic politics of place in rural Ceredigion.

But of course, the most significant examples of a more localized politics of place at this time – with regard to the context behind the formation of Cymdeithas yr Iaith – are to be found in the town of Aberystwyth. In this respect, we need to ask why Aberystwyth acted as such a propitious location for fostering a more militant attitude towards the preservation of the Welsh language, with the formation of Cymdeithas yr Iaith being an organizational representation of this. We have already touched on what we believe to be Aberystwyth's significant geography in Chapter 3. It is a relatively small and intimate town located in a convenient position for those travelling north and south through Wales. At the same, it has been the location of a number of different organizations, which possess either nationalist or quasi-nationalist aims. We do not wish to re-hash these broad arguments in this chapter. Rather, we want to focus on the specific contexts within which the town of Aberystwyth has been linked to Welsh linguistic nationalism. We see more specific evidence of the significance of Aberystwyth as a local context within which the broader group-making project of a Welsh linguistic nation was played out in a number of different contexts. In the first place, it is evident that Aberystwyth was a place within which informal networks of people had already met to discuss the fate of the Welsh language and its role as a key badge of Welsh identity. One such group or network was entitled 'Cymru ein Gwlad' (Wales our Country). Cynog Dafis recalls his experiences of attending the meetings of Cymru ein Gwlad, held in the Belle Vue Hotel in Aberystwyth:

> *Oedd 'na anfodlonrwydd cyffredinol yn nechrau'r chwechdegau ynghylch cyfeiriad y Blaid. Ac mi fues i'n mynd i fynychu rhyw gyfarfodydd gan fudiadau . . . neu grwpiau 'fringe', megis grwp Cymru Ein Gwlad. Rwy'n cofio mynd i gyfarfod yn y Belle Vue gan y rheini. Beth oedd oedd diffyg amynedd mewn ffordd, ac anfodlonrwydd ynghylch cynnydd y mudiad cenedlaethol ac arafwch cynnydd etholiadol y Blaid.*

> [There was a general sense of unhappiness at the beginning of the sixties about the direction being taken by Plaid Cymru . . . And I attended some meetings held by movements . . . or 'fringe' groups, such as the group

Cymru ein Gwlad ... I remember going to a meeting that they organised in the Belle Vue ... There was an impatience as it were, and a lack of acceptance of the slow progress of the nationalist movement and the slow electoral progress of Plaid.]

It is important to note, too, that Cymru ein Gwlad advocated a more confrontational and extra-constitutional approach to securing a greater status for the Welsh language (Phillips 1998: 30). While the Cymru ein Gwlad group's discussions did not lead to much in terms of action, it is evident that they represented an early example of how new organizations were beginning to consider an alternative to the constitutional route to self-government advocated by Plaid Cymru. At the same time, their attempt to promote a more radical and active approach to nationalist politics would act as somewhat of a precedent for the subsequent formation of Cymdeithas yr Iaith.

As well as being a place of discussion, it is clear that Aberystwyth also emerged as a place of action with regard to the emerging linguistic movement of the early 1960s. In February 1962, Gareth Miles committed a minor offence on Aberystwyth promenade (along Marine Terrace). The following account is based largely the interview conducted with Gareth Miles:

Rhyw barti Nadolig hwyr oedd hi, y Geltaidd ... rhoiais i 'pass' adref ar y beic i'r ferch ifanc 'ma ... dyma'r plisman ma'n llamu allan o'r tywyllwch ... canlyniad hyn oedd ein bod ni'n cael gwys ... mae'n siwr bod hynny'n uchafbwynt i'w wythnos!

[It was a late Christmas party, the Geltaidd [society][3]. . . I gave this young girl a lift home on the bike ... this policeman jumped out of the darkness ... as a consequence, I received a summons ... that must have been the highlight of his week!]

Gareth Miles subsequently decided to follow the lead of other nationalist campaigners, who had recently refused to answer summons written solely in English as a way of demonstrating the lack of status afforded to the Welsh language within the legal system in Wales (Davies 2000: 217). Not surprisingly, such a lack of status for the Welsh language had acted as a source of severe discontent for many Welsh nationalists, not least Gareth Miles. As a result of his intransigence in not responding to the court summons, Gareth Miles spent one night in a police cell and the fine was collected from his person at the end of the night. According to one of our interviewees, the majority of Welsh-language campaigners in Aberystwyth were familiar with Gareth Miles and, not surprisingly, supported his actions. In addition, it is notable that the act of civil disobedience received the full backing of the local Aberystwyth branch of Plaid Cymru.[4] The Gareth Miles episode also set a precedent for other acts of civil disobedience by Welsh Language Society activists, in Aberystwyth and further afield.

Aberystwyth, therefore, was a place within which a Welsh linguistic politics was discussed and acted upon during this period. As one would expect, both these aspects fed off each other in productive ways. Returning to Davies' (1976: 5) account of the early years of Cymdeithas yr Iaith, we find an interesting description of a conversation that he had with Gareth Miles on the steps of the National Library of Wales in Aberystwyth at the beginning of the summer of 1962. In the conversation, Miles stated that he would be willing to refuse the English-medium summons (discussed above), with which he would shortly be presented, in order to illustrate the lack of status afforded to the Welsh language within the legal system in Wales. We begin to see here how discussions concerning the parlous status of the Welsh language could lead to instances of direct action while, at the same time, active campaigning could lead an energising or reframing of linguistic debates within the town. What is also significant in Davies' account is Miles' explanation for his adoption of a radical stance; Saunders Lewis' radio lecture, which was broadcast earlier that year. Once again, complex scalar connections – between a national radio broadcast and the actions of an individual in the townscape of Aberystwyth were crucial for the linguistic nationalism emerging during this period.

Nowhere do we better witness the scalar connections that helped to shape the emergence of Cymdeithas yr Iaith than in the actual mechanics of the formation of the organization. As we have already seen, part of the rationale for the formation of Cymdeithas yr Iaith was the perceived inability of Plaid Cymru to engage with the kind of concerted direct action that many nationalists believed was necessary to effect a change in the status and fortunes of the Welsh language. The national scale also featured in the radio broadcast made by Saunders Lewis. In addition to these two impetuses at the national scale, it is clear that the actions of Gareth Miles on the promenade in Aberystwyth were also contributory factors. His actions inspired other activists to take similar stances in other parts of Wales and, more fundamentally, led directly to the first moves in favour of a more permanent campaigning structure to improve the status of the Welsh language. Davies (1976: 6–7), a founder member of Cymdeithas yr Iaith, describes his own recollections of the genesis of the new organization. Miles' protest, according to Davies, galvanized the

Aberystwyth branch of Plaid Cymru to instigate the procedures necessary to form a new, autonomous political movement to campaign solely on the basis of Welsh language policy issues. Twelve individuals, from Aberystwyth and further afield, attended Plaid Cymru's Summer School and Conference, held in Pontarddulais at the end of July 1962, and submitted a motion under the leadership of Tedi Milward and John Davies in order to create an independent organization that would campaign wholeheartedly in favour of an increased status for the Welsh language within Wales (Davies 1973: 250; Phillips 1998: 199). Tedi Milward informed us how *'fe basiwyd y cynnig yn frwd iawn, yntife, yn unfrydol os cofia'i'n iawn*/the motion was passed very enthusiastically, with full support if I remember rightly' by Plaid Cymru's Executive Committee. Milward added that:

> Fe gwrddon ni wedyn, y bobl oedd y tu ôl i'r cynnig, pobl Aberystwyth a rhai eraill, yn yr ysgol haf . . . A bod angen grŵp o bobl oedd yn fodlon . . . dwyn y pwnc i sylw cyhoeddus ac yn y blaen, a gweithredu'n anghyfansoddiadol ac yn di-drais. Ac yn y fan 'na y sefydlwyd Cymdeithas yr Iaith.

[We met then, the people behind the motion, Aberystwyth people and others, in the summer school . . . And there was a need for a group of people that were willing to . . . draw the subject to public attention and so on, and act unconstitutionally and non-violently. And Cymdeithas yr Iaith was created there.]

The genesis of Cymdeithas yr Iaith, in this respect, clearly demonstrates the intermeshing of various scales ranging from a national lecture, executive bodies and organizations, through to local branch activities of nationalist organizations and the isolated activities of one individual on the promenade in Aberystwyth.

The final paragraphs of this section have begun to focus our attention on the specific politics of place that were at work in Aberystwyth during the 1960s. There is no finer example of the tangled politics of place and how it intermeshes with the broader politics of the nation than the protest on Trefechan bridge, which took place in February 1963 and we turn our attention to this event in the following section.

Wyt ti'n cofio Pont Trefechan?[5]

Pont Trefechan is one of the key historic events that help to structure the Welsh nation-building project, especially in linguistic terms. Indeed, it has entered the Welsh national consciousness to such an extent that it is difficult to tease out the historic fact from the mythologized fiction. Our goal in this section is to show how the politics of place within Aberystwyth – and the events that took place on one day in February 1963 – contributed to the reproduction of a Welsh nationalist discourse centred on the Welsh language.

The protests of 2 February 1963 took their inspiration at one level from Saunders Lewis' lecture and, at another, from the act of civil disobedience perpetrated by Gareth Miles the previous year on the promenade in Aberystwyth. In this respect, John Davies, who was involved in the day's protests, was keen to emphasize the almost coincidental choice of Aberystwyth as the location for the protests. At one level, Aberystwyth was a convenient location in which protestors from different parts of Wales could gather. At the same time, Aberystwyth also seemed a 'natural' choice since it was the location of Gareth Miles' earlier act of civil disobedience:

Ar ryw olwg, damwain oedd mai yn Aberystwyth y bu'r protest gyntaf. A damwain wir oedd y ffaith bod e'n fater o dor cyfraith o'r cychwyn. Beth 'sbardunodd ni' . . . oedd [gweithred] Gareth Miles . . . Gan bod e' wedi digwydd yn Aberystwyth, oedd e'n amlwg bod eisiau protest ar y mater yn Aberystwyth, achos yr ergyd oedd yn erbyn ynadon Ceredigion, Aberystwyth.

[In some respects, it was an accident that the first protest was held in Aberystwyth. And it was certainly an accident that it was a matter of breaking the law from the outset. What spurred us on was Gareth Miles' actions . . . Since it happened in Aberystwyth, it was obvious that we needed a protest in Aberystwyth, since the targets were the Ceredigion magistrates in Aberystwyth.]

In this context, the protestors' goal was to follow Gareth Miles' lead by committing acts of civil disobedience that would lead to an arrest or arrests. The monolingual character of legal procedure could, then, be used to publicize the lack of status afforded to the Welsh language within the British legal system. But despite the impact of the 'Trefechan Bridge protest' on recent Welsh political history it is ironic that the first and, originally, only target for the day's activities was Aberystwyth Post Office. The key, in this regard, was to break the law without recourse to any violence. The daubing of posters on the walls of Aberystwyth Post Office, according to one organizer of the protest, was deemed to be an ideal compromise. Our interviews with key activists involved in the protests on this day illustrate an almost military air to the whole exercise. For instance, the headquarters of the day's activities was the upstairs room of the Home Café on Pier Street. In addition, the protesters' march on the Post Office had been planned carefully. As Tedi Millward, one of the leaders of the protest explained to us, groups of protesters were to advance on three fronts in order to circumvent opposition from the police. The outcome of the protest, nonetheless, was deemed to be somewhat of an anticlimax. Admittedly, society members were able to put up posters bearing the slogans *'Statws i'r Iaith'* (Status for the Language) and *'Defnyddiwch yr Iaith Gymraeg'* (Use the Welsh Language) on the walls of the Post Office (see Plate 4.1). According to one report, 'phone kiosks, letter boxes, Inland Revenue and Council Offices were plastered' (*Welsh Nation* 1963). However, the day's protests were not as successful as they could have been since the police had decided to adopt a low-key, accommodative strategy towards the Society's activities. Reports in the *Daily Herald* (4 February 1963) and *The Express* (3 February 1963) respectively chart the day's development in entertaining detail (original emphases):

> Seeing the 6ft. 4in. of Inspector L. T. K. Williams leaving the police station, [E. G.] Millward stood in his path and announced: 'We have broken the law. We have stuck posters all over your police station.' The inspector smiled, shrugged his shoulders and walked on.

> The poster-carrying demonstrators, mainly students, moved off from their Home Café rendezvous WITHOUT A POLICEMAN IN SIGHT. They plastered the post office with slogans. Irate staff started tearing down the posters. STILL NO POLICEMAN TO BE SEEN . . . The town hall was 'attacked' [with posters] – then the police station itself. BUT THE POLICE DID NOT SEEM TO SEE . . . Dismayed, the society held a council of war [in the Home Café]. Some felt they had done enough for the day. But 25 minutes later about 40 [society members] blocked Trefechan Bridge.

The key development, as noted in the above quote, was the decision made by some of the campaigners to block the road leading into Aberystwyth from the south (see Plate 4.2) (Phillips 1998: 228). Tegwyn Jones recalls his experiences as part of the protest on the bridge as follows:

> *A 'wi'n cofio eistedd yn groes yr hewl. Dim byd yn digwydd, bysus yn stopio, a gyrrwyr yn mynd yn wallgo ac yn y blaen, gandryll, ond dim plisman o unrhyw fath. Doedd 'na ddim byd. Wedyn dwi'n cofio rhywun yn gofyn i fi, ac . . . Elenid Jones o Lanelli, i fynd i ffonio. Aethon ni lan wedyn, a'r ffôn agosa' oedd i fyny top y dre . . . ffonio'r heddlu . . . dweud 'ylwch, 'da ni'n trio croesi Pont Trefechan, ond 'y'n ni'n methu gwneud. Beth y'ch chi'n mynd i wneud?' 'O, da'n ni'n gwybod syr am y drafferth, ry'n ni'n mynd i edrych mewn iddo fe'.*

> [And I remember sitting across the road. Nothing happening, buses stopping, and drivers going crazy and so on, berserk, but no policeman of any kind. There was nothing. And then I remember somebody asking me, and . . . Elenid Jones from Llanelli, to make a phone call. We went up then,

and the nearest phone was at the top of town . . . phoning the police . . . saying 'look, we're trying to cross Trefechan Bridge, but we can't. What are you going to do about it?' 'Oh, we know about the trouble sir, we're going to look into it'.]

However, despite the increasing tension and scale of the protests, still no arrests were made. Nevertheless, the blocking of the road on Trefechan Bridge through a sit-in protest was decisive and successful, in that it had attracted the unprecedented attention of the news media on both Welsh and British national scales. Davies recalled in a later account (Davies 1976: 14):

Cafwyd cyhoeddusrwydd neilltuol; tudalennau yn y Cymro, colofnau a lluniau yn y Western Mail, y Daily Post, yr Express a'r Sunday Citizen, hanner tudalen yn y Daily Herald . . . a phytiau yn yr Observer, y Times a'r Guardian . . .

[Excellent coverage was had; pages in the *Cymro* [a Welsh weekly newspaper], columns and pictures in the *Western Mail*, the *Daily Post*, the *Express* and the *Sunday Citizen*, half a page in the *Daily Herald* . . . and short pieces in the *Observer*, *The Times* and the *Guardian* . . .

The significance attributed to the media coverage of the protest illustrates clearly the importance of national media for shaping the broader currents of the reproduction of Welsh nationalism at the time (Anderson 1983; Billig 1995). It is significant, too, that the Trefechan Bridge protest had succeeded in cementing the importance of Aberystwyth as a focal point for future Welsh language campaigning and as a key place in the production of Welsh nationalism. Tedi Millward's words in *The Times* (4 February 1963) emphasize this point:

Today one of the society's secretaries, Mr. Edward Glynne Millward, a lecturer[6] in Welsh at the University College Aberystwyth, said 'the society will meet again and there will probably be future demonstrations. We are making Aberystwyth a focal point for this campaign'.

This rather bald account of the day's activities can give an impression of a carefully laid set of plans, which, despite a small hiccup, proceeded largely according to plan. The narrative provided above can also give an impression of a nationalist movement, which was totally united in its support of the day's activities. The linguistic group-making project facilitated by the protests on 2 February 1963, however, was riddled with internal tensions and contradictions. First of all, we need to appreciate that the day's protest, although staged in Aberystwyth and led by individuals based in Aberystwyth, also drew large-scale support from people outside the town. Activists were attracted from various parts of

Wales in order to contribute to the day's activities. The presence of activists from other locations in Wales, we would argue, does not detract from the arguments made in this chapter. Rather, it demonstrates the importance of Aberystwyth as a meeting point for all those concerned with the state of the Welsh language and nation at this time (Massey 1994). The *Daily Herald* (4 February 1963), in its account of the planning stages of the protest, makes this point clearly:

> Students from Bangor, Cardiff, Merthyr and Pontypridd joined a home contingent in an upper room in Aberystwyth to consider how the 'language of heaven' could be returned to honour.[7]

Furthermore, the presence of these different individuals on the streets of Aberystwyth on this day contributed to certain divisions within the Welsh nationalist movement. This derived, at least in part, from a certain conflict between nationalist campaigners drawn from the town's indigenous population – including its students in residence – and other 'outsiders' who had been attracted to Aberystwyth in order to take part in the day's protests. Following the 'failure' of the day's earlier protests, there was much heated discussion between the various activists (Plate 4.3). Significantly, some have argued that the main impetus for the subsequent protest on Trefechan Bridge derived from those activists who had travelled to Aberystwyth for the day. Tegwyn Jones, for instance, argued as follows:

> *Fe aeth pawb i'r Home Café i gael rhyw bwyllgor mawr, a fan ni penderfynwyd 'mae'n rhaid i ni wneud rhywbeth drastig' achos roedd pobl wedi dod lawr o Fangor a dod i fyny o Gaerdydd ond doedden nhw ddim yn mynd nôl heb unrhyw ganlyniad o gwbl, a felly dyna pam aethpwyd i Bont Trefechan.*

> [Everyone went back to the Home Café to have some sort of a big committee, and we decided there 'we have to do something drastic' because people had come down from Bangor and up from Cardiff and they didn't want to go back without any result at all, and that's why we went to Trefechan Bridge.]

The leaders of the day's protest – largely people who were resident in Aberystwyth – did not see the same need to persevere with the protest. Whether this was as a result of a lack of conviction on their part is a moot point. There is some evidence, however, that the leaders of the protest exhibited a greater sense of social responsibility than some of the 'foot-soldiers' and that this may have militated against them encouraging others to push the protest into more radical and, perhaps, dangerous realms. Tedi Milward, for instance, stressed as follows:

I ddweud y gwir 'o'n i'n teimlo'n gyfrifol am . . . fyfyrwyr . . . [ro'n i'n] ofni beth fyddai'n digwydd iddyn nhw a ddweud y gwir . . . ro'n i'n meddwl bod pwnc y Swyddfa'r Post yn ddigon . . . fe gawson ni sylw eang iawn ar ôl hynny.

[To tell the truth I felt responsible for . . . students . . . I was scared about what would happen to them, to tell the truth . . . I thought that the subject of the Post Office was enough . . . we had a lot of broad coverage after that.]

He went on to argue that the Trefechan Bridge protest was *'answyddogol, ddim wedi ei threfnu* / unofficial, it hadn't been organised'. One can almost hear the sense of grievance in his voice. Whatever the reason for the lack of 'official' support for the second unplanned stage of the day's protests, it is clear that other individuals, who were part of the influx of campaigners into Aberystwyth on that day, were critical of lack of support of some of the Aberystwyth contingent towards the new plan of action. One of the more critical activists argued as follows:

Dach chi'n gyfarwydd ag Aberystwyth. Cerdded i lawr rwan o'r Home Café, mynd yn hollol syth i lawr heibio'r Lion, a dach chi ar Bont Trefechan. Ond rhywsut neu'i gilydd, mi aeth pobl [o Aberystwyth] ar goll o'r Home Café i Bont Trefechan. Beth ddigwyddodd iddyn nhw, does neb yn rhyw wybod.

[You're familiar with Aberystwyth. Walking down now from the Home Café, going totally straight past the Lion, and you're on Trefechan Bridge. But somehow or other, people [from Aberystwyth] became lost between the Home Café and Trefechan Bridge. What happened to them, nobody really knows.]

Our interviewee elaborates here on the perceived lack of commitment of Aberystwyth-based students to the Trefechan Bridge protest. Clearly, such sentiments speak of a certain dissent between different factions of the campaigning movement on that day. In effect, these factions envisaged different ways of promoting the importance of the Welsh language for the nation-building project in Wales.

Of course, more serious divisions existed between the campaigners and other residents of the town. Large swathes of the population of Aberystwyth were, by no means, supportive of Cymdeithas yr Iaith and its ideological stand. In this respect, the majority of the town's population would have found much common ground with the popularly held view that Cymdeithas yr Iaith represented somewhat of a 'lunatic fringe' conducting a 'madcap campaign' that were to be, at best, humoured, and, at worst, ridiculed (see Davies 1973: 258; Phillips 1998; more broadly, see Jones 2000). The documentary evidence suggests that the immediate local reaction to the Welsh language protest was far from positive. To start with, we focus on reports of the local reaction to the protests around Aberystwyth on 2 February 1963. At the Post Office, the site of the original protest, 'demonstrators met resistance from local teenagers, who stood on each other's shoulders to tear down the fifty posters' (*Liverpool Daily Post*, 4 February 1963). Reaction to the sit-down protest on Trefechan Bridge was even more hostile. Opposition to the sit-in came from irate drivers wanting to cross the bridge, along with local bystanders who found the protest either to be a source of good sport, or annoyance, or a combination of both. An 'elderly bystander', for instance, was quoted in the *Cambrian News* (5 February 1963) thus: 'I think these students need a damn good spanking'. The local reaction to the protest was to become far more menacing, however, as the patience of the various onlookers evaporated:

> Angry motorists pleaded, then threatened and finally nudged their chargers into the mass. Not one student flinched ... A crowd of local lads watched for half an hour. In the end it was an economic grievance which roused them. 'Do we keep you in college for this?' shouted one rabble rouser ... A companion looked down at the icy waters of the River Rheidol 40ft. below and suggested: 'Throw them all in'. Instead the native youths rushed into the students, fists flying ... Two girl students were knocked unconscious ... (*Daily Herald* 4 February 1963)

The sit-in lasted some three-quarters of an hour and was finally ended as police intervened to separate protestors from a combination of hostile local bystanders and angry drivers. The divide between campaigners and the majority of the residents of the town has been encapsulated in Dafydd Iwan's protest song, *Daw fe ddaw yr awr* (Iwan 1992: 80):

Wyt ti'n cofio Pont Trefechan
A'r brotest gynta'i gyd
A'r Cardis yn ffaelu deall
Pam roedd Cymry'n blocio'u stryd.

[Do you remember Trefechan Bridge
And the first ever protest
And the Cardis[8] failing to understand
Why the Welsh were blocking their street.]

Dafydd Iwan, a long-standing nationalist campaigner and current President of Plaid Cymru, makes an important comment on the politics of place within Aberystwyth, the broader Ceredigion and the lack of general support for the nationalist and linguistic aims of Cymdeithas yr Iaith in his portrayal of the day's events.

It is noticeable that one important way in which this hostility became manifest was in the context of antistudent sentiment. This is not surprising given the strong connection between students attending the University College of Wales, Aberystwyth and the development of nationalist sentiment within the town, a connection that still holds true today, as we will witness in later chapters of this book. In this way, the locals' taunts highlight the complex spatial and social relationships that exist between town and gown in many university towns. These relationships are surely heightened in a town as small and as intimate as Aberystwyth. The antistudent sentiment reoccurs in evidence from a subsequent Cymdeithas yr Iaith protest in Dolgellau, Gwynedd, in November 1963. According to *Y Cymro* (2 December 1963),[9] locals heckled Cymdeithas protestors with the following taunts:

Meddyliwch ein bod ni'n talu i gadw'r stiwdants 'ma yn y colegau i wneud ffyliaid ohonom.

[Just think that we're paying to keep these students in college just for them to make fools of us.]

Ewch yn ôl at Aberystwyth 'na.

[Go back to that Aberystwyth place.]

The above quotes suggest a perception arising elsewhere in Wales, that Cymdeithas yr Iaith was a creation of Aberystwyth and, more specifically, the University College of Wales, Aberystwyth.

When viewed as a whole, the evidence discussed in this section illustrate the complex politics of place in Aberystwyth that was to be instrumental, as the following section shows, in the development of a particular linguistic form of nationalism in Wales. The political activities and practices of key protagonists within the town, the networks of association between different groups of activists, the conflicts and contestations within groups of activists and between activists and locals, were all key elements in a politics of place within the town. Furthermore, the discussion in this section has illustrated the need to focus on certain sites within the town – the Post Office, Trefechan Bridge and the upstairs room in the Home Café – as ones that helped to 'anchor' the campaigning activities of the period, in both physical and metaphorical contexts. Viewed as a whole, these various factors, we would argue, show the need to examine the potential role of the politics of local places in reproducing nationalist discourse. But in order to demonstrate the validity of this claim fully, we need to reconnect the politics of place within Aberystwyth – as illustrated on this one frosty day in February

1963 – with the broader politics of the nation. These scalar relationships between localized places and national places, as they were manifest in the linguistic politics of the later 1960s, are discussed in the final empirical section of this chapter.

The legacy of Trefechan Bridge

The immediate legacy of the Trefechan Bridge protest was the instigation of *ad hoc* responses to the thorny issue relating to English-medium summonses. Some of our interviewees contended that the Trefechan protest had led to some magistrates and civil servants fearing the administrative headaches and negative publicity that would come in lieu of mass acts of civil disobedience in other parts of Wales. As an example, there is some evidence that Cardiff Magistrates' Court began to issue summonses in Welsh in reaction to the protests that had taken place in Aberystwyth. John Davies explains as follows:

> *Y ddadl bennaf oedd gyda . . . [cynghorydd cyfreithiol Cyngor Caerdydd] wrth berswadio'r adran berthnasol yng Nghaerdydd i ala'r gwys Gymraeg oedd 'Os nag y'ch chi'n gwneud, fe gawn ni brotest fan hyn'. A dyw gweision sifil a swyddogion cynghorau ddim eisiau protest ar drothwy eu drws, mae'n 'ala nhw i edrych yn ddwl, a mae e'n gyhoeddusrwydd gwael.*

> [[The legal adviser to Cardiff Council's] main argument in persuading the relevant department in Cardiff to send the summons in Welsh was 'If you don't do this, then we'll have a protest here'. Civil servants and council officials don't want protests on their doorstep, it makes them look stupid, and it's bad publicity.]

Trefechan Bridge, in this respect, clearly forced local legal-administrative agencies into thinking on their feet, and producing an *ad hoc* policy response within a matter of days. What is interesting, in this respect, is the way in which the change of procedure within Cardiff finally led magistrates in Aberystwyth to a similar change in tack. John Davies puts it aptly as follows: '*pan roedd Caerdydd, a'r* . . . Western Mail . . . *yn dweud* "Capital shows the way" *ac yn y blaen, fe ildiodd Aberystwyth yn weddol buan ar ôl hynny*/when Cardiff, and. . . the *Western Mail* . . . said "Capital shows the way" and so on, Aberystwyth gave in relatively soon after that'. The adaptation of these new linguistic legal procedures, as such, diffused throughout many parts of Wales and illustrates the way in which the influence of local protests within Aberystwyth, and subsequent policy responses in Cardiff, could lead to further widespread procedural changes on a broader national scale (Jones and Fowler 2007b).

Another possible impact of the Aberystwyth protests was their contribution to a governmental re-evaluation of the role of the Welsh language in public life in Wales. As Dafis (Davies 1973: 251) has noted, Sir Keith Joseph, the Minister for Welsh Affairs, announced in 1963 that the government was to appoint a committee to explicate the legal status of the Welsh language. The committee was to be chaired by Sir David Hughes-Parry and commenced its work in September 1963 (Davies 1976: 26). To what extent was this a reaction to the formation of Cymdeithas yr Iaith, along with the Trefechan Bridge protest? There is no evidence that the Committee was formed as a direct response to the creation of the Society and the Aberystwyth protests (though see Phillips 1998: 289). Indeed, Davies concedes that the committee may have owed its formation to the legal ambiguity occasioned by an earlier controversy in 1962 surrounding the language used in nomination papers for a local by-election in Ammanford, Carmarthenshire (Davies 1976: 26). This point of detail does not, however, detract from an implicit feeling among the Cymdeithas yr Iaith ranks that the creation of the Committee was a reaction, at least in part, to the activities of the organization in 1962/63. More important, in our view, is the fact that Cymdeithas yr Iaith, with their roots in Aberystwyth, perceived themselves to be a legitimate player in a political process on the national scale. Phillips (1998: 206) notes how the Society supplied information to the members of the Committee, something that that they would continue to do with subsequent Committees formed to enquire into the status of the Welsh language. Indeed, an item of personal correspondence from John Davies to Gareth Miles suggests that the Hughes-Parry committee and Cymdeithas yr Iaith Gymraeg were certainly on cooperative terms, and that the committee was even 'eager' to receive a delegation from Cymdeithas yr Iaith.[10] Building on this theme, John Davies recalls his experience of cooperating with the Committee as follows:

> *Aethon ni i weld Pwyllgor Hughes-Parry ym Mangor, fi a Tedi Millward a Harri Pritchard-Jones . . . cawson ni groeso brwd iawn, boneddigaidd iawn.*

> [We went to see the Hughes-Parry Committee in Bangor, me and Tedi Milward and Harri Pritchard-Jones . . . we received a very warm welcome, very noble.]

The Hughes-Parry report itself mentions the genteel informality of the process: 'The Committee's task was made easier and more pleasant by the friendly manner in which they were received by all in the course of their visits' (Welsh Office 1965: no page).

As well as witnessing an emerging influence of Cymdeithas yr Iaith – and, we would argue, a politics of place based in Aberystwyth – on the evolving politics of linguistic nationalism in Wales in this example, it is significant that the formation of the Hughes-Parry Committee also impinged on the local campaigning strategies of Cymdeithas yr Iaith. The Society's response to the formation of the committee was to call a moratorium on confrontational civil disobedience activities, focusing instead on less contentious strategies such as letter-writing and the gathering and presentation of evidence to the Hughes-Parry Committee (Phillips 1998: 228–9). While Dafis (Davies 1973: 251) latterly criticized this 'astonishingly moderate' decision, it is clear that Cymdeithas activists at the time were well aware of the strategic advantages accruing to their cause through cooperating with the committee's activities.[11] Despite the cessation of confrontational activities, the activities of Cymdeithas campaigners during this period still illustrate the productive role for place within the reproduction of Welsh linguistic nationalism. We think here, in particular, of John Davies' so-called 'innocent Welsh letter' campaign. The campaign involved writing personally to 158 district and borough councils in Wales, asking a spurious question concerning *'hynafiaethau'* (historic monuments) in their local area. Davies received 83 non-responses, 49 English-language responses and just 39 Welsh-language responses (Phillips 1998: 80–81). The campaign provided ammunition for Cymdeithas yr Iaith to disprove previous government findings, which had claimed that most Welsh councils already answered Welsh-language correspondence through the medium of Welsh (Phillips 1998: 205; Davies 1976: 23–4).

The tangible outcomes of these negotiations and more muted forms of campaigning, admittedly, are not particularly impressive. Dafis (Davies 1973: 253) laments the lack of progress made by the Society's various campaigns during the 1960s and his words are worth quoting at length:

> A great deal of quiet work had led to very little. Not one genuine victory had been achieved; the Welsh summonses then issued, for instance, were typed and available only on request, often in grossly incorrect Welsh; when certificates of registration of births were issued later on, parents were presented with a choice of registering either in English or bilingually, but not in Welsh alone. Nothing approaching equal status for Welsh had been granted even in the limited spheres where there was any recognition at all.

Dafis was equally damning of the Welsh Language Act 1967, which was based in part on the recommendations of the Hughes-Parry Committee. At face value, the Hughes-Parry Committee's report was supportive of the Welsh language. It argued that the English-dominated UK state had ignored the Welsh language, save for the sole exception of education. The legal system and public administration bore no imprint of the Welsh language and there was a severe need to transform this situation (Welsh Office 1965). And yet while the Report, which acted as the basis of the subsequent Welsh Language Act 1967, 'recommended that Welsh be accepted as equally valid with English in law', it did not state that the right to use the Welsh language should be incorporated in legislation (Davies 1973: 254). Another respected commentator has argued that the Act 'lacked teeth' since the 'decision whether to adopt equal validity, and if so, to what extent, was discretionary' (Davies 2000: 243). The perceived weakness of the Act has led the vast majority of language campaigners, such as Cynog Dafis, to distance themselves from the Act, viewing it as something that was *'cwbl, cwbl anfoddhaol/* totally, totally unsatisfactory'.

A judgement on the merits of the Society's various campaigns during this period, as well as of the Welsh Language Act, lie beyond the scope of this chapter. We want, rather, to make two broader points regarding the efforts to ascribe an important linguistic element to the Welsh nation-building project at this time. First, it is evident that the linguistic nation-building project was then one that was highly variegated and contingent in nature. Different individuals, whether within Cymdeithas yr Iaith or within local and central state bureaucracies were intimately involved in the gradual incorporation of the Welsh language into legal procedures. In addition, it is clear that different places contributed to this process in different ways. While activities and activists in Aberystwyth may have played a disproportionate role in shaping the linguistic and nationalist agenda of the 1960s, it is clear that other places were also involved in this geographical matrix of linguistic campaigning. We have already seen how individuals within Cardiff Borough Council reacted reasonably positively to the changing legal landscape by issuing a Welsh-medium summons. Within the ranks of Cymdeithas yr Iaith, too, it has been argued that certain individuals, based in certain locales, acted as driving forces behind the Society's activities during its early years in existence. Reference has been made, here, to the unstinting work carried out by Owain Owain, for instance, the leader of the Society's Bangor cell (Davies 1973: 252). In this respect, the efforts to produce a Welsh linguistic nationalism at this time were, in addition to the important role played by campaigners in Aberystwyth, predicated upon a networked group of individuals located in various towns and cities throughout Wales.

Second, and somewhat paradoxically, there was an ongoing effort to embed the Welsh linguistic nation in a set of more formal structures and accompanying discourses existing at the national scale. Cymdeithas yr Iaith, despite its amorphous character during its first few years in existence, increasingly sought to create a more bureaucratic structure in order to underpin its campaigning activities. A Central Committee was formed in 1965 in order to bring some semblance of administrative efficiency to the organization and this was superseded by a Senate and a series of committees in 1970 (Phillips 1998: 82). One can also view the Welsh Language Act 1967, despite its limitations, as another instance of the growing embeddedness of the Welsh language at the Welsh national scale. The Act, in this respect, should be conceived of as a product of a series of different politics of place and scale. The Act was the logical conclusion, or at least an interim staging-post, of a process that commenced with Saunders Lewis' *Tynged yr Iaith* lecture some five years earlier, a process which received significant impetus from the activities of a small group of individuals on the streets of Aberystwyth and from the coordinated and strategic campaigning of the national organization of Cymdeithas yr Iaith. Viewed as a whole, the reproduction of a linguistic Welsh nationalism at this time cannot be fully appreciated without understanding its complex place-based and scalar politics.

CONCLUSIONS

This chapter has provided one snapshot of the initial role played by Cymdeithas yr Iaith in seeking to promote a more linguistically orientated form of nationalism in Wales during the 1960s. Their commitment to this cause has not wavered since this early period, as numerous authors have demonstrated (e.g. Davies 1973; Davies 1976; Phillips 1998). Various campaigns from this period onwards sought to increase the status afforded to the language in a number of different contexts including education, broadcasting and community-based policies. A review of all these areas of policy contestation is beyond the reach of this chapter, although some of these issues are discussed at greater length in subsequent chapters of this book. Our comments in this conclusion centre on two broader themes relating to the reproduction of a linguistic form of nationalism in Wales in the period subsequent to the 1960s, along with the role played by Cymdeithas yr Iaith within this process.

As we hinted in the above paragraphs, one noticeable aspect of the role of Cymdeithas yr Iaith in the period after 1970 has been its increased bureaucratization. Whereas there was a highly haphazard and contingent feel to the activities of the organization during the 1970s, it is clear that the Society from this period onwards developed more of a formal and systematic campaign strategy. One way in which we can think about this shift is through examining the growing territorial extent of the Society's activities as it sought to reach out to all parts of Wales. One measure of this transformation was the Society's campaign against monolingual road-signs. As Phillips (1998: 231) notes, the campaign had started in an unstructured and uncoordinated manner. The signs at 'Trevine' in Pembrokeshire were removed in 1964 and replaced with signs bearing the Welsh name 'Trefin'. The campaign, if one can call it so at this early stage, resumed in 1968, when students from the University College vandalized road signs in the area around Aberystwyth, significantly, without the permission of the Central Committee. The tenor of the whole campaign changed after the General Meeting held later that year, when it was agreed that the Society should actively seek to improve the status of the Welsh language in all aspects of local government in Wales. A key aspect of the campaign would revolve around the whole issue of road signs. Detailed instructions were published by the Society in the January 1969 issue of *Tafod y Ddraig*, the Society's magazine, in which Society members were advised on the types of road sign that should be painted, which paint to use and so on. Legal advice for those taking part in the campaign was published in the July edition of the same edition. The above information testifies to the increasing sophistication of the road-sign campaign but it is clear, too, that the campaign also became far more systematic in its territorial reach throughout the 1970s. Phillips (ibid), in this respect, has shown that by 1970 a total of 185 court cases had been held against Society members who had painted road signs and that these had taken place 'throughout Wales'. We discuss this theme at greater length in Chapter 5.

As an indication of this growing territorial reach of the Society's campaign and of the long-term success of its policies there is no better example than the erection of bilingual road signs *throughout* Wales, a feature that is discussed with evident pride in the following quote by John Davies, a long-time language activist:

> *Ond erbyn hyn, yn sgil buddugoliaethau'r Gymdeithas, rwy'n teimlo rhyw wefr o groesi Pont Hafren tua cyffiniau Cas-Gwent, a 'Cas-Gwent' mae'r arwyddion yn*

dweud. A 'Chasnewydd' a 'Dim Parcio' ac yn y blaen. O'r union bwynt y ffin [pwyslais gwreiddiol]. I gymharu a beth oedd yn bodoli hanner canrif yn ôl, mae'n ymylu ar fod yn wyrthiol.

[But by now, as a result of the victories of the [Welsh Language] Society, I feel a certain exhilaration as I cross the Severn Bridge near to Cas-Gwent [Chepstow], and it's 'Cas-gwent' [Chepstow] that the signs say. And 'Casnewydd' [Newport] and 'Dim Parcio' [No Parking] and so on. From *the very boundary* [of Wales] (original emphasis). To compare that with what existed fifty years ago, it's nigh-on miraculous.]

Such developments begin to illustrate a second key implication of what we have discussed in this chapter, namely the way in which the campaigning activities of Cymdeithas yr Iaith have contributed to the increased embeddedness of the Welsh language within the institutional fabric associated with the Welsh nation and British state within Wales. In this respect, a group-building project associated with Welsh linguistic nationalism has been successful up to a point. A place-based and scalar politics, which began in the early 1960s, and which has continued through until today, has contributed to the gradual evolution of a place of the Welsh linguistic nation (Taylor 1999) as particular linguistic norms began to be applied throughout the country in socio-legal contexts (Williams 2001). This does not mean that the process of defining a Welsh linguistic nation in more material terms should be conceived of as something that is uncontested or in any way finalized. There is a continuing politics of place and scale operating with regard to the production of the Welsh linguistic nation. Political debate regarding the 'true' extent of the Welsh linguistic nation rages, for instance, between Cymdeithas yr Iaith and Plaid Cymru, who view the linguistic nation as something that applies to the whole of the territory of Wales, and Cymuned, who seek to focus political energy on the safeguarding of the so-called Welsh 'heartland' in the north and west of the country (see Jones and Fowler 2007a). This is a theme that we take up at further length in Chapter 7. The existence of this current debate within Welsh nationalist circles should not detract from the role played by the protests that took place in Aberystwyth during the 1960s in shaping a new national linguistic place of Wales. The debate shows, however, that the process of producing a national (linguistic) territory – and the politics of place and scale that characterize this – is clearly emergent and ongoing in character.[12]

NOTES

1   Translated from *'Canys nid oes na ffordd na modd well yn y byd i warchadw iaith rhag ei cholli na gwneuthur Gramadeg iddi ac ohoni'*.
2   At the same time, Dafis (Davies 1973: 252–3) makes clear that the debate about the role of the Welsh language within Welsh nationalism also possessed geographical implications, most notably with regard to the need to preserve the Welsh-speaking 'heartlands' from further linguistic erosion. This theme is taken up in more detail in Chapter 7.
3   The Geltaidd Society was, and still is, a society for Welsh-speaking students in the University (College) of Wales, Aberystwyth.
4   National Library of Wales, PPC Rhan. Cered = Papers of Plaid Cymru, Ceredigion Rhanbarth (Regional Committee): 27.
5   Do you remember Trefechan Bridge?
6   Tedi Milward was, in fact, a tutor in the University College's Welsh Department at this time.
7   NLW, PCYIG = Papers of Cymdeithas yr Iaith Gymraeg: 68/3.
8   A colloquial term for the inhabitants of Cardiganshire, now renamed Ceredigion.
9   NLW, PCYIG Cang. Cered = Papers of Cymdeithas yr Iaith Gymraeg Ceredigion Branch: A 1990/132.
10 NLW, PJD = Papers of John Davies: 1/10.
11 NLW, PCYIG = Papers of Cymdeithas yr Iaith Gymraeg: 40/16
12 In a related context, it would be possible to show how different Welsh speakers, living in different parts of Wales, have attempted to promote alternative visions of the Welsh linguistic nation, depending on their own place-based vernacular versions of Welsh. This theme is discussed in Jones and Desforges (2003).

5

Educating a Welsh nation

INTRODUCTION

The link between nationalism and educational systems has been a long-standing focus of academic enquiry. Work by classical theorists of nations and nationalism, in particular, has shown how state education systems may serve to encourage a greater adherence to nationalist ideals amongst a nation's youth. The famous work conducted by Gellner (see especially 1973; 1983) on nationalism stands out in this respect. As part of his effort to connect the emergence and reproduction of nationalism with the broader transformations associated with modernity, Gellner focused on the key role played by state education systems in creating literate and numerate individuals who could contribute to the reproduction of national states and national economies. The critical issue at stake here is the kinds of demands placed by modern capitalist economies on workers. Instead of stressing the value of manual labour, as had been the case in pre-modern society, capitalist states now required a literate and numerate workforce that could make sense of the standardized procedures that were becoming increasingly important within the world of work, whether on the factory floor or in the offices of state bureaucracies. The only organization with the ability to ensure a standardized education of school children, of course, was the state itself and so it is in this respect that state education systems – namely 'public, standardized, academy-supervised and diploma-conferring institution[s]' (Smith 1998: 31) – were created as a means of inculcating 'the skills, techniques and values of modernity' in a nation's youth.

The development of these public and state-sanctioned education systems impacted in significant ways on the cultures of the inhabitants of the nation. Gellner (1983: 50–2) notes, specifically, how the 'low cultures' or 'wild cultures' of pre-modern society were increasingly replaced by the 'high cultures' or 'garden cultures' of the nation. As part of a process of cultural and linguistic standardization, state education systems sought to distance a nation's youth from their inherited cultural customs and encourage or coerce them into engaging with the new cultural norms associated with the national project. As Gellner (ibid: 55) puts it, the 'general social conditions' associated with modernity 'make for standardized, homogeneous, centrally sustained high cultures, pervading entire populations and not just elite minorities' and which lead to a situation in which 'well-defined educationally sanctioned and unified cultures constitute very nearly the only kind of unit with which men [*sic*] willingly and often ardently identify'. There are strong connections here, of course, between Gellner's ideas and Anderson's (1983) work on the emergence of national print cultures during the modern period, which helped to reinforce notions of linguistic and cultural separation between different nations and which provided the raw cultural material with which schools could educate a nation's youth into its 'high culture'. The most compelling example of such a process, it has been argued, is France. As part of a deliberate nation-building project, the state education system in France sought to inculcate French citizens with a common high culture and the *langue d'oïl* and, at the same time, attempted to eradicate the more vernacular and localized languages and cultures that existed within the state's boundaries (see Calhoun 1997: 75–6; Scott 1998: 72–3). As part of a process that Weber (1977) has described as 'domestic colonization', 'peasants' were transformed – albeit gradually and with no little contestation and conflict – into 'Frenchmen' (see also Sahlins 1989).

Several importance threads can be disentangled from this work. First of all, part of the significance of Gellner's ideas is how they draw attention to the importance of the general experience of a state education system for the creation of a particular type of national citizen. The standardization of experiences within state educational systems, of necessity, can be viewed as a mechanism through which a nation-building project seeks to create a homogeneous nation, united in its loyalty to a national culture (Gellner 1983: 36). The fact that a nation's youth has undergone similar experiences within the state education system, in this way, acts as a common source of reference for all members of the nation. Moreover, as Gellner shows, these common experiences within schools and universities are ones that can be translated into an individual's forms of interaction with the other key institutions of modernity. The discipline learnt within the school environment, for instance, acts as a common reference point for clerks within state bureaucracies, workers on factory floors and soldiers within national armies (more broadly, see Bourdieu 1996; Foucault 1977; 1991). Second, the language used within school environments is an especially important mechanism through which a nation-building project can lead to the reproduction of a 'high culture'. Similarly, the language used as a medium of communication within state education systems can become a source of cultural tension and conflict, especially when minority groups seek to resist the imposition of a perceived alien language upon them. This is a theme that is, of course, especially pertinent to the Welsh example and it is one that will be explored at greater length below. Third, much has been made of the significance of particular subjects that occupy crucial positions within the nation-building project associated with state education systems (see Philippou 2005; Saigol 2005). The subjects of history and geography have been deemed to be especially relevant in this context; history because of its emphasis on glorious national pasts and geography because of its role in teaching children about the bountiful resources of all kinds associated with a particular nation. Hobsbawm (1983: 270–9), in this respect, has shown how the state education system in France, especially in the period after the Franco-Prussian war, took on the important role of communicating a series of national historic traditions to its schoolchildren in school textbooks and through particular practices and rituals. Finally, a focus on state education systems can act as one important way of illustrating how a state elite seeks to transmit a national culture to the mass of the population. The third stage of Hroch's (1985) portrayal of the production of nations in Eastern Europe, for instance, is characterized by the transmission of the national ideology to the general population through organizations such as state education systems and it is this process that enables the nation to take on the form of a mass movement.

Classical theorists' focus on the role of state education systems in forming nations highlights, at least implicitly, the saliency of an educational group-making project that is processual in character. In this way, such work echoes the more fluid conception of the nation that appears in social constructivist work. Social constructivists, in this respect, have furthered this work by attempting to show how a national group-making project is furthered by state education systems. State education systems, in this way, are critical elements within a project of national integration, as is explained by Calhoun (1997: 15–16; see also 79):

> This effort grew alongside the development of censuses and related efforts
> to count and describe the inhabitants, and alongside the building of better
> roads, then railways, and better communications systems (which along
> with more popular education helped to encourage standardization of
> national languages). All of this fostered national integration, making it

meaningful for a map to treat France, say, as a single unit rather than focusing on the divisions among various feudal duchies and baronies.

But, at the same time, we need to be wary of how we conceive of this process of national integration. There is a danger of falling foul of classical theorists' ideas regarding the homogeneous qualities of the nation, which are reproduced on the basis of the dominant nationalist discourse that is perpetuated within state education systems. Obviously, there is some value in stressing such themes since the whole point of a state educational system is its attempt to confer a sense of cultural homogeneity on a disparate group of people. There is still a need, however, to show how different 'subordinated' people – varying in terms of their ethnicity, gender, culture, geographical location and so on – engage within state educational systems in different ways. Some social constructivist accounts of nationalism have implicitly sought to counter such assertions. We think here, for instance, of the work of Yuval-Davis (1997: 32; see also Özkırımlı 2000: 207) on the connections between the social categories of gender and nation. She has shown, for instance, how a woman's constructed position with a nationalist discourse is dependent, at least in part, on her educational achievements.[1]

Other fascinating work has been conducted that begins to show, in a more explicit sense, the variegated relationship between different groups of students and state education systems. With regard to religion, for instance, Kong (2005) has examined the way in which madrasah schools engage with the state education system in Singapore. As part of a nation-building project within Singapore, schools seek to promote two types of discourse. The first is based on a series of ideologies and practices that further a multiracial and multicultural vision of Singapore, which is said to lead to a process of national integration. The aim of this discourse is to promote a common experience for all schoolchildren in Singapore, in which 'multicultures occupy and interact in common space on terms specified by the state' (ibid: 621). The second discourse is based on the construction of state schools as 'sites of modernity, in which students are provided with education aimed at enabling them to partici-pate effectively in the modern economic life of the country' (ibid). The economic relevance of state education is of especial significance in this respect. The fascinating and most pertinent aspect of Kong's work is the way in which she is able to show how madrasahs offer an alternative understanding of the role of education within Singapore. The primary consideration of madrasah schools is to produce the Muslim religious leaders of the future but they are also viewed as sites of a more 'holistic' type of education, in which moral and religious issues are deemed to be of equal importance to purely academic training (ibid: 622). Such work, we would argue, shows how different groups of people – based on religious beliefs in this case – can alter and refract the nation-building project associated with state education systems.

Work conducted in Wales, too, has examined such themes. Research by Desforges and Jones (2000; 2001; 2004), for instance, attempted to chart the engagements of students with higher education through a detailed case study of the University of Wales, Aberystwyth. In particular, they showed how students possessing different linguistic skills – either bilingual Welsh and English or monolingual English – were able to construct differing interpretations of the higher education that they encountered. The linguistic abilities of students, in this respect, determined to a certain extent the way in which students engaged with higher education and its associated nation-building project. Another study, conducted by Scourfield and Davies (2005) within primary schools, attempted to show how schoolchildren articulated different attitudes towards ideas of race and Welshness. Despite a National Curriculum that seeks to promote an inclusive attitude towards ideas of nationhood and multiculturalism, Scourfield and Davies (2005) discovered that primary schoolchildren exhibited a range of different attitudes towards the alleged connections between race and national identity. Most telling in the context of the present discussion was their effort to relate these differing attitudes to the geographical location of schools (ibid: 94–5). Children in schools located in the north and west of Wales, for instance, articulated more exclusive versions of Welshness than children attending primary schools in the more urbanized areas of the south and east. Geographical location, in this respect, was one factor that enabled a differential engagement of schoolchildren with the nation-building project promoted in and through a state-sanctioned education system.

Despite the value of these studies, we maintain that there is considerable scope to supplement this work by showing how various types of people – differentiated in terms of their ethnicity, gender, culture and geographical location – engage with this nationalist project. Our aim in this chapter is to begin to fill this relative lacuna by showing the engagements of Welsh speakers with the British and Welsh nation-building projects in Wales. The following section examines the nationalist politics associated with Welsh-medium education in Wales over the twentieth century and focuses in particular on those instances which illustrate most clearly the significant place-based and scalar processes that were fundamental to this political agitation. We then proceed to concentrate on the important role played by people, organizations and processes in Aberystwyth for the reproduction of a Welsh linguistic nationalism within the higher education sector. Two case studies are used to structure this discussion. The first, which illustrates the significance of place-based processes for a Welsh linguistic politics within the field of higher education in Wales, discusses the campaign for the designation of a Welsh-medium hall of residence within the University. The second case study builds on this theme by examining how Pantycelyn Hall, since its establishment, has acted as a focus of nationalist discourse and practice. In particular, we show how recent protests within the town of Aberystwyth have renewed a politicized and nationalist interpretation of higher education in Wales. In discussing these themes, we seek to show, once again, how a focus on the geographical concepts of place and scale can serve to bring new life to social constructivist interpretations of nations and nationalism.

EDUCATION AND THE REPRODUCTION OF WELSH NATIONALIST DISCOURSE

The role of education in reproducing Welsh identity has been a source of debate over a number of years. For many Welsh nationalists, the most infamous discussion of the connections between the Welsh language, the Welsh identity and education came in the form of the Report of the Royal Commission on Education in Wales (HMSO 1847). Forty years later, it seemed as if the British state's attitude towards the place of the Welsh language within the education system in Wales had undergone somewhat of a transformation. The Royal Commission on Elementary Education in 1886, for instance, stated – without irony – that there was no reason why Welsh should not be taught in schools in Wales, either as a subject or as a medium of education (Williams 1973: 98). Similar state proclamations have been made since this time and have reflected and produced considerable debate concerning the role of the Welsh language within education. For the most part, these debates have centred on the need to reproduce the Welsh language for future generations but they have also been part of broader discussions concerning the role of the education system in reproducing a Welsh national identity. We do not have the time or space to discuss all of these debates in this brief section. Rather we want to focus on the few debates that illustrate the scalar tensions between a nationalist agenda that sought to promote a greater role for the Welsh language within education and more localized educational and nationalist politics of place. The discussion of this secondary material, thus, acts as an appetizer for the more empirical themes that we discuss in the following section.

A key development with regard to the promotion of both the Welsh language within the state education system and an education system that was more Welsh in outlook was the establishment of the Welsh Department of the Board of Education in 1907, under the leadership of His Majesty's first Chief Inspector of Schools in Wales. The formation of this state organization gave a certain 'institutional shape' (Paasi 1991) and legitimacy to Welsh and Welsh-medium education. Under the leadership of O. M. Edwards, it reaffirmed the prescriptions of the earlier Royal Commission on Elementary Education when it stated that 'any of the subjects of the curriculum may be taught in Welsh' and that 'provision should be made for the teaching in every school of Welsh history and the Geography of Wales and Welsh literature' (quoted in Williams 1973: 98). The reference to the subjects of geography and history is significant, in this respect, and echoes some of the broader statements that have been concerning the role played by these subjects in reproducing nationalism within schools (Saigol 2005).

Unfortunately, the impact of these positive statements was limited. Few schools taught the Welsh language and even fewer taught other subjects through the medium of Welsh. The reasons for this lack of enthusiasm are numerous but they testify, in different ways, to the significance of more localized cultures and important gatekeepers within particular communities. As Evans (2000: 344) has shown, the supportive and nationalist prescriptions of individuals such as O. M. Edwards often clashed with the apathy or intransigence of individuals such as headteachers, local authority councillors or parents. But such clashes may well also have reflected different nationalist and educational ideological stances. Jones (1982: 18), for instance, has shown the divide that existed at this time between a Welsh public, which was concerned with securing the economic prosperity and social mobility of its children, and a nationalist educated intelligentsia, who were more concerned with the esoteric connections between a people's language, culture and moral progress (see Chapters 4 and 7). It was for pragmatic reasons such as these that individuals such as the headteacher of the Tonypandy Higher Elementary School could introduce French and Latin into the school curriculum rather than Welsh (Evans 2000: 344). The economic and social needs of his pupils were far more important than the abstract cultural needs of the Welsh nation.

Other scalar tensions became apparent in the academic discussions that were taking place at this time concerning the value of bilingual education. It is significant, too, that much of this research was conducted in the Department of Education of the University College of Wales, Aberystwyth. Work by D. J. Saer, Frank Smith and John Hughes, in particular, had begun to argue that monoglot English speakers were at an educational advantage when compared with their bilingual counterparts (Evans 2000: 349). The research conducted in Aberystwyth generated a more state-centred response from the Welsh Department of the Board of Education. Under the aegis of its Permanent Secretary, Alfred T. Davies, the Department commissioned a report into the role of the Welsh language within the education system in Wales. Significantly, the report, in addition, was charged with offering 'advice to the President of the Board of Education on . . . [the] promotion [of the Welsh language] in all types of educational institutions' (ibid: 351). The report, *Y Gymraeg mewn Addysg a Bywyd* (Welsh in Education and Life), was published in 1927 (HMSO 1927) and proved to be highly significant for the Welsh language. It stated that the Welsh language was in a perilous situation and that its traditional defences had been weakened. Welsh-medium education would, therefore, need to play a crucial role in preserving and regenerating the Welsh language (Evans 2000: 351; Williams 1973: 99). Importantly, strong connections were drawn between the Welsh language and the broader culture of the Welsh nation. The report stated, for instance, that 'the language of a people is the outward expression of its individuality. With the loss of its language some essential part of its character is at least obscured' (HMSO 1927: 180).

And yet, despite this national reassertion of the key role to be played by the Welsh language within education in Wales, there was very little that the Welsh Department of the Board of Education could do practically in order to encourage the greater use of Welsh, either as topic or medium of education. We witness here a recurring tension between the prescriptions made by national organizations and the intransigence of local authorities, headteachers or parents (or a combination of all three). In this respect, Evans (2000: 368) has noted the peculiarity of the state education system in Wales and the broader UK for much of this period: 'the keynote of educational policy-making and administration was the partnership of central government and local education authorities'. But if local intransigence in the face of nationalist prescriptions explains the lack of support for Welsh-medium education at this time, local support for the Welsh language also explains its few isolated successes. Key here

was the opening of the first Welsh-medium primary school in Aberystwyth in 1939 as an independent school sponsored by the Urdd (Williams
1973: 100; Janet Davies 1993: 77). The school was very successful and,
indeed, was to have a 'profound impact on the growth of Welsh-medium
education in the post-war years' (Evans 2000: 357). Local support,
especially in areas of Wales that were becoming increasingly Anglicized,
led to the designation of other Welsh-medium schools. The first primary
school supported by public funds, Dewi Sant, opened its doors in
Llanelli in 1947. Others soon opened in different areas of Wales but what
was common to these various ventures was the way in which they came
about as a result of concerted local support and agitation. Dewi Sant was
opened as a result of agitation by local Welsh-speaking professionals,
while a number of schools were established in Flintshire as a result of the
support of Dr B. Haydn Williams, the Director of Education in the local
education authority (ibid: 361). Local demand, as well as the existence of
some institutional support within local education authorities, also
explains the more gradual expansion in the number of Welsh-medium or
bilingual secondary schools; Ysgol Glan Clwyd opened its doors in 1956
and was followed in 1961 by Ysgol Maes Garmon – both in north-east
Wales – and by Ysgol Gyfun Rhydfelen in the south Wales valleys in
1962 (ibid: 363–4; Janet Davies 1993: 80).

The final instance of a localized politics of place and an associated
scalar relationship with a national education system became apparent in
the localized protests conducted against Welsh-medium education in
different parts of Wales. During the 1970s academics in the university
towns of Aberystwyth and Bangor established the Language Freedom
Movement as a way of protesting against the growing tide of Welsh-
medium education within the Welsh heartland (Janet Davies 1993: 79).
Similarly the local government reorganization that took place in 1974
acted as a spur for some local authorities to consolidate and rationalize
its approach to Welsh-medium education. Gwynedd, in particular, used
the opportunity as a means of strengthening its commitment to Welsh-
medium education, an act that led to considerable consternation for the
Language Freedom Movement. Dyfed, on the other hand, sought to
systematize its approach to Welsh-medium education by designating
different categories of school, which would subsequently incorporate the
Welsh language into their curricula to different degrees. Importantly, the
more formal act of categorizing schools led to a significant and vocal
minority of disaffected parents forming a movement called Education
First, which called for the curtailing of Welsh-medium education on

social and material grounds (ibid: 79). The Language Freedom Movement and Education First, it has been argued, 'seldom disguised their hostility to the Welsh language' and 'equated it with social elitism and the promotion of an unhealthy nationalism' (Evans 2000: 368). What is important in the context of this book is the way in which a particular politics of place and scale are crucial explanatory mechanisms for their formation. Both movements were formed in response to a growing support for Welsh-medium education at both a national and local scale. In addition, both movements derived their support from a politics of place: the presence of an Anglicized academia in the towns of Aberystwyth and Bangor and their conflict with an indigenous Welsh-speaking population in the case of the Language Freedom Movement; the contentious categorization of local primary schools and an associated localized linguistic politics in the case of Education First.[2]

In this section, we have tried to show how debates concerning the promotion of Welsh within the state education system in Wales throughout the twentieth century have been characterized by a particular politics of place and scale. There has been a long-standing tension within the country between the supportive statements made by national organizations concerning the role of the Welsh language – as a subject and medium of instruction – and the apathy that has been apparent in some localities. Indeed, the growth in the provision of Welsh-medium education at primary and secondary level has come about, largely, as a result of those few instances in which national support has been matched by local agitation. One sphere of education that was noticeable by its absence in the above discussion, of course, is that of higher education and we turn to focus at length on this theme in the following section.

ABERYSTWYTH AND THE REPRODUCTION OF A WELSH-MEDIUM HIGHER EDUCATION

It is tempting to view debates surrounding the use of the Welsh language within higher education as ones that existed separately from those taking place at a primary and secondary level but, of course, they were related in large measure. The designation of new Welsh-medium primary schools throughout Wales from the late 1940s onwards impacted in a direct fashion, for instance, on the establishment of two teaching training colleges – in Trinity College, Carmarthen and Coleg Normal, Bangor – which would possess responsibility for training teachers through the medium of Welsh (Williams 1973: 102; Evans 2000:

363). Similarly, the gradual establishment of Welsh-medium secondary schools from the late-1950s and 1960s onwards led to demands by pupils taught within those schools for similar linguistic provision within higher education. More broadly, campaigns for the greater use of Welsh-medium education in primary and secondary schools, in an indirect sense, also created a general atmosphere within which similar demands for a Welsh-medium higher education could take root and flourish.

With this context in mind, therefore, it is no surprise that demands were made for an increased use of the Welsh language within higher education. Much of the activism of the period centred on the need to increase the number and extent of courses taught through the medium of Welsh. Individuals in the Department of Welsh in the University College of Wales, Cardiff had begun to teach courses on Welsh language and literature, fittingly, through the medium of Welsh in the 1920s and by the 1940s, a similar practice was in place in each of the constituent colleges (Janet Davies 1993: 81). The most contentious issue, however, was the expansion of a Welsh-medium education into other subject domains. Evans (2000: 364) notes how Departments of Education, especially the one in the University College of Wales, Aberystwyth fostered a gradual expansion of Welsh-medium education in subjects other than Welsh Language and Literature during the early 1950s. Welsh-medium courses had also been provided within the Department of Philosophy in the same institution (Williams 1973: 104). These developments were given further impetus as twenty-four lecturers were appointed to posts in the constituent colleges of the University of Wales to teach other subjects through the medium of Welsh (Jenkins 1993).[3] This commitment was strengthened in 1968 with the appointment of further Welsh-medium lecturers. The Welsh-medium provision by this time, however, had also become increasingly targeted, in both geographical and thematic terms. The largest numbers of Welsh-medium lecturers were appointed in the University Colleges of Wales at Aberystwyth and Bangor, located within the Welsh-speaking 'heartland' (Morgan 1997: 127; see Desforges and Jones 2001: 335). Deeming Aberystwyth and Bangor to be the most appropriate locations for the development of Welsh-medium courses, we would argue, helped to reinforce long-standing conceptions concerning an alleged – and almost necessary – link between the Welsh language and the rural areas of Wales (see Chapter 7; Bowen 1959; Gruffudd 1994; Jones and Fowler 2007a). In thematic terms, the Welsh-medium education that was being promoted during this period was largely centred on arts and social science subjects. Williams (Williams 1973: 104) notes that appointments were made in Aberystwyth to teach in the subject areas of philosophy, history, geography and French, whereas the Welsh-medium appointments in Bangor were made in the faculties of social science and theology (Jones and Fowler 2007c).[4]

Despite these criticisms, it is evident that these developments represented a welcome expansion of Welsh-medium education at the tertiary level. Significantly, these new appointments also had an indirect positive impact on Welsh-medium teaching within secondary schools as lecturers developed a growing corpus of Welsh terms within particular subject areas (Williams 1973: 105). And yet the nationalist and linguistic campaigning of the post-war period – and especially the activism that took place during the late 1960s and early 1970s – also encompassed other important issues relating to the role of the Welsh language within higher education. One particularly contentious campaign revolved around the need to increase the use of the Welsh language within meetings and official correspondence of the University of Wales' and its constituent colleges. Morgan (1997: 128), for instance, describes how Alwyn D. Rees, the Head of the Department of Extra-Mural Studies in the University College of Wales, Aberystwyth and Warden of the Guild of Graduates of the University of Wales as a whole used his official status as a means of provoking the University of Wales' central authorities to accede to the use of the Welsh language within its meetings. Similar debates took place within the constituent colleges (for Aberystwyth, see Ellis 1972: 321). The issue was not finally resolved until the introduction of simultaneous translation technology during the early 1970s. The other key campaigning issue with regard to Welsh higher education during the late 1960s and early 1970s, especially in locations such as the University Colleges of Aberystwyth and Bangor, was the perceived need to designate Welsh-medium student halls of residence. The need for a Welsh-medium hall of residence in Aberystwyth, for instance, was deemed to especially crucial since it was perceived that the diffuse distribution of Welsh-speaking students throughout a number of different halls within the University College was leading to a gradual waning of the Welsh language and identity within the student population. In many ways, the need to designate a Welsh-medium hall of residence within Aberystwyth can be equated with a nation's desire for a national territory or homeland, within which the culture of the nation can be protected (see Anderson 1988). A Welsh-medium hall of residence, therefore, was viewed as something that could act as a product and a producer of a Welsh identity and the Welsh language within the University College of Wales, Aberystwyth.

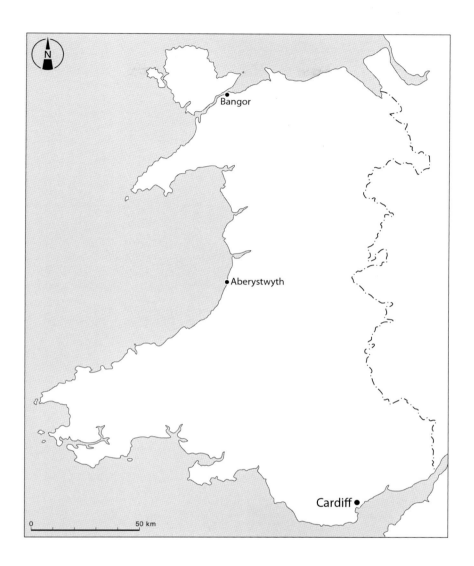

PLATE 3.1. The location of Aberystwyth within Wales
© Institute of Geography and Earth Sciences, Aberystwyth University

PLATE 3.2. An aerial view of Aberystwyth
© Aberystwyth University

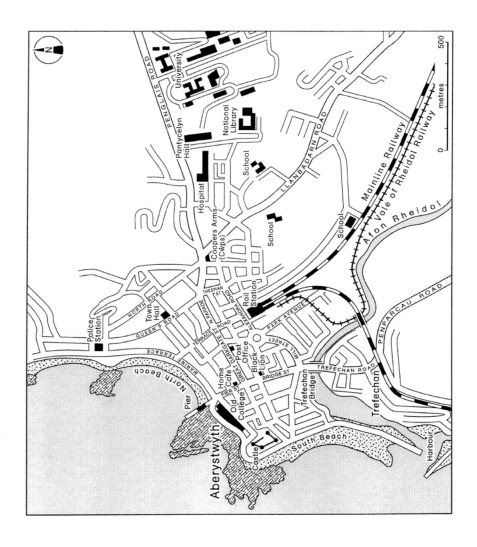

PLATE 3.3. Map of Aberystwyth showing key locations
© Institute of Geography and Earth Sciences, Aberystwyth University

PLATE 4.1. The protest at the Post Office
© National Library of Wales

PLATE 4.2. The protest on Trefechan Bridge
© National Library of Wales

PLATE 4.3. The 'council of war' in the Home Café
© National Library of Wales

PLATE 5.1. Alwyn D. Rees, leader of the campaign?

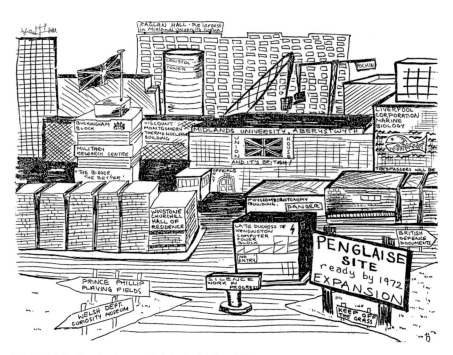

PLATE 5.2. Student complaints in *Llais y Lli*
© Undeb Myfyrwyr Cymraeg Aberystwyth

PLATE 5.3. Pantycelyn Hall © Aberystwyth University

PLATE 5.4. Recent student protests in Aberystwyth © *Cambrian News*

CYMRU WERDD - BYD GWYRDD!

GREEN WALES - GREEN PLANET!

CYFARFOD CYHOEDDUS - *PUBLIC MEETING*

8.00 p.m.

Nos Lun - *Monday*

Mawrth - 16 - *March*

Yr Hen Goleg - *Old College*

Aberystwyth

Siaradwyr - *Speakers*

JONATHON PORRITT

a - *and*

CYNOG DAFIS

Trefnwyd gan: Plaid Werdd Ceredigion a Phlaid Cymru

Called by: Ceredigion Green Party and Plaid Cymru

PLATE 6.1. The Cynog Dafis/Jonathon Porritt meeting
© Plaid Cymru

PLATE 6.2. 'Something in the air'? Aberystwyth prior to polling day © Iolo ap Gwynn

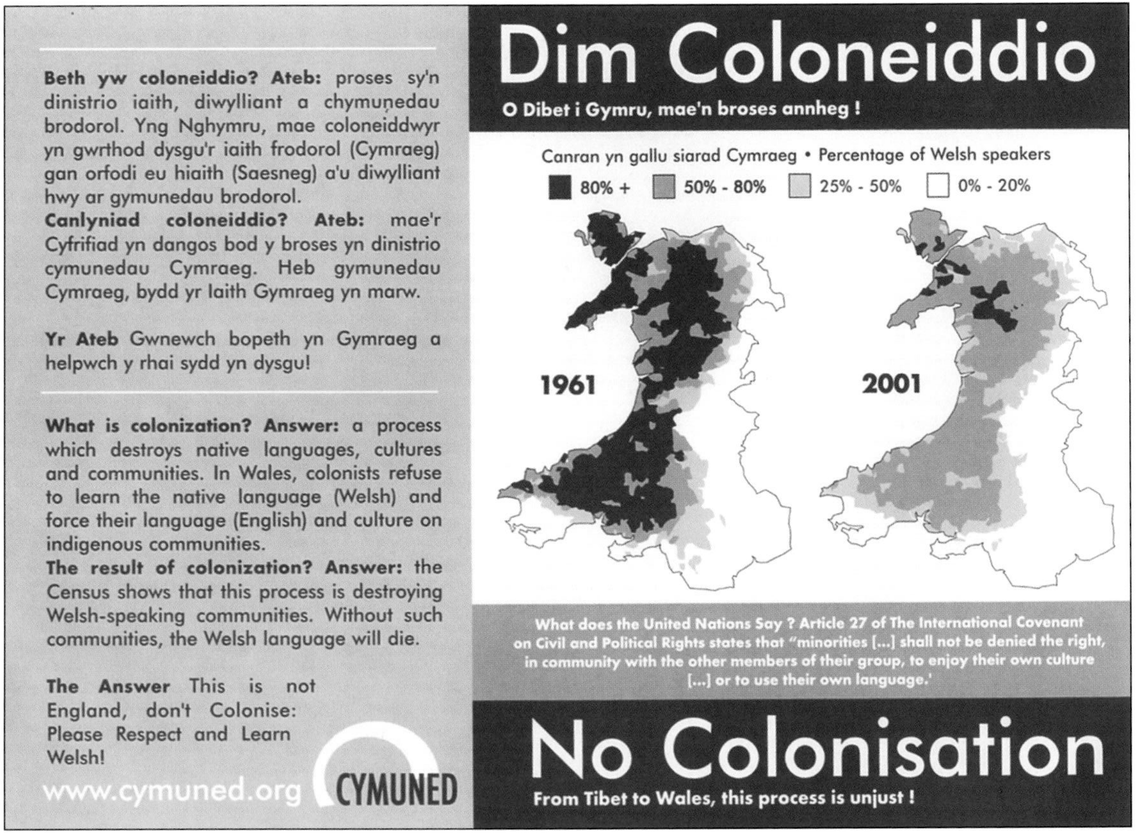

PLATE 7.1. The process of colonization said by Cymuned to be affecting the Welsh heartland © Cymuned

PLATE 7.2. Inscribing the landscape ... defining the heartland © Cymuned

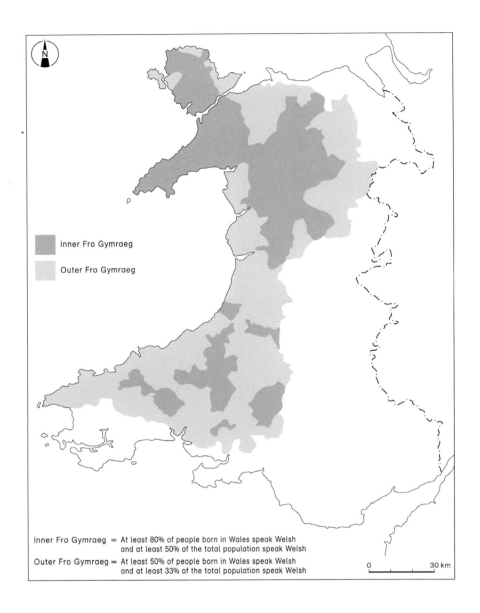

Inner Fro Gymraeg

Outer Fro Gymraeg

Inner Fro Gymraeg = At least 80% of people born in Wales speak Welsh
and at least 50% of the total population speak Welsh
Outer Fro Gymraeg = At least 50% of people born in Wales speak Welsh
and at least 33% of the total population speak Welsh

0   30 km

PLATE 7.3. Map of the Welsh heartland
© Institute of Geography and Earth Sciences, Aberystwyth University

The tangled politics of the designation of such a hall within the University College of Wales, Aberystwyth is discussed in the following section. We then proceed to focus on how the Hall acted as a key site of nationalist politics in Wales, particularly with regard to debates concerning the need to support and expand the proportion of Welsh-medium education being provided in Aberystwyth and a broader Wales. Both these case studies, we maintain, shed considerable light on the politics of place and scale with regard to the reproduction of Welsh nationalism within higher education and of the crucial role played by people, organizations and places within the town of Aberystwyth in shaping this discourse.

Finding a place for Welshness: The campaign for a Welsh-medium hall of residence

There is no doubt that the campaign to establish a Welsh-medium hall of residence was informed by Aberystwyth's emerging status as a key location of nationalist practice and the production of nationalist discourse within Wales. Not surprisingly, students within the University who had been part of broader campaigns to increase the status of the Welsh language in public life were more than ready to translate these concerns into more specific demands that were targeted at the University authorities. This point was made clear by Hywel Roberts, a former editor of *Llais y Lli*, the Welsh language student newspaper of the period, when he argued that the fact that Aberystwyth was the 'home' of Cymdeithas yr Iaith and had been the location of their first official protest acted as a key context for the campaign for the Welsh-medium hostel. But as we have already indicated, the demand for a Welsh-medium hall of residence in Aberystwyth also derived from a belief that the expansion of the University College of Wales from the 1960s onwards, and the distribution of Welsh-speaking students throughout the campus, was having a detrimental effect on the Welsh language within the University and the town. Hywel Roberts, again, expanded on this theme:

> *Roedd y Brifysgol wedi mynd trwy gyfnod o ehangu, ehangu sylweddol . . . mwy na thebyg mi roedd Aberystwyth wedi dyblu yn ei faint . . . Nid yn unig ehangu o ran niferoedd ond ehangu daearyddol hefyd . . . ac mi roedd 'na raglen adeiladu neuaddau preswyl oedd yn raglen sylweddol . . . Y gred oedd wrth gwrs fel oedd y coleg yn ehangu o ran niferoedd, bod canran y Cymry a chanran y Cymreictod, os mynnwch chi, yn lleihau . . . wedi gwasgaru yn y 'digs' neu yn y neuaddau*

preswyl eraill i gyd ... a chymharol fychan fyddai eu dylanwad nhw ar y neuaddau hynny. A chymharol fychanfyddai eu gobaith nhw o ennill unrhyw bleidlais o safbwynt Gymreictod.

[The University had gone through a period of expansion, significant expansion ... Aberystwyth had probably doubled in size ... Not only expansion in terms of numbers but geographical expansion as well ... and there was a programme of building halls of residence which was a significant programme ... The belief was of course that as the college was expanding in terms of numbers, the percentage of Welsh and the percentage of 'Welshness', if you like, was decreasing ... scattered in digs or in the halls of residence ... their influence within those halls would be comparatively small. And their hopes of winning any vote in terms of Welshness would be fairly small.]

The expansion – in terms of physical scale and size of the student population – led to concerted calls to designate a Welsh-medium hall of residence within the University. The campaign for a Welsh-medium hall of residence extended over a period ranging from 1966–73 and involved countless forms of political campaigning; from street demonstrations and student union meetings to heated discussions in the University College's Court, Senate and Council. Our oral history research demonstrates the existence of a complex politics of place, which finally led to the designation of Pantycelyn Hall as the Welsh-medium hall of residence in 1973.

At one level, we need to consider the massive contribution made by individual staff members to the campaign. Alwyn D. Rees, who we have already met, Jac L. Williams, a Professor of Education, and Hywel Moseley, a Professor of Law, were all heavily involved during the early stages of the campaign and they received additional support from Goronwy Daniel, the University College's Principal from 1968 onwards. It is unlikely, in this respect, that the decision to establish single-sex Welsh-medium halls of residence in 1967 would have come about without the advocacy of Rees and Williams. Latterly, Goronwy Daniel would be similarly influential in presiding over the decision in 1972/73 to establish Pantycelyn Hall as the unified, mixed-sex Welsh-medium hall of residence that exists today. But if the campaign to designate a Welsh-medium hall of residence should be viewed as a team effort, it is obvious that the team's leader or captain was Alwyn D. Rees (see Plate 5.1). He was credited by many of our interviewees as being the key instigator of the campaign. Tegwyn Jones, a student at the time, recalls as follows:

Ro'n ni gyd yn teimlo ... dros y pethau yma, heb wybod yn iawn pam ro'n ni'n teimlo dros y pethau yma. Ond roedd Alwyn Rees yn gallu rhoid y peth mewn geiriau ... Fe oedd yn llefaru i ni ... Ac oedd meddwl bargyfreithiwr gyda fe. Roedd e'n gallu gosod achos allan, chi'n gwybod, '1; 2; 3; 4;' ac ar y diwedd 'o'ch chi'n dweud 'wel ie, yn hollol, dyna fel 'o'n i'n teimlo'.

[We all felt . . . in support of these things, without really knowing why we felt for them. But Alwyn D. Rees could put these things in words . . . He spoke for us . . . And he had the mind of a barrister, Because he could set out a case, you know, '1; 2; 3; 4;' and at the end you would say 'well yes, exactly, that's how I felt'.]

Further confirmation of Alwyn D. Rees' critical role within the campaign was provided by John Davies, who would, in turn, become the first Warden of Pantycelyn Hall:

Yn sicr, roedd [Alwyn D. Rees] gyda'r dadleuwyr penna' ar gyngor y coleg a senedd y coleg ac, yn wir, roedd y ffordd oedd e'n gallu defnyddio logic, ro'n i wastad yn teimlo 'wel, dwi'n falch mai ar ein hochr ni mai e' ac nid yr ochr draw, neu bydde fe'n argyhoeddi fi bod popeth dwi wedi gwneud erioed yn wrong!'

[[Alwyn D. Rees] was definitely amongst the best debaters on the college council and senate and, indeed, the way in which he could use logic, I always felt 'well, I'm glad that he's on our side and not the other side, or he would convince me that everything that I had done was wrong!']

In addition, a key enabler of Alwyn D. Rees' activism – and other supporters of the campaign within the body of staff – was their permanence on University structures, as opposed to student cohorts who would change from year to year. Rheinallt Llwyd lamented that the campaigns would lose continuity as students moved on from university, 'but the one person who was there for the duration was Alwyn D. Rees'.

Staff activists, and especially Alwyn D. Rees, were not averse either to promoting their demands on a broader agenda. Alwyn D. Rees, as we have already seen, had sought to make bilingualism a characteristic of committees and meetings for the University of Wales centrally (Morgan 1997: 128). But he also was able to shape this inchoate nationalist educational agenda both within the University and in a broader Welsh context through his journalistic exploits in the Welsh media: the *Western Mail* and the Welsh language periodical, *Barn*, which he edited. John Davies, for instance, told us that Alwyn D. Rees' articles ranked as 'the most powerful and commendable journalism that was ever had in Wales'. Moreover, as Geraint Evans – a student at the time and also a

subsequent warden of Pantycelyn Hall – recalls, Rees' articles provided
an important form of leadership for the students:

> *Rwy' wedi sôn am y trafodaethau oedd yn digwydd yn y neuadd. Ond doedden*
> *nhw ddim yn digwydd mewn gwagle. Mae'n amlwg yr oedden nhw'n digwydd yn*
> *erbyn canfas ehangach. Mi roedden ni hefyd yn darllen ambiti'r peth . . . roedd*
> *llawer iawn o lythyru, erthyglau yn y wasg ac yn y blaen ac yn y blaen. Ac mi*
> *fydde chi'n gallu darllen y* Western Mail, *byddech chi'n edrych ar* Barn, *hynny*
> *yw Alwyn D. Rees, dyna oedd ei blatfform.*

[I have told you about the discussions that were happening in the halls.
But it didn't happen in a vacuum. It was obvious that it was happening
against a broader canvass. We were also reading about it . . . there was a lot
of letter-writing, articles in the press and so on and so on. And you could
read the *Western Mail*, you would look at *Barn*, in other words, Alwyn D.
Rees, that was his platform.]

An additional air of mystery was added to the campaign by the
regular appearance of articles in *Barn* on Welsh-medium provision in
higher education, and the Welsh halls issue, under the pseudonym
Isambard. It has since been established that both Alwyn D. Rees and Jac
L. Williams were responsible for articles written by *Isambard* (Morton
2002). We would argue that these articles, when viewed as a whole, are
highly significant for they illustrate the way in which the campaign for a
Welsh-medium hall of residence in Aberystwyth drew succour from a
broader set of nationalist discourses being promoted at this time by
individuals such as Alwyn D. Rees, Saunders Lewis and so on, as well as
by key organizations such as Cymdeithas yr Iaith. Moreover, the campaign for a Welsh-medium hall of residence also provided additional
fuel for the broader linguistic and nationalist debates taking place
throughout Wales at this time. A student petition in favour of the
designation of a Welsh-medium hall of residence, was, for example,
elaborated upon by *Isambard* – most likely Alwyn D. Rees – in subsequent issues of the *Barn* monthly periodical. In the May edition, *Isambard*
noted, for instance, that a petition had been submitted and that a report
was expected back from the University authorities in June (*Barn* 1967;
see also *Barn* 1968).

But while certain staff members were key advocates of the campaign
for a Welsh-medium hall of residence, it is clear that a large proportion
of the staff were ill-disposed to the proposal. We should not underestimate the preponderance of English-speaking and English staff within
Aberystwyth at this time. It was individuals such as these, for instance,
that established the Education Freedom Movement in Aberystwyth and

Bangor during the early 1970s (Evans 2000: 368). In this respect, University committees of all kinds became a critical battle ground between supporters and opponents of the campaign for the designation of a Welsh-medium hall. Indeed, the climate within University committees during debates on this issue could be incredibly acrimonious (Janet Davies 1993: 82). The opponents of the campaign to designate a Welsh-medium hall of residence drew on a series of different discourses. First of all, a number of individuals maintained that the designation of a Welsh-medium hall of residence would run contrary to the ethos of university life (Ellis 1972: 321). John Davies elaborated on this argument:

> *Ro'ch chi'n cael y syniad bod e'n gul, bod chi'n corlannu ryw grŵp ethnig bach 'da'i gilydd, a'ch bod chi'n hiliol, yn wir. Bod chi'n dewis pobl nid ar sail yr universitas y dylai prifysgol gynrychioli, ond ar ryw sail oedd yn gwbl amherthnasol i unrhyw werthoedd academaidd.*

> [You had this idea that it was narrow, that you were herding some small ethnic group together, and that you were, really, racist. That you were choosing people not on the basis of the universitas that a university should represent, but on some basis that was totally irrelevant to any academic values.]

A second, more extreme, version of this argument was that the designation of a Welsh-medium hall of residence was tantamount to linguistic apartheid or a process of linguistic ghettoization (Morgan 1997: 129), as is explained in the following quote by Hywel Roberts:

> *Y dadleuon yn syml iawn oedd yr hyn a elwyd yn apartheid ieithyddol. Mi roedd e'n derm emosiynol iawn ar y pryd, oherwydd dyma'r cyfnod pan oedd apartheid ar ei anterth yn Ne Affrica, Mandela wedi mynd i garchar, ac yn y blaen . . . ghetto oedd y gair arall oedd yn cael ei ddefnyddio. A rhywsut neu'i gilydd oedd hynny'n gwneud i ni deimlo'n bobl annigonol, negyddol iawn. Dadl ni wrth gwrs oedd mai dyna oedd ein hawl foesol ni, ynde, yn ein prifysgol ni ein hunain, yn ein gwlad ni ein hunain.*

> [The arguments, simply, were ones that were called linguistic apartheid. It was a very emotional term at the time, because this was the period when apartheid was at its height in South Africa, Mandela had gone to gaol, and so on . . . ghetto was the other word that was being used. And somehow or other that made us feel that we were inadequate people, very negative. Our argument of course was that that was our moral right, as it were, in our very own university, in our very own country.]

A third set of arguments revolved around the fact that the campaign for the designation of a Welsh-medium hall of residence was constituted on the basis of improper relationships between certain staff and students. At a time in which many believed in the need to maintain a large social divide between staff and students, the campaign for a Welsh hostel was accused of fostering unhealthy connections between staff and students. Individuals such as Alwyn D. Rees were accused, in this respect, of inspiring a nationalist campaign amongst the students. The following memorandum of 28 March 1973 from certain members of the University Senate to the University Council, for instance, maintained that:

> We feel that politically motivated groups, mainly from outside college, but with some internal support, have influenced policy decisions in ways that we think improper in university institutions . . . We are convinced that any further support given to the Welsh extremists will bring irretrievable harm to the college. (NLW PADR: A13/36)

The key words in this memorandum are 'some internal support', which was a coded reference to the influence of the members of staff that we have mentioned above – Alwyn D. Rees, Jac L. Williams, Hywel Moseley and Goronwy Daniel. Indeed, opponents of the designation of a Welsh-medium hall of residence perceived these individuals as being in league with the students on a whole range of nationalist issues. Finally, and especially when the possibility of designating Pantycelyn Hall as a mixed-sex Welsh-medium hall of residence was being discussed, many opponents were critical of the actual choice of building as the Welsh-medium hostel. Geraint Evans noted the importance of this argument, especially during the early 1970s, when he stated that Pantycelyn *'oedd y neuadd orau . . . o ran ei chyfleusterau . . . [a]. . . a bydden nhw'n colli hwnna a bydde hynny yn mynd i'r Cymry/*was the best hall in terms of its facilities . . . [and] . . . they would lose that and that would go to the Welsh'.

It could be argued, therefore, that the campaign to designate a Welsh-medium hall of residence was played out in various committee rooms and the national press by members of a Welsh nationalist elite and their various opponents. But to focus solely on the role played by University staff in this campaign would be to do a disservice to the active and productive contribution of students to the process. The campaign derived much of its emphasis from protests and activities carried out amongst the Welsh-speaking student population. The initial sparks of the campaign emanated from some of the more mundane aspects of student life. One respondent, for instance, drew attention to their inability to secure enough popular support in mixed-language halls to purchase Welsh-medium literature such as *Y Faner* and *Y Cymro*. But the main source of linguistic discontent arose because of differential access to televisual choices. This situation is recalled by both Hywel Roberts and Bobi Jones:

> *Ym Mhantycelyn pan oeddwn i'n fyfyriwr, un lolfa deledu oedd 'na. A wedyn 'oedd pawb yn mynd i weld* Top of the Pops *a* Dr Who. *A bydde ddim gobaith efo chi o safbwynt byth cael mwyafrif o blaid cael* Heddiw *neu . . . beth bynnag. Byddech chi bob amser mewn lleiafrif. (Hywel Roberts)*

> [In Pantycelyn [Hall][5] when I was a student, there was one TV lounge. So everyone went to watch *Top of the Pops* and *Dr Who*. And you would have no hope in terms of gaining a majority in watching *Heddiw* [literally 'Today', and one of the few regular Welsh-medium television programmes at the time] or . . . whatever. You would always be in a minority.] (Hywel Roberts)

> *Wedyn un digwyddiad mawr mewn blwyddyn byddai, dwedwch chi, drama gan Saunders Lewis ar y teledu. Ac wedyn fyddai myfyrwyr Cymraeg yn tyrru i'r neuadd lle roedd y set deledu – yr unig set deledu ar y pryd! – ac wedyn mi fyddai myfyrwyr Saesneg a oedd yna ar y pryd ishe rhywbeth fel* Coronation Street, *chi'n gweld, ynde.* (Bobi Jones)

> [Then one big occasion in a year would be, say, a drama by Saunders Lewis on the television. And then the Welsh-speaking students would pile in to the hall where the television set was – the only television set at the time! – and then English students that were there at the time would want something like *Coronation Street*, you see.] (Bobi Jones)

Such statements illustrate how a highly localized politics of place was crucial to the emergence of the campaign for a Welsh-medium hall of residence. In addition, this evidence chimes with other work that has sought to emphasize the significance of small-scale and mundane processes occurring within specific localities for the reproduction of nations. Conflicts taking place within particular localities are reworked into local forms of nationalist conflict (Billig 1995; Jones and Desforges 2003; see also Thompson 2001).

Tensions such as these led to a raft of different forms of protest being instigated during this period, including petitions, meetings and protests. There is documentary evidence from the period, which testifies that the student campaign began as early as 1965. The Welsh-language student newspaper, *Llais y Lli*, provided a prominent focal point for the grievances of Welsh-speaking students. The halls issue was first raised explicitly on 12 January 1965 under the rhetorical headline 'A Welsh Hall For Aber?' (*Llais y Lli* 12 January 1965). The agenda was carried forward in general terms in an editorial column on 2 October which dwelt on the social and cultural fabric of the University and of Welshness therein (*Llais y Lli* 2 October 1965). A more direct attack on University policy occurred on 15 November, in a front page which exclaimed: 'Expansion! But what about the Welsh?' (*Llais y Lli* 15 November 1965). The editorial lambasted the University authorities for following an expansionist agenda with little reference to its possible impacts on the status of the Welsh language. It was argued: '*yn ôl pob tebyg bydd yn ddu iawn ar Gymreictod y coleg os byth y cawn ni chwech neu hyd yn oed pedair mil o fyfyrwyr yma*/more than likely it will be very black for the Welshness of the college if we have six or even four thousand students here'. Indeed, the editor believed that: '*mae'r Cymry yn cael eu boddi fel y mae hi*/the Welsh people are being drowned as it is' (ibid). The editorial was followed by a satirical diagram of the envisaged campus (see Plate 5.2), complete with 'Prince Philip Playing Fields', 'Winstone [*sic*] Churchill Hall of Residence' and a modern towerblock proclaiming 'Midlands University, Aberystwyth', as well as a parody of R. Williams Parry's famous ode to *Eifionydd*:

> Mae golwg hagrwch cynnydd
> Ar wyneb trist Penglais,
> Bu'n fro rhwng môr a mynydd
> Heb arno graen na Sais,
> Ond daeth peiriannau ar y ffridd
> I rwygo coleg neis o'r pridd.

> [The haggard look of progress
> Lies on the sad face of Penglais,
> It was a land betwixt sea and mountain
> Without lustre nor English person,
> But machines came on the meadow
> To rip a nice college from the soil.]

Further articles published in *Llais y Lli* in December 1965 and February 1966 illustrate the complex connections between the very localized politics of place in Aberystwyth at this time and the broader currents within which Welsh nationalist discourse was being reproduced. The two articles were penned by D. J. Williams, an eminent writer and founder member of Plaid Cymru, and expressed concern at the encroachment of 'Englishness' within the University. His endorsement of the students' campaign was seen as something of a coup for the student leaders (*Llais y Lli* 13 December 1965; 28 February 1966). In November 1966, D. J. Williams, once again, expressed his specific personal support for a Welsh hall of residence (*Llais y Lli* 15 November 1966).

The student campaign reached its zenith during the 1966–7 term. On 1 March 1967 a petition signed by 149 students, referred to above, was presented to the University authorities (Interview, Rheinallt Llwyd). A copy of the petition still exists (NLW PADR: A13/3) and includes the names of some of our prominent interviewees, such as Hywel Roberts, Geraint Evans and Rheinallt Llwyd. The petition reads:

> We, the undersigned, are eager to see the establishment of a Welsh hostel and declare our willingness to reside in it ourselves where possible. We should wish that a certain proportion of the residents are learners.

The wording of the petition is significant, in this respect, since it alludes to the students' perceived need to counter the allegations of linguistic apartheid by portraying the proposed hall as a place that would be open to outside influences in the form of Welsh learners. Efforts were made, in effect, to ensure that the Welsh nationalist discourse implicitly connected with the campaign to establish a Welsh-medium hall was as inclusive as possible. In any case, the petition generated a certain momentum for the cause and this was augmented by the more supportive members of the University staff. The matter of a Welsh-medium hall was officially brought to the attention of the Finance and General Purposes Committee of the University on 22 November 1965 in a memorandum submitted by Jac L. Williams. The memorandum called for the designation of a mixed-sex Welsh-medium hall. The Committee responded to the memorandum in a positive, if rather convoluted, fashion:

> it was Recommended . . . That consideration might be given in the future planning of halls of the designation of units as Language Halls, in which a language other than English would be the official language and the expected medium of conversation. (UCWA 1965)

A working party was established in order to address the issue of a Welsh-medium hall and it reported its findings on 17 April 1967 (UCWA 1967a). It was recommended within the report that a steering committee should conduct a questionnaire amongst all those students entering the University in October 1967 to enquire whether they would want to reside in a Welsh-medium hall or Welsh-medium halls. Council minutes indicate that lengthy discussions took place in Council meetings in November and December 1967, and again in March 1968. A delegation from Y Geltaidd (the Welsh Language Society within the University) was present in each of these meetings (UCWA 1967b; 1967c; 1968a). The first stage of the campaign formally came to a close in the Council meeting held in June 1968, in which support was given for the establishment of two single-sex Welsh-medium halls of residence:

> It was reported that at a special meeting of the Court of Governors a resolution had been adopted calling for the 'designation of two Halls of Residence as Welsh Halls from October 1968 onwards, for the admission of students who have expressed a preference for a Welsh Hall. The two Halls which might be so designated are Ceredigion (Men) and Neuadd Davies Bryan (Women). (UCWA Council Minutes 1968b; see also Morgan 1997: 129)

The experience of students in the two single-sex halls of residence was overwhelmingly positive and, before long, demands for the establishment of a mixed-sex Welsh-medium hall resurfaced. The decision to establish such a hall was made in a Senate meeting in October 1973 and this decision was finally ratified by the University Council in November of the same year. In spite of the positive decision, several protestations by opponents of the scheme were noted. The Committee on Student Residences, by a narrow majority, favoured the establishment of such a hall in Penbryn. A letter from the Secretary of the Non Professorial Staff, too, regretted the fact that the Senate had supported a proposal for Pantycelyn to be designated as the Welsh hostel. Furthermore, a petition was signed by 488 staff and students objecting to the use of Pantycelyn as a mixed-sex Welsh language hall. This petition also expressed 'the view that the setting up of linguistically segregated residential accommodation is contrary to the spirit and purpose of university education' (UCWA Council Minutes 1973). It has been argued that the key figure in ensuring that the Senate's decision was ratified in Council was Goronwy Daniel, the College Principal at that time (Morgan 1997: 129). Many of our interviewees maintained that he showed a remarkable sense of leadership at this difficult time. But despite the resistance to the planned designation of Pantycelyn as a mixed-sex Welsh-medium hall of residence, it is surprising how quickly the Hall became an accepted part of the life of the University College (see Plate 5.3). The following material comes from a leaflet that was distributed to all prospective students of the College in February 1975 and gives a clear sense both of the reasoning behind the campaign for such a hall in the first place and the degree to which it had already assumed a degree of permanence and, indeed, banality:

> Pantycelyn Hall has been designated a Mixed Welsh Hall since 1974. There are enough Welsh-speaking students in this Hall to ensure that the day-to-day-language of the hall is Welsh. The object is to give to the Welsh-speakers a home in the College which is compatible with their

background, to promote cultural activities using the medium of the Welsh language, and to provide a suitable atmosphere for those who wish to learn Welsh or to improve their knowledge of the language . . . A welcome is also extended to those who have no firm desire to learn Welsh but would like to broaden their understanding of the life and culture of Wales. This could be of special interest to overseas students. (UCWA Senate's Halls' Committee Minutes 2 February 1975)

The campaign to establish a Welsh-medium hall of residence in Aberystwyth, we would argue, illustrates some of the important connections that we have been seeking to discuss in this book. The whole tenor of the campaign was based around the need to designate a 'protected place' for the Welsh language and those who associated themselves with a Welsh national identity. In this way, the campaign echoed the broader debates taking place during the 1960s and 1970s concerning the need to protect the Welsh-speaking heartland from a process of linguistic and cultural erosion (see also Chapter 7). The early stages of the campaign, too, were based on a close interaction between a highly localized politics of place and the broader linguistic and nationalist discourses being promoted by individuals such as Alwyn D. Rees and D. J. Williams. And, as we show in the following section, the formation of Pantycelyn as a mixed-sex Welsh-medium hall of residence was to have a significant impact on the reproduction of Welsh-nationalist discourse in the years that followed.

Pantycelyn, nationalist agitation and Welsh-medium education

In the period subsequent to its establishment, Pantycelyn has developed into a fruitful seedbed for nationalist agitation and the production of nationalist discourse within Wales. In many ways, the Hall has succeeded in bringing together – and mixing – various types of individuals and various types of nationalists from different parts of Wales. Its success as a general 'melting pot' of people from different parts of Wales is made clear in the following quote by Geraint Evans, a former Warden of the Hall:

Roedd pobl o gymoedd y de a Pwllheli yn cael eu bwrw at ei gilydd fel 'na . . . A felly roedd Pantycelyn mewn ffordd fechan, efallai, yn gallu gwneud cyfraniad i'r cenedligrwydd 'na . . . Dychmygwch y 'scenario': mae rhywun o Treorci yn dod ac maen nhw'n mynd lawr i'r Cwps ac mae'n nhw'n cwrdd â rhywun o Borthmadog, reit? Dyw hi ddim yn or-ddweud, oherwydd dwi wedi clywed pobl yn dweud hyn, o'n nhw prin yn deall ei gilydd yn siarad. Ond, maen nhw'n dod yn ffrindiau mawr, ac yn ffrindiau mawr, ac yn ffrindiau pennaf.

[There were people from the south Wales valleys and Pwllheli being brought together like that ... And therefore Pantycelyn in a small way, perhaps, was able to make a contribution to that sense of nationalism ... Imagine the scenario: someone from Treorchy coming and they go down to the Cŵps and they meet someone from Porthmadog, right? It's not an overstatement, because I've heard people say this, they could hardly understand each other talking. But, they become big friends, big friends, and best friends.]

The significance of the above quote is the way in which it illustrates a common theme within theories of nationalism, namely how particular common experiences act as important lubricators of the emergence of nationalism. Tilly (1975), for instance, has discussed the significance of the formation of standing armies for the development of nationalism as different individuals come together, and are mixed together, as part of a national cause. In the same way, Pantycelyn can be viewed as a specific location that has enabled a mixing of different kinds of Welsh people so that they came to view each other as members of the same nation (Desforges and Jones 2000). Moreover, it was argued that Pantycelyn's location in Aberystwyth meant that it was particularly successful in mixing individuals from both south and north Wales, in contradistinction to other Welsh-medium halls of residence, such as Neuadd John Morris Jones in Bangor.[6] Individuals from certain parts of south Wales, in particular, were deemed to bring a particular verve to Welsh nationalism and related campaigns for an increase in Welsh-medium education, as the following quote from John Davies, one-time Warden of the Hall, indicates:

Maen nhw [pobl o gymoedd De Cymru] wedi cael y profiad yna yn yr ysgol. Mae 'na rywbeth wedi digwydd iddyn nhw, wedi cael eu tanio ... maen nhw'n dod o gymuned ddi-Gymraeg ... yn dilyn testunau trwy gyfrwng y Gymraeg yn yr ysgol, maen nhw'n dod i Pantycelyn, maen nhw am fyw yn y neuadd, mae eu Cymreictod nhw yn cryfhau ac yn y blaen ac yn y blaen, oherwydd, un rheswm yw ble maen nhw, a wedyn 'ny cam naturiol yw bod nhw'n disgwyl hynny i gael ei adlewyrchu wedyn 'ny mewn ffordd ehangach o fewn y coleg.

[They've [people from the south Wales valleys] have had that experience in school. Something has happened to them, been fired up ... they come from a community which isn't Welsh-speaking ... following subjects through the medium of Welsh in school, they come to Pantycelyn, they want to live in the hall, their Welshness strengthens and so on and so on, because, one reason is where they are, and then a natural step is for them to expect that to be reflected in a broader way within the college.]

But as well as being a 'clearing house' for Welsh people and Welsh nationalists of different hues, it is evident that Panctycelyn over the years was able to act as a source of Welsh nationalist activists, activities and broader discourses. For Hywel Roberts, one of the early campaigners for the designation of a Welsh-medium hall of residence, Pantycelyn had become a *'ffatri ddeinamig*/dynamic factory' of Welshness and a '"nucleus" *o weithgaredd, p'run ai ydy e'n wleidyddol neu'n ddiwylliannol*/a nucleus of activity, whether it is political or cultural'. During the 1970s, for instance, students from Pantycelyn were extremely active in the campaigns for Welsh roadsigns and a Welsh television channel. John Davies, Warden of the Hall at the time, explained the centrality of Pantycelyn students within these events:

Amser yr ymgyrchoedd mawr ar arwyddion ffyrdd, a'r brotest teledu, roedd ymweliadau cyson gan yr heddlu . . . tri o'r gloch y bore. Rwy'n cofio adeg pan 'o'ch chi'n teimlo [os] oedd hi'n werth mynd i'r gwely, achos 'oedd ryw gnoc ar y drws am dri . . . roedd y myfyrwyr, yn ddigon teg, yn mo'yn i rywun fod yn eu 'stafelloedd nhw, pan 'oedd yr heddlu yn ymchwilio . . . mater o eistedd dwy awr tra 'o'n nhw'n chwilota 'stafelloedd, a mynd i beilo mas, a dweud gair da drostyn nhw yn y llys ac yn y blaen, 'oedd e' gyd yn eithaf cyffrous.

[At the time of the large campaigns concerning road signs, and the television protest, there were frequent visits by the police . . . three o'clock in the morning. I remember a period when you wondered [whether] it was worth going to bed at all, because there was a knock on the door at three . . . the students, understandably, wanted someone to be in their rooms when the police were searching . . . a matter of sitting for two hours while they searched rooms, and going to bail out, and say a few words for them in court and so on, it was all quite exciting.]

Students residing within the Hall were also active during the 1980s, particularly in the various campaigns and protests being promoted by Cymdeithas yr Iaith. Llyr Huws Griffiths, for instance, remembered how Pantycelyn students were viewed as 'flying pickets' within many of these activities. He went on to argue as follows:

Os oedd 'na rali yn rhywle, os oedd 'na gyfarfod cyhoeddus yn rhywle, neu os oedd 'na weithredu mwy uniongyrchol yn digwydd . . . peintio slogannau, neu godi posteri, y math yna o beth, yn sicr mi oedd 'na griwiau yn mynd o Bantycelyn i bob cwr o Gymru i gyflawni gwahanol dasgau. Felly bydden i'n meddwl bod 'na 'impact' wedi bod yng nghyd-destun cael argraff ar ymgyrchoedd cenedlaethol, yn sicr.

[If there was a rally anywhere, if there was a public meeting anywhere, or if more direct action was taking place . . . painting slogans, raising posters, that sort of thing, certainly there were crews going from Pantycelyn to every part of Wales to complete different tasks. Therefore I would have though that there had been an 'impact' in terms of having an impression on national campaigns, certainly.]

The above quote illustrates how students based within Pantycelyn were instrumental within broader nationalist campaigns. At the same time, of course, individual students based within the Hall were influenced by the nationalist discourses being promoted by different organizations. As an example, we can focus on the late 1980s and early 1990s, which was a period of considerable nationalist discontent and discord. One instance of this discord revolved around the fire-bombing campaign conducted by Meibion Glyndŵr (Gruffydd 2004). A particularly ardent group of nationalists within the Hall at this time were labelled the 'MG Mob' by their peers. At one level, therefore, particular political identities within the Hall were being shaped by the broader currents of Welsh nationalism. At the same time, these selfsame individuals sought to contribute to the broader nationalist debate surrounding Meibion Glyndŵr. In 1991, the well-known actor and singer Bryn Fôn was arrested on suspicion of being a member of Meibion Glyndŵr and this event led to a demonstration of mass support for Meibion Glyndŵr by individuals in Pantycelyn; the 'MG Mob' among them, as Llyr Huws Griffiths explains:

Ac mi welwyd yn ystod fy nghyfnod i yn y coleg wrth gwrs, arestio Bryn Fôn a rhai ffigurau eraill. A be' dwi'n credu lwyddodd hynny i wneud oedd symud Pantycelyn lan y Richter Scale 'ambiti ddwy notch, yntife . . . arwr gwerin gwlad yn cael ei arestio, ac mi oedd 'na 'undercurrents' o gefnogaeth cryf i Feibion Glyndŵr ar draws y wlad, dwi'n meddwl . . . A dwi'n credu bod hynny'n cael ei adlewyrchu ym Mhantycelyn yn yr ystyr pan gafodd Bryn Fôn ei arestio, o fewn pedair awr ar hugain roedd 'na ddau, tri llond car o fyfywyr wedi mynd lan i bicedi tu fas i orsaf heddlu Dolgellau, lle oedd Bryn Fôn yn cael ei gadw. Ac o fewn tri, pedwar diwrnod roedd na rhai cannoedd o bobl yn picedi tu fas, gan gynnwys nifer o unigolion . . . o Bantycelyn.

[And during my time in college, of course, we saw Bryn Fôn and some other figures being arrested. And I think what that did was move Pantycelyn up the Richter Scale about two notches . . . a Welsh folk-hero being arrested, and there were 'undercurrents' of support for Meibion Glyndŵr across the country, I think . . . And I think this was reflected in Pantycelyn in the sense that when Bryn Fôn was arrested, within twenty-four hours two, three cars full of students had gone up to picket outside Dolgellau police station, where Bryn Fôn was being held. And within three, four days there were some hundreds of people picketing outside, including many people . . . from Pantycelyn.]

Here, Pantycelyn is portrayed as both the product and producer of broader nationalist discourse and practice in Wales. Another indication Pantycelyn's significance for the production of nationalist discourse and practice in Wales in the way in which it helped to create a generation of nationalist activists who subsequently became key leaders of different organizations associated, admittedly in various measures, with Welsh nationalism. The following list, we maintain, is indicative of the broader impact of Pantycelyn on the reproduction of Welsh nationalism: Dafydd Trystan, resident in the early 1990s, who subsequently became Chief Executive of Plaid Cymru; Simon Thomas, Elfyn Llwyd (MPs) and Helen Mary Jones (AM), who became elected representatives of Plaid Cymru; Simon Brooks, Lefi Gruffudd and Siôn Jobbins, who were resident in the Hall in the late 1980s and early 1990s and who later became leading figures in Cymuned; Jim O'Rourke, resident in the 1970s, who became Chief Executive of the Urdd; and; a number of different individuals who have subsequently become members of Cymdeithas yr Iaith's governing body.

But we would be remiss if we did not highlight the significance of Pantycelyn Hall for the promotion and reproduction of particular campaigns in favour of Welsh-medium education. We witness the clearest instance of such activism in the context of recent demands for greater investment in Welsh-medium higher education. It is significant that this campaign has centred on both the local and national contexts for Welsh-medium higher education; in this regard, successive vice-chancellors of the University of Wales, Aberystwyth and the National Assembly's Minister for Education, Jane Davidson, have been the subject of the student's ire. At one level, the context for the current round of activism has been the establishment of a National Assembly and the increased social and cultural expectations that have come in its train. And yet, the emergence of more militant student activity in Aberystwyth over recent years has also derived from interactions between Aberystwyth and national organizations as well as changed circumstances within the town and University itself. With regard to connections between the local and the national scale, it is clear that student militant activity, particularly with regard to issues of language and education, emerged as a result of the University's efforts to develop and implement a language scheme, as it is required to do under the Welsh Language Act 1993 (see Welsh Language Board 2000). The University of Wales, Aberystwyth was criticized from many quarters because of its allegedly half-hearted efforts to develop and implement a scheme.[7] Allied to the Welsh Language Board's criticism of the University was a growing feeling amongst Welsh-medium students that more needed to be done to improve the status of the Welsh language within University administration and teaching. At the same time, particular developments within Aberystwyth itself also contribute to the emergence of an increasingly active student body. In this regard, we cannot underestimate the role of student leaders within Aberystwyth. Gwion Evans, the President of Undeb Myfyrwyr Cymraeg Aberystwyth (UMCA), the Welsh student union, in 2001–2, for instance, was credited by his successor as an individual who 'wedi *plannu hadau pwysig ofnadwy*/sowed extremely important seeds' with respect to student campaigns in favour of Welsh-medium activism. More sustained activism occurred, however, with the election of Catrin Dafydd as President of UMCA. She was described by her fellow students as someone with '*bach o* "go" *arni*/a bit of "go" in her'.

Given the above comments, it is not surprising that the majority of the students' campaigns in the period between 2002 and 2004 centred on the perceived linguistic fallibility of the University of Wales, Aberystwyth. Catrin Dafydd explained how the publication of the University's proposed Welsh-language scheme provided considerable impetus in this regard:

> '*O'n ni gyd yn gwybod yn y drydedd [flwyddyn] bod y Cynllun Iaith ar fin dod mas, a 'o'n ni'n gwybod yn iawn bod e'n annigonol, felly 'oedd e'n sail wych i ni allu mynd amdani . . . Tri chwarter awr oedd y brotest yna, ond fi'n credu gafodd e gymaint o effaith achos bod pobl methu credu bod ni'n 'actually' dechrau gwneud e' eto, a bod 350 o fyfyrwyr wedi dod mas.*

> [We all knew in the third [year] that the Language Scheme was about to be published, and we all knew that it was lacking, so it was a brilliant reason for us to go for it . . . That protest was for three quarters of an hour, but I think it had so much of an effect because people couldn't believe that that we were actually starting to do it again, and that 350 students had come out.]

This quote is fascinating, we believe, since it shows the extent to which the re-emergence of instances of direct action amongst the student body came as a surprise to both the students themselves and, presumably, the University authorities. It also shows the extent of the support for student action, in terms of physical numbers, at this time. Protests continued against the University throughout this period. On 9 February, 2004, for instance, over 100 students blocked the main entrance into the University campus. Osian Rhys, the Welsh-language officer in the main Student Guild, was quoted by the BBC in this protest. He argued that 'Welsh-speaking students are being treated unfairly' and went on to contend that 'education through the medium of Welsh here is very patchy and is minute in comparison to what is available in English'.[8]

What is really significant about these protests is the way in which they have also set their sights on the broader national agenda for Welsh-medium higher education. Catrin Dafydd, who led much of the campaigning at this time, explained the importance of this 'two-pronged approach':

> *Cawson ni glywed, trwy rhywun oedd ddim fod dweud, bod Jane Davidson [Gweinidog Addysg Llywodraeth y Cynulliad Cenedlaethol] yn dod yma. Wrth gwrs, 'oedd hynny'n gyfle euraid i ni allu ganolbwyntio ar y Cynulliad yn hytrach na'r Brifysgol am ychydig. Achos mae'n 'two-pronged approach' mewn ffordd, achos mae gyda ti'r Cynulliad a'r Brifysgol i dargedu. Y Brifysgol yn gwneud yn wael gyda'r adnoddau presennol. Ond mae'r Cynulliad yn erchyll o ran faint o arian maen nhw'n rhoi i hynny [addysg cyfrwng-Cymraeg].*

> [We got to hear, from someone who wasn't supposed to say, that Jane Davidson [the National Assembly Government's Minister for Education] was coming here. Of course, that was a golden opportunity for us to be able to concentrate on the Assembly for a while rather than the University. Because it's a two-pronged approach in a way, because you've got to target the Assembly and the University. The University doing poorly with the current resources. But the Assembly is awful in terms of the amount of money they give to that [Welsh-medium education].]

On 11 March 2004, students confronted the Minister in Aberystwyth and demanded an increased financial support for Welsh-medium education from the Assembly (see Plate 5.4). The students discussed the lack of support offered by the Assembly to the Welsh language within higher education in Wales. They referred specifically to the figure of 0.3 per cent, which represented the proportion of moneys allocated to the higher education sector in Wales that was spent on Welsh-medium provision. It is significant that in the months following this protest, Jane Davidson was able to announce that extra moneys would be made available from the Assembly's Reconfiguration and Collaboration Fund to support Welsh-medium higher education, specifically through the establishment of a Welsh-medium postgraduate scholarship and fellowship scheme.[9] There is no direct evidence to connect the establishment of this scheme with the protests that took place in Aberystwyth but student activists, not surprisingly, were convinced of the instrumental role that they had played in facilitating this significant development, as Catrin Dafydd makes clear below:

> *Ar ôl y protestiadau hynny, wnaeth hi ddweud bod arian allan o . . . y peth ail-gyflunio 'ma . . . dyna pam oedd hi'n cwrdd â Derec Llwyd Morgan*

[Is-Ganghellor Aberystwyth ar y pryd] . . . yn y lle cyntaf. Dywedodd hi mai dim oherwydd y myfyrwyr oedd e', ond bod hi wedi penderfynu bod na pot o arian yn y strwythur ail-gyflunio bydde hi'n gallu rhoi i addysg Gymraeg . . . Wnaeth hi ddweud taw dim oherwydd y myfyrwyr ond fi'n gwybod yn iawn na fydde hi ddim wedi gwneud unrhyw beth oni bai bod y 400 . . . wedi lleisio pa mor gryf oedden nhw'n teimlo.

[After those protests, she said that money out of . . . this re-configuration thing . . . that was why she was meeting with Derec Llwyd Morgan [the Vice-Chancellor of Aberystwyth at the time] . . . in the first place. She said it wasn't because of the students, but that she had decided that there was a pot of money in the re-configuration structure that she would be able to give to Welsh education . . . She said that it wasn't because of the students but I know for sure that she wouldn't have done anything apart from the fact that 400 . . . had stated how strongly they felt.]

The above quote suggests that the students themselves believed strongly that they had been able to shape the agenda for Welsh-medium higher education at a national Welsh scale. Further evidence that students in Aberystwyth adopted a national perspective at this time emerges in their efforts to organize a national campaign for Welsh-medium higher education that would extend throughout the whole of Wales. Students from Aberystwyth, for instance, were instrumental in arranging a national student rally in Cardiff at the beginning of March 2004. Catrin Dafydd, in the following quote, explains how this rally formed part of a conscious rescaling of political activity on behalf of the students:

Ro'n i wedi bod yn trefnu ers tri mis . . . y Rali Genedlaethol, achos 'o'n i'n meddwl bod rhaid . . . i fi wneud rhywbeth . . . i ddangos bod fi yn rhywun oedd mo'yn gwneud rhywbeth fel ymgyrch oedd yn mwy na jyst yn blwyfol, a bod e' yn apelio at nifer o wahanol fathau o bobl. Achos mae fyfyrwyr sydd yn fyfyrwyr yng Nghaerdydd, mae eu cwynion nhw yn hollol wahanol i ni ond mae'r brif gwyn yna, mae rhywbeth yn gyffredin.

[I had been arranging for three months . . . the National Rally, because I thought that . . . I had to do something . . . to show that I was someone who wanted to do something like campaign that was more than just parochial, and that it appealed to a variety of different kinds of people. Because students who are students in Cardiff, their complaints are totally different to us but that main complaint, something is in common.]

Student activists in Aberystwyth were keen at this time, therefore, to demonstrate that their concerns were not parochial in character but rather extended into a regard for the future of the Welsh language in the higher education sector throughout the whole of Wales. The Rally drew support from various organizations, such as Plaid Cymru, UCAC (the Welsh Union of School Teachers) and Rhieni Dros Addysg Gymraeg (Parents for Welsh Education).[10] This protest, in many ways, gave further impetus for Jane Davidson's announcement of the marked increased in financial support for the Welsh language in higher education in Wales, made in 2004 (see above). Students within Aberystwyth, in particular, have sought to further their national and, we would argue, nationalist agenda by demanding the establishment of a Welsh Federal College, which would act as a centre for enhancing the provision of Welsh-medium courses in higher education.[11] While the exact nature of this Federal College has been the subject of considerable debate over a number of years (e.g. see R. W. Jones 2001b; 2004), students demanded that it should include branches in a number of different higher education institutions in Wales, along with a separate administrative system and independence with respect to granting degrees.[12] Recent studies conducted by the University of Wales have rejected the feasibility of the creation of such an institution but the concept of a Welsh Federal College still retains considerable appeal among student activists concerned with the long-term health of the Welsh language within the higher education sector in Wales.

CONCLUSIONS

In this chapter, we have focused on the connections between education and nationalist discourse. Much has been made in the literature on nationalism about the key role of state education systems in reproducing nationalist discourse. They are, moreover, key features of the nation-building project: they take young members of the nation and educate them concerning their position within a world of nations; they also teach the youth of the nation about national cultures, histories and geographies, which assume the status of a 'common (national) knowledge'. And yet, state education systems are also places of nationalist debate and discord, as illustrated by the evidence discussed from Wales. From the mid-nineteenth century onwards, concerns about the relative roles of the English and Welsh languages within the different sectors of the education system in Wales have been apparent. This concern has been centred, largely, on the need to reproduce the Welsh language but it has also extended outwards into themes relating to political identity. The Welsh language, according to many Welsh nationalists, is needed in order to maintain the distinctiveness of the Welsh people and nation.

Educating a Welsh nation

Such debates were obviously apparent in the campaign to establish a Welsh-medium hall of residence in Aberystwyth. Students during the late 1960s and early 1970s felt that they were becoming 'swamped' by the large numbers of English-speaking students attending the University. The campaign to designate a Welsh-medium hall of residence, furthermore, was fuelled by the broader changes affecting Welsh society and the Welsh language during the 1960s. The emergence of a broader linguistic politics of the Welsh nation provided a broader context for some of the more specific campaigning activities taking place in Aberystwyth. At the same time, the campaign for a Welsh-medium hall of residence was used within the broader nationalist discourse being reproduced at this time, particularly by Alwyn D. Rees. We have also shown how Pantycelyn Welsh-Hall of Residence, following its establishment in 1973–4, has acted as a key location for the reproduction of Welsh nationalist discourse in Aberystwyth; among the student population at least. The local political culture existing in Pantycelyn Hall, in this respect, has contributed to the reproduction of nationalist discourse and practice in educational and other fields. At the same time, the political culture associated with the Hall has been shaped by the broader nationalist politics within which it is positioned. Nowhere is this connection between the local and the national exhibited more clearly than in the context of the recent campaigns for an increase in the provision of Welsh-medium higher education; in Aberystwyth and at a broader Welsh scale. Students from Aberystwyth, in this respect, have been key players in the successful reproduction of a Welsh linguistic nationalism within higher education. Many student activists believe that the recent scheme to provide Welsh-medium postgraduate scholarships and fellowships would not have occurred were it not for the sustained protests on the streets of Aberystwyth and Cardiff Bay by students from Aberystwyth. In this way, we see how networks of people within the Hall have been instrumental in the production of new nationalist discourses and organizations within higher education in Wales. For over thirty years, therefore, Aberystwyth, and specifically Pantycelyn Hall, has been a key product and producer of a Welsh nationalist discourse centred on issues relating to education.

NOTES

[1]   Another social constructivist strand that has examined the significance of state education systems in largely implicit terms has been Billig's (1995) work on the banal reproduction of nations. We think, in particular, of his

account of the mundane practices of nationalist commemoration that take place every morning in schools in the United States. Similarly, work within educational studies has examined the differential interaction between various kinds of pupils and/or students and education systems but has failed to address explicitly issues relating to the group-making project associated with nationalism (Monk 2000; with regard to gender, see McDowell and Bowlby 1983; Bondi and Peake 1988; for sexuality, see England 1999; Knopp 1999).

2   A more muted politics of place and scale, within the context of Welsh-medium education, has been apparent in the implementation of the National Curriculum for Wales. Welsh is supposed to be a core subject within the National Curriculum throughout the whole of Wales but localized campaigning and protests led to certain schools in the south of Pembrokeshire and along the border with England being excepted from the curriculum's linguistic requirements (see Janet Davies 1993: 80–1).

3   Up until recently, the University of Wales has operated as a federal university. This has meant that it has been able to plan the implementation of Welsh-medium education at an all-Wales level. The mooted abolition of the University Wales and the redesignation of the constituent colleges as independent universities in their own right has the potential to undermine any national strategic direction of Welsh-medium education, apart from the more informal guidance offered by the Higher Education Funding Council for Wales (HEFCW) and the National Assembly for Wales (NAfW).

4   The increase in the numbers of Welsh-medium lecturers during the late 1960s was funded through the large expansion in the numbers of students attending University Colleges in Wales during this period. The funding of Welsh-medium education since 1994 has been channelled through a Welsh-medium teaching premium (26% more funding than for an equivalent English-medium module) (see http://194.81.48.132/index.htm, accessed 4 April 2007).

5   Pantycelyn Hall was a single-sex bilingual hall of residence before its designation as a mixed-sex monolingual hall in 1973.

6   Some of our respondents argued that Neuadd John Morris had not provided the same breeding ground for nationalists as had Neuadd Pantycelyn, despite their similarities. In addition to not providing the same cultural mix as Pantycelyn, Neuadd John Morris Jones was said to suffer because of the fact that most students returned to their homes for the weekend. Aberystwyth's relative isolation, in this respect, has meant that students have tended to reside in Neuadd Pantycelyn on most weekends, thus providing an additional intensity to student relations and forms of political action.

7   For criticism from the Welsh Language Board, see http://www.bwrdd-yr-iaith.org.uk/cynnwys.php?pID=241&langID=2&nID=227 and http://news.bbc.co.uk/1/hi/wales/mid/3582091.stm, accessed 8 December, 2006.

8   http://news.bbc.co.uk/1/hi/wales/mid/3472081.stm, accessed 8 December 2006.

9   http://www.hefcw.ac.uk/Sector_Management/rc_fund.htm, accessed 8
     December, 2006.
10   http://news.bbc.co.uk/welsh/hi/newsid_3490000/newsid_3499300/
     3499376.stm, accessed 8 December, 2006.
11   For example, see http://news.bbc.co.uk/welsh/low/newsid_6080000/
     newsid_6087900/6087996.stm, accessed 8 December, 2006.
12   http://news.bbc.co.uk/welsh/low/newsid_6080000/newsid_6087900/
     6087996.stm, accessed 8 December, 2006.

6

Aberystwyth, Ceredigion and the electoral politics of Plaid Cymru

INTRODUCTION

In the previous two chapters we have discussed two important arenas of Welsh nationalist agitation that have either been centred in Aberystwyth or have drawn ideological and practical support from people within the town. We turn in this chapter to examine another area of nationalist campaigning that has been important over the past 50 or so years, namely that relating to electoral politics. We want to show how the electoral politics of place within Aberystwyth has both shaped, and been shaped by, broader political and nationalist concerns at both Welsh and British scales.

Studies of electoral politics within the social sciences have long emphasized the significance of the particularities of place as well as the scalar connections between places and processes occurring at a broader, national scale. These studies, as such, echo some of the broader theoretical concerns that inform this book. First, consider the attention that has been directed towards the role played by places in shaping political and electoral behaviour. Political geographers since the late 1960s have stressed that place-based processes of socialization affect the choices that are made by voters within elections. Two key advocates of a more sustained geographical interpretation of elections, Johnston and Pattie (2004: 53), have argued that 'geography is not epiphenomenal: it provides the arena (at a variety of scales) within which electoral decisions are made'. The most notable context within which such geographical studies have been conducted is with regard to the so-called 'neighbourhood effect'. Voters within particular localities are disposed to vote in particular ways as a result of their embeddedness within local political cultures. 'Political learning', according to Johnston and Pattie (ibid: 51), is based upon 'interpersonal interaction – at home, school and college, at

the workplace, and in the local neighbourhood and formal organizations'. As an early example of this work, Butler and Stokes (1969) noted
that whereas 91 per cent of working-class people living in British mining
areas voted for the Labour Party during national elections, only 48 per
cent of the working-class voted for the Labour Party in middle-class
seaside resorts. While some have disputed the validity of geographical
claims such as these – on methodological and empirical grounds (e.g.
Prescott 1972; in a related context, see Denver and Hands 1997) – there is
no doubt that many political geographers accede to the importance of a
process of 'conversion through conversation' (Miller 1977: 67; see also
Johnston and Pattie 2004, Taylor and Johnston 1979: 221–69) within local
electoral politics. In this sense, the processes of political socialization
occurring within particular places are of critical importance in determining voting behaviour and the outcomes of electoral politicking.

Second, much has been made by social scientists of the need to
examine the connections between local electoral politics and processes
taking place at other geographical scales. At one level, scholars have
sought to examine how local electoral politics may be shaped by
processes occurring at the national scale. Rokkan (1970), for instance, has
shown how political cleavages have formed within particular countries
in Europe as a result of conflicts and alliances between different factions
within those countries. In Britain, for instance, a nation-building group
allied itself with the landed gentry and the church (the Tories/
Conservatives) and contested elections with another alliance formed
between dissenters, industrialists and minority groups (the Whigs/
Liberals). The significance of Rokkan's work for the present argument is
that these political cleavages and alliances that have been played out at a
national scale have impacted on the electoral politics that have evolved
within certain localities (see also Taylor and Flint 2000: 238–9; Taylor and
Johnston 1979: 107–29). National alliances and conflicts, in this respect,
are seen to shape local politics and voting patterns. Another, more
socio-economic, account of the impact of national processes on local
electoral politics can be found in the work carried out by geographers on
the so-called spatial division of labour. Massey (1984), for instance, has
highlighted how a Marxist social division of labour also possesses a
spatial manifestation as people occupying different socio-economic
strata become differentially located. This process takes place at a variety
of different scales, ranging from the regional down to the intra-urban.
The significance of such a spatial division of labour for electoral politics
is obvious. As different classes of people become clustered in particular
constituencies, so electoral politics are affected. Writing back in 1979, for

instance, Taylor and Johnston (1979: 233; 164–217) noted how the 623 constituencies located within England, Scotland and Wales were characterized by a different 'socio-political environment, comprising a characteristic social structure with which certain social and political attitudes [were] associated'. What helped to determine these manifold socio-political environments and the subsequent local electoral politics, of course, were economic processes and governmental policies taking place at the national scale.

As an offshoot of such Marxist-inspired work, another important research thread has revolved around the incorporation of world-systems theory into electoral studies. Drawing on the work of Wallerstein (1974; 1980; 1989), Taylor (see Taylor and Flint 2000) has attempted to show how electoral politics at both the national and local scales are, ultimately, shaped by the persistent structural socio-economic disparities that exist within a global world economy. According to this work, the type of electoral systems – and thus the type of electoral results – that are formed in different countries are conditioned by that country's relative location within the world economy. The emergence of liberal democracies in the countries of the north and the west over the twentieth century, for instance, has been facilitated by their relative economic strength within the world economy. Their economic success has enabled these countries to engage in a meaningful reallocation of resources, governed through largely democratic electoral contests (ibid: 252–7). The creation of effective and meaningful liberal democracies in countries located in the periphery of the world economy, on the other hand, has been hampered by these countries lack of economic viability. But as well as shaping the form – and success or failure – of electoral systems at a national scale, it is also argued that these global economic processes, in the last instance, help influence the types of political engagement that can emerge at the scale of the constituency within particular countries. The types of political debate that can take place within certain constituencies, for instance, depend on the resources that can be redistributed within that particular state. The global processes at work within the world economy, in this respect, influence the electoral politics that can legitimately exist within particular places.

While there is much to be gained from this work that has examined the connections between local electoral politics and processes taking place at larger geographical scales, it can unfortunately give the impression that local electoral politics should be viewed as merely the product of processes occurring at other scales. Such a stance is clearly at odds with the more recursive association between the politics of place and the politics of nationalism portrayed in this book. We want to suggest that local electoral politics, as well as being the product of broader social processes, can also help to shape wider nationalist and/or electoral politics. If we are to take seriously the fact that 'places are not inert settings' and that 'they have cultures: shaped by people, significant for the shaping of people, and then re-shaped by people in a continuing dialectic' (Johnston and Pattie 2004: 50), we would argue that we also need to consider how places, and the local electoral politics contained within them, can shape people's attitudes and cultures over a whole range of geographical scales. Our aim in this chapter is to show how a local electoral politics within Aberystwyth and the constituency of Ceredigion and Pembroke North have possessed broader implications for the reproduction of nationalism in Wales.

PLAID CYMRU AND ELECTORAL POLITICS

Our discussion of electoral politics, of necessity, is based largely on the political activities of Plaid Cymru, the Welsh nationalist party. We outlined the broad significance of Plaid Cymru for the reproduction of Welsh nationalism in Chapter 3. It is important, nonetheless, for us further to contextualize the relationship that has existed between Plaid Cymru and electoral politics. At one level, we need to draw attention to the perennial tension that characterized Plaid Cymru's relationship with parliamentary politics. One important way in which this tension has been manifest has been in debates concerning the status of Plaid Cymru as either a pressure group or an electoral party (McAllister 2001: 91–126). As Phil Williams, one-time party chair, noted:

> The distinction is important: a pressure group is dedicated to specific aims and seeks to achieve those aims by influencing the people who hold power; a political party seeks to hold power itself (quoted in McAllister 2001: 94).

In the last instance, as McAllister has noted, Plaid Cymru has sought to combine these two roles. The tension between these two roles was at its most apparent during the 1960s and 1970s (ibid: 95) and was characterized, among other things, by the differing attitudes taken by various party members towards direct action. Direct action was viewed as a legitimate campaigning strategy by some individuals who viewed Plaid Cymru mainly as a pressure group but would not be countenanced by those other individuals who wished to see it evolve as a serious political party, whose success would be judged on purely electoral terms. While the debate about the appropriate nature of Plaid Cymru's role may have led to some consternation within the party itself, the relationship between the party's role as a campaign group and as an electoral force was not without its benefits. Gwynfor Evans, for instance, recalls the electoral impetus provided to Plaid Cymru by its involvement in the Parliament for Wales Campaign, launched in 1950 (ibid: 100). Despite the underlying ambivalence demonstrated by members of Plaid Cymru towards electioneering, it is clear also that the Party's attitude towards elections has become more favourable and proactive through-out the twentieth century. In this regard, many commentators have noted that Plaid Cymru was far more concerned with linguistic and moral issues during its early years than it was with achieving electoral success. Davies (1983: 73), for instance, has noted that linguistic issues dominated Plaid Cymru's prospectuses during its years in existence. Indeed, for Williams (1982: 152), the Plaid Cymru of this period was 'primarily a cultural nationalist pressure group' that was far more concerned with securing a separate linguistic identity for Wales than it was with political independence as such (see also Gruffudd 1994). The upshot of such a stance was a half-hearted approach to electioneering. This attitude is crystallized by Davies (1989: 42; see also Combs 1977) when she argues that:

> While party policy consistently advocated working through the electoral system to win self-government and thereby ensure the survival of the Welsh language, the predominantly middle-class, nonpolitical membership was reluctant to enter the political fray.

And yet, at the same time, there were some efforts within Plaid Cymru to engage with electoral issues. After all, the party still believed that self-government or home-rule was essential as a mechanism for ensuring the linguistic well-being of Wales (Davies 1983: 73). Accord-ingly, the party contested a small number of seats (Caernarfonshire, Caernarfon Boroughs, Neath and the University of Wales) in parliamen-tary elections during the period between 1929 and 1945 (Williams 1982: 160). Although some electoral support was gained, most notably for Saunders Lewis' candidature in the University of Wales seat in 1931 (where he gained 17.9 per cent of the votes), and although the number of seats that the party fought had doubled by 1945, Plaid Cymru struggled to make a meaningful electoral breakthrough (ibid; McAllister 2001: 97). The immediate post-war period witnessed more heartening electoral results for the party and in the 1959 general election, Plaid Cymru succeeded in enhancing its political support. Twenty candidates man-aged to poll 77,571 votes (Williams 1982: 161) Further political success was to follow, with the party winning the Carmarthen seat in a by-election in 1966 (McAllister 2001: 114–15; Williams 1982: 164; Combs 1977: 246–7). As a sign of the political maturity attained through the success of 1966, Plaid Cymru contested every Welsh seat from the general election of 1970 onwards, despite suffering from a lack of political support in the majority of constituencies in the east of the country (McAllister 2001: 97). As well as expanding its political reach throughout Wales, Plaid Cymru during this period also sought to consolidate the political gains that it had made in the Welsh-speaking north and west of Wales. By the second general election of 1974, for instance, the party had gained control of the constituencies of Caernarfon, Meirionnydd and Carmarthen (Williams 1982: 180). Although Plaid Cymru lost the Carmarthen seat in the general election of 1979 – largely due to the party's association with the unsuccessful devolution referendum that had been held earlier that same year – it bounced back during the 1980s and 1990s. The general election of 1992 witnessed Plaid Cymru's representation within Parliament rise to four MPs for the first time, with the party controlling the constituencies of Ynys Môn, Ceredigion and Pembroke North, Caernarfon and Meirionnydd Nant Conwy. Plaid suffered the loss of Ynys Môn in the 2001 general election but gained some compensation for this by winning the seat of Carmarthen East and Dinefwr. Plaid lost the Ceredigion Westminster seat at the 2005 general election but currently holds the National Assembly for Wales seat (for more detailed accounts, see Williams 1982; McAllister 2001; Combs 1977).

While Plaid Cymru's engagement with British parliamentary politics has been characterized by a gradual if not steady rise in political support and electoral success, it is clear that the creation of the National Assembly for Wales has also provided the party with an alternative political context within which it can seek to exercize its influence. We do not want to explicate Plaid Cymru's electoral efforts with respect to the National Assembly for Wales at this stage since this theme will act as an important context for the themes discussed in the following chapter, in which we elaborate on the role of Aberystwyth in reproducing Welsh nationalism in more recent years. We want, rather, to move on to the empirical themes that form the main substance of this chapter. The following sections elaborate in detail on one particular time period during which an electoral politics of place in Aberystwyth was especially important in shaping broader nationalist and electoral agendas. We focus in particular on the period during the late 1980s and early 1990s in order to show how

Aberystwyth and the electoral constituency of Ceredigion and Pembroke North first became a Plaid Cymru/Green Party constituency. Our account of the election of the first Plaid Cymru/Green Party MP is organized as a linear narrative in order to highlight the complex connections between the politics of place and the politics of scale that were apparent during this period. This empirical account is then followed by an extended conclusion in which we discuss in a more conceptual manner the internal politics of place within Aberystwyth during the late 1980s and the early 1990s, as well as the series of fascinating scalar connections that existed at this time between one electoral candidate, the town of Aberystwyth, the Welsh nation and the British parliament.

ABERYSTWYTH AND THE CONSTITUENCY OF CEREDIGION AND PEMBROKE NORTH

The political tradition of Aberystwyth and the broader constituency of Ceredigion and Pembroke North lies in a particular form of Liberalism with its roots deep in the nineteenth century. Ceredigion, as such, can be said to have been part of the dominant political culture of Wales in the period between 1868 and 1920. As we discussed in Chapter 3, 'old' Welsh liberalism's cultural base was nonconformist Protestantism and its policy planks included educational reform, land reform and the disestablishment of the Church in Wales (Morgan 1980 [1963]; Evans 1989). Significantly, it is also evident that Welsh liberalism was also closely associated with issues of home-rule and national self-determination. Home-rule for Wales, admittedly, did not emerge as a critical issue to the extent that it did in Ireland. Nevertheless, Welsh Liberals were quite happy to describe their political and constitutional stance as 'Welsh nationalist'.

The Liberal Party's star waned during the inter-war years. The Labour Party's increasing electoral dominance of the south Wales coalfield caused the Liberal Party in Wales to retreat into a few rural bastion constituencies. One such constituency was Ceredigion, which remained an isolated pocket of Liberal support after 1945. Ceredigion's unbroken Liberal tradition was infringed between 1966 and 1974 by the success of Elystan Morgan in becoming the county's first Labour MP. Labour's success in Ceredigion can be attributed, in large measure, to forces of local and even familial networks rather than an explicit political shift towards socialist doctrine. Elystan Morgan explained how voters supported his candidature in 1966 as a result of ties of kinship: 'I remember many people . . . saying "I never was in favour of the 'Labours' [sic] but I can't vote against my own blood!"' The Liberal Party's ascendancy in Ceredigion resumed in February 1974 with the victory of Geraint Howells, a local farmer. In 1983, a large section of northern Pembroke- shire (a traditionally Conservative county) was appended to the south- ern part of Ceredigion in a constituency boundary change. The boundary change might have been expected to have been enough to return Ceredigion to the Tories for the first time in democratic times, given the surprise Conservative gains elsewhere in Wales during the Thatcher era. The fact that the Conservative Party did not gain control of the seat, however, was due in large part to the presence of Geraint Howells. Indeed, Howells was praised by Cynog Dafis, his successor as the constituency's MP, for being an 'obstacle to the Tories winning the seat'. Howells' success as an MP was based on his ability to combine his home-grown knowledge of agricultural issues with assiduous local networking skills. Two long-standing political figures in Ceredigion, Elystan Morgan and Iolo ap Gwynn respectively, described Howells' social, cultural and political virtues as follows:

> Sylfaen fawr Geraint yn gymdeithasol wrth gwrs oedd ei amaethyddiaeth e'. Nid dyn oedd yn chwarae ffarmio oedd e'. Roedd e'n ffarmwr o'r iawn ryw. Mi roedd e' hefyd yn un o sefydlwyr Undeb Ffermwyr Cymru.

> [Geraint's major social base of course was his agriculture. He wasn't a man who played at farming. He was a farmer of the right ilk. He was also one of the founders of the Farmers Union of Wales.]

> Roedd o'n rwydweithiwr da. 'Oedd o'n mynd i bob angladd oedd yn digwydd, hyd yn oed os nag oedd e'n 'nabod y teulu, 'oedd Geraint yno, yn yr angladd. Ac wrth gwrs trwy wneud hynny 'oedd o'n rhwydweithio ac yn creu y math o gefnogaeth bersonol 'ma oedd ganddo fo.

> [He was a good networker. He went to every funeral that was happening, even if he didn't know the family, Geraint was there, in the funeral. And of course through doing so he was networking and creating the sort of personal support that he had.]

By the 1980s, Geraint Howells' degree of embeddedness within the political culture of Ceredigion and Pembroke North had led some Plaid Cymru activists to believe that he was 'to all intents and purposes, immovable'. The concatenation of circumstances that led to his ousting by a Plaid Cymru/Green Party alliance were, indeed, remarkable, as were the circumstances that led to the break-up of the alliance some five years later. The formation of the alliance and its subsequent dissolution show how complex place-based politics could be linked, through a process of scalar articulation, to events, processes and institutions operating at a national scale. We trace the empirical nature of these connections in the following sections before discussing their theoretical implications at further length.

The Plaid Cymru/Green Party alliance: intellectual roots and electoral imperatives

The figure of Cynog Dafis looms large in an account of the intellectual roots of the formation of the Plaid Cymru/Green Party alliance. Nowhere was his role more evident than in the way in which he managed to reconcile the different intellectual traditions of nationalism and environmentalism, as espoused by Plaid Cymru and the Green Party. Dafis was an established local candidate, having previously contested the constituency in the General Elections of 1983 and 1987. Dafis was also a veteran of the Welsh nationalist movement, having played a key part during the 1960s in the formative years of Cymdeithas yr Iaith Gymraeg. Cynog Dafis was unusual within Welsh nationalism, however, since ideas relating to the environment and to sustainability had played a major role in his political philosophy over a number of years (Dafis 2005b: 174–5). Dafis admitted to us, for instance, that:

> '*Oedd gen i, ers ugain mlynedd, ddiddordeb mawr yn natblygiad y mudiad gwyrdd, y Blaid Ecoleg yn y lle cyntaf, ac wedyn y Blaid Werdd, 'o'n i wedi bod yn watcho hwnna i gyd, 'o'n i wedi bod yn darllen cylchgronnau fel yr* Ecologist *felly 'o'n i'n gwybod am y sîn yna'n dda iawn.*

> [I had held, for twenty years, a great interest in the development of the green movement, the Ecology Party in the first instance, and then the Green Party, I had been watching all of that, I had been reading magazines such as *The Ecologist* so I knew that scene very well.]

Importantly, Cynog Dafis had already put his concerns for sustainable development into action at an early stage. Dafis and some companions had formed a co-operative farm in Talgarreg, Ceredigion in 1964 as part of an attempt by individuals within the Welsh nationalist movement to counter the urbanization of Welsh speakers by developing small-scale enterprizes in rural, Welsh-speaking areas of Wales (Phillips 1998: 149). Cynog Dafis' credibility as an individual who possessed both nationalist and environmental concerns was crucial to the emerging dialogue between Plaid Cymru and the Green Party during the late 1980s.

But as well as helping to shape a particular environmental and nationalist mentality in Ceredigion, it is also clear that Cynog Dafis –

and, indeed, some of his nationalist colleagues – was the product of a wider strand of thought within west Wales, which had incorporated and promoted ideas of environmentalism and sustainability over a number of years. This thinking is represented in concrete form by the Centre for Alternative Technology near Machynlleth, some twenty miles north of Aberystwyth. We would also contend that Aberystwyth, a centre of the University of Wales, provided a meeting-point from the 1970s onwards for intellectuals of both nationalist and environmentalist tendencies. Iolo ap Gwynn noted the significance of an active brand of environmentalism within west Wales at this time:

> *Roedd nifer ohonon ni wedi bod â diddordeb yn ochr amgylcheddol. 'O'n i yn ymwybodol iawn o wleidyddiaeth werdd, cofio darllen Blueprint for Survival nôl yn y cyfnod hwnnw, a teimlo wel, ie, mae hyn yn bwysig. Ac wrth gwrs 'oedd Canolfan Dechnoleg Amgen wedi sefydlu yn y cyfnod yna yn y 70au.*

> [A number of us had held an interest in the environmental side. I was very conscious of green politics, [I] remember reading Blueprint for Survival back in that period, and feeling, well, yes, this is important. And of course the Centre for Alternative Technology had been established in that period in the 70s.]

The existence of certain Welsh nationalists possessing environmental credentials had led to some interaction between Plaid Cymru and the Green Party during the late 1980s. On the policy front, the two parties had engaged in an amicable, low-level exchange on policy differences after the 1987 general election. There is no doubt, however, that the decisive electoral impetus was provided by the Green Party's success in the June 1989 European elections. The factors governing the electoral surge in favour of the UK Green Party in 1989 (and the Greens' subsequent retreat) have been documented in detail elsewhere and relate to an increased public concern about prominent environmental issues such as acid rain, global warming and the depletion of the earth's ozone layer (Curtice 1989; Carter 1992; Porritt and Winner 1988; McCormick 1991). A more personal insight is provided by the former leader of the UK Green Party, Jonathon Porritt:

> The whole area of sustainability and climate change and things had just come onto the mainstream political agenda in a big way in the late 80s. Mrs. Thatcher helped significantly in that process by her short-lived persuasion that greenery was really important to the Tory party. The media had really cottoned on to that, I mean there was a lot of coverage in the media at the time. And, quite honestly, the European Election as we know is not a big deal for a very large number of people. So those of a green sensibility who had the vote thought 'Well, I am really worried

about this, there are Green Party candidates. I may not know a great deal about the manifesto they're standing on but I know what "Green" means. And sure as hell I'm going to have a punt on this one'. And I suspect that they were, a lot of them at that stage, joining environmental organisations like Friends of the Earth, Greenpeace, WWF and so on, and I guess they saw a Green Party candidate as the embodiment of the NGO activity that was becoming much more prevalent at that time. So the Green Party was the beneficiary of that.

The upsurge of public support in favour of the Green Party in the 1989 election had meant that Plaid Cymru (12.3 per cent) had only just managed to scrape into third place ahead of the Green Party (11.3 per cent) in Wales as a whole (Lynch 1995: 204). The situation for Plaid Cymru was even more acute in Mid and West Wales (including Ceredigion), where the Greens (13.2 per cent) had edged into third place ahead of Plaid Cymru (11.6 per cent) (see Jones 1999: 157). The main and unintended consequence of the Green performance in Wales was to galvanize Plaid Cymru both at a national and constituency scale. We take up the action inside the 1989 count of the Mid and West Wales European Parliamentary constituency, from the perspective of Cynog Dafis and Alun Williams (Green Party) respectively:

Wel, 'oedd twf y Blaid Werdd yn sioc, wrth gwrs, ac oedd eu llwyddiant etholiadol yn sioc. Ac mi ymladdodd y Blaid yn llwyr, yn gyfangwbl, yn yr etholiadau yna. Dwi'n cofio bod yn y cyfri' ... a'r ffaith ... bod y Blaid Werdd wedi dod yn agos iawn ... [i ddisodli Plaid Cymru o ran pleidlais Gymru'n gyfan].

[Well, the growth of the Green Party was a shock, of course, and their electoral success was a shock. And Plaid Cymru fought totally, wholeheartedly, in those elections ... I remember being in the count ... and the fact ... that the Green Party had come very close [to displacing Plaid Cymru in terms of the Welsh national vote].

It had a big influence I think from Plaid's perspective ... in that we did ever so well. In Mid and West Wales we beat Plaid Cymru ... I was at the count and Cynog said to me 'Look, you've really hammered us. We have to get together.' But it wasn't just that. Cynog was interested in working with the Greens in any way. And myself and certain others were interested in working with Plaid Cymru ... So there was a desire anyway, but it was the 1989 European Election result that really gave the impetus for that.]

The upshot of these discussions and the electoral result was the instigation of a series of formal and informal meetings between Plaid Cymru and the Green Party in 1989 and 1990. There was certainly a belief amongst certain members of Plaid Cymru – notably Phil Williams,

Iolo ap Gwynn and Cynog Dafis – that the party would benefit immeasurably from engaging more wholeheartedly with ecological thinking. At one level, these individuals believed that a fusion of nationalist and ecological concerns would facilitate a greater understanding between Plaid Cymru and the Green Party in Ceredigion and Pembroke North, which would enable them to compete more effectively in elections. More broadly, doing so would also encourage a fundamental and much-needed 'greening' of Plaid Cymru's policies in a national context.

Plaid Cymru invited the Green Party to a formal debate at the 1989 Plaid Cymru annual conference in Denbigh (Plaid Cymru 1989: 82–101) in which Alun Williams, on behalf of the Green Party, engaged in a sympathetic critique of the lack of green thinking present in Plaid Cymru's General Election Manifesto from 1987 (Dafis 2005b: 175). Whether as a result of this debate or the broader impetus provided by certain key individuals within the party, by the time of their annual conference in 1990, Plaid Cymru had passed a green economic policy (Plaid Cymru 1990: 19–26; Dafis 2005b: 176). In addition, a motion was passed enabling Plaid Cymru to engage in dialogue with the Green Party at constituency level about the possibility of local electoral pacts. In Ceredigion, the local Plaid Cymru and Green parties signed what was termed the 'Llandysul Accord' on 10 April 1991, which constituted a formal agreement of coalition between the two parties in the constituency of Ceredigion and Pembroke North. A joint press release exclaimed: 'Plaid Cymru – Green agreement "creates winning combination"' (NLW PCD: 10). The impact of the creation of the alliance can be charted through the results of a series of internal polls conducted between 1990 and 1992. Standing as separate parties, Plaid Cymru and the Greens had polled a combined total of just 17.9 per cent at the 1987 general election, a figure that seemed to confirm the nationalists' opinion that Geraint Howells was 'immovable' as MP. An independently conducted poll, commissioned by Plaid Cymru within the constituency in 1990, merely confirmed Plaid Cymru's 1987 level of support. Moreover, the poll highlighted existing perceptions that Plaid Cymru's support was heavily weighted towards Welsh speakers. The poll had also confirmed a marked increase in Green Party support (Dafis 2005a: 3). A subsequent poll was conducted in July 1991, after the Plaid Cymru/Green Party agreement had been concluded. The poll showed 37 per cent intending to vote for Plaid Cymru/Green Party, with the Liberal Democrats on 32 per cent (Dafis 2005a: 6). At least as important as the headline figures in this poll was the data that was gathered on linguistic composition of party preference. Cynog Dafis' election agent in 1992, Gwyn Jenkins, illustrated the linguistic significance of this poll as follows:

Ac mi ddangosodd e' bod ni, o ran y cytundeb a'r Blaid Werdd, bod ni ddim wedi colli pleidleisiau o gwbl o ganlyniad i'r cytundeb. 'Oedd hynny wastad yn bryder, ynde. Beth ddangosodd e' hefyd oedd bod na symud mawr wedi bod. 'Oedd e' i weld yn y proffil o safbwynt iaith ... bod ni wedi torri trwyddo ymhlith y di-Gymraeg, o ganlyniad i'r cytundeb ... Dwi'n dweud 'o ganlyniad i'r cytundeb'. 'O'n ni ddim yn gwybod, wrth gwrs, ond dyna yr unig ffordd oedd o ddehongli beth oedd wedi digwydd.

[It showed that we [Plaid Cymru], in terms of the agreement with the Green Party, that we hadn't lost votes at all as a result of the agreement . . . What it also showed was that a big change had occurred. It was to be seen in the profile from the perspective of language . . . that we had broken through in terms of the non-Welsh speakers, as a result of the agreement . . . I say 'as a result of the agreement'. We didn't know, of course, but that was the only way of explaining what had happened.]

The 1991 opinion poll suggested that the formalization of a Plaid Cymru/Green Party pact had had a profound impact upon the party political landscape of Ceredigion and on the perceptions of voters. Crucially, for one nationalist interviewee, a concept of 'Plaid Cymru plus' had made nationalism palatable to the raft of non-Welsh speaking voters in Ceredigion (see also Dafis 2005b: 176).

'Towards a Green Welsh future': a joint Plaid-Green programme for Ceredigion and Pembroke North

While members of Ceredigion Green Party had convincingly backed the alliance in March 1991, by forty-nine votes to seven (AW Papers, no date, no page), it was, if anything, the local Plaid Cymru membership which appeared most reticent during the early stages, thus revealing something about Plaid Cymru's traditional socio-cultural perspective in the process. Gwyn Jenkins recalled as follows:

Dwi'n meddwl 'oedd gan bobl amheuon ymhlith y Blaid [Plaid Cymru]. Dwi'n meddwl bod rhai ddim yn siwr a oedd yn syniad da yn wleidyddol i wneud hyn. Nid bod pobl yn erbyn syniadaeth y Blaid Werdd. Ond a oedd e mewn gwirionedd yn beth doeth i wneud ... i ymuno efo ... plaid oedd yn cael ei gweld fel plaid oedd yn Seisnig, yn ei ffordd, a ddim cefnogaeth o gwbl ymhlith y Cymry Cymraeg?

[I think people had doubts within the Blaid [Plaid Cymru]. I think that some weren't sure if it was politically a good idea to do this. Not that people were against the Green Party's philosophy. But was it in truth a

wise thing to do . . . to join with . . . a party that was seen as, in their own
way, an English party, and no support whatsoever amongst the Welsh?]

Perhaps because of these potential tensions between Plaid Cymru and
the Green Party, there was a concerted effort to set out the many
synergies that could come about as a result of the formation of the
alliance. In a broad ideological context, for instance, Cynog Dafis was at
pains to highlight the common ground that existed between nationalist
and green discourses. Dafis, as we have already noted, had been a keen
follower of ecological forms of politics since the 1970s and it is interesting that he viewed such ideas as an ideological foundation and justification for his own nationalist thinking. The Green movement's emphasis
on subsidiarity, sustainability and the devolution of political power and
means of production to small-scale communities, in particular, tallied
well with much of Dafis' own nationalist thinking (Dafis 2005b: 174).
Cynog Dafis and other advocates of the alliance were able to use this
common frame of reference, which was present within nationalist and
green discourses, to outline a series of principles that could unite the
followers of both parties. The three principles that they outlined were
(PC&GPCPN 1993: 2, original emphasis):

> *First,* the need to find ways to live in harmony with our natural
> environment. *Secondly,* that we take back control of our lives through
> achieving genuine local democracy and the establishment of a Parliament
> for Wales, and through the development of a more self-reliant economy.
> *Thirdly,* we want a social order whose priority is a decent quality of life for
> all our people in the context of our global responsibilities. This includes
> the celebration of diversity, of place, culture, language and lifestyle.

In many ways, these three principles helped to spell out in a slightly
more concrete way the similarities of outlook between Plaid Cymru and
the Green Party. The key challenge, of course, arose in the context of
identifying specific policies or strategies that could speak in equal
measure to these two electoral constituencies. Alun Williams discussed
some of the more specific policy issues, which had to be ironed out
during this period prior to the 1992 election:

> Transport was talked about a lot . . . Plaid Cymru were keener on road
> building though than the Greens. So that was something that had to be got
> over. Fox-hunting was an issue for a lot of Greens – Cynog's sort of quite
> keen on it actually – and obviously Greens are dead against it and so we
> had to kind of work out a very fine middle-way there. That was a bit
> difficult at times, but we got through that one. The nuclear power issue, it
> wasn't so much Cynog . . . it's just obviously there's the Trawsfynydd
> issue. For example, we wouldn't have been able to have an agreement

with Plaid Cymru in Meirionnydd because of Trawsfynydd. But Trawsfynydd isn't a particular issue in Ceredigion so it wasn't really a problem. In fact, Plaid members and Green members were all at one really on the nuclear issue. But there was a little bit of concern about that, I guess. Those are the issues that particularly spring to mind.

The 'Trawsfynydd' issue noted above refers to one of two nuclear power stations that are located within Plaid Cymru-held constituencies in north-west Wales. In both cases, Plaid Cymru has had to reconcile its traditional anti-nuclear policy stance with the imperative of safeguarding jobs within local constituencies. Indeed, it was suggested by one Plaid Cymru activist that Plaid Cymru's ambiguous stance on the Wylfa and Trawsfynydd power stations partially explains the Green Party's localized hostility towards Plaid Cymru in north Wales. Documentation from the period demonstrates the creative manner in which some of these policy differences were overcome (PC&GPCPN 1993). Nuclear power was condemned as a 'dangerous dead-end which can have no place in these policies', but without reference to the two north Wales power stations. The parties compromised on the need for 'some upgrading of the existing road system' in west Wales. Fox hunting was omitted as an issue altogether, leaving individual members to follow their conscience.

Having hammered out the policy, the coalition embarked on the election campaign itself. The literature from the election is symptomatic of the respective Liberal Democrat and Plaid Cymru/Green Party campaigns (NLW WPE BA 4/13). The Liberal Democrats' (fairly drab) leaflets relied heavily on the established persona of Geraint Howells. Their catchphrase was: 'Everyone knows someone who has been helped by Geraint Howells'. In contrast, the Plaid Cymru/Green coalition produced a series of eye-catching policy-oriented documents under the theme of *Something Worth Voting For* (PC&GPCPN 1993) with specific leaflets targeted at young voters, small businesses and farmers respectively. A more substantial document, entitled *Together: Building a Future* (ibid), underlined the policy emphasis of the Plaid Cymru/Green Party partnership. It outlined a mixture of long- and short-term issues in a detail quite uncharacteristic of a regular constituency campaign. The document's themes included: The Rio Summit; equal opportunities for women; global consumption; the NHS; housing; devolution; agriculture; regional economic development; education; the Welsh language; transport and a targeted, local message for 'Fishguard and district', i.e. the 'Pembroke North' appendage to the traditional Ceredigion constituency.

There was a further, tactical imperative for a policy-based campaign. The myriad possible incongruities between environmentalism and nationalism demanded that the Plaid Cymru/Green Party partnership spelt out their policies in a more detailed form than might otherwise be expected of conventional party manifestos. In 1997, Tony Blair was able to sell Labour policy by way of a five-point 'pledge card'. This may be contrasted to the Plaid Cymru/Green Party experience of 1992. Alun Williams explained the need for such a detailed elaboration of the alliance's policies:

> The Green/Plaid Cymru thing had to be presented very well and very clearly. Because a lot of people, obviously, were very surprised to see Plaid Cymru and the Greens getting together. And so that had to be explained very carefully and very clearly to a lot of people, supporters, who may have been quite doubtful on both sides, and also to the media as well. So there were an awful lot of policy documents written and papers on various aspects of our philosophy, if you like. We were trying to put across a sort of philosophy, I suppose, that was possibly a little more intelligent than the things that parties normally try to convey at elections. And so we had to spend a lot of time explaining and developing policies in a way that was understandable to the media, to our supporters and then to the wider Ceredigion public who we were hoping would vote for us. So there was an awful lot of small publications and leaflets and presentations and things. And of course a lot of our meetings, we would have to have people from both parties there, to present the united front.

Electing the UK's first Plaid Cymru/Green MP

The general election date was set by Prime Minister John Major for 9 April 1992. The campaign at UK level was an intense, two-party contest between John Major's governing Conservative Party, and the Labour Party led by Neil Kinnock. Notwithstanding Labour's tentative commitment to a Welsh Assembly (Wales Labour Party 1992: 3), Welsh election issues did not register on the mainstream agenda of the general election (Butler and Kavanagh 1992: 75). Instead, a small number of marginal constituencies assumed an almost totemic status among media pundits. Foremost among these key marginals was the seat of Basildon, Essex (Butler and Kavanagh 1992: 207–9). By road, Ceredigion is some 250 miles from Basildon. In ideological terms, the two constituencies might as well have been on separate continents. In Basildon – and in the UK general election as a whole – the campaign centred on material growth: recovery from economic recession and the related issues of individuals' jobs and mortgages. In Ceredigion and Pembroke North, the political agenda was set by issues such as regional democracy, sustainable agriculture policy and global climate change. It was, furthermore, a localized contest between the personalities of Geraint Howells and Cynog Dafis, so that the constituency election came to resemble, in one campaigner's words, a 'by election', in which UK issues were an afterthought. Gwyn Jenkins echoed this sentiment when stating that '*Dwi'n meddwl bod yr ymgyrch yn . . . wahanol*/I think the campaign was . . . different' and that 'Labour v Conservative *oedd hi ym Mhrydain ond doedd y frwydr ddim yn berthnasol rhyw ffordd, oedd yn cael ei anghofio yng Ngheredigion*/it was Labour v Conservative in Britain but that contest wasn't relevant somehow, it was being forgotten in Ceredigion'.

The main campaign events in Ceredigion and Pembroke North were the public interventions of two public figures in favour of Cynog Dafis' campaign. First, Dai Jones 'Llanilar', a farmer and a Welsh language radio and television broadcaster from the hamlet of Llanilar, Ceredigion, publicly professed his support of Cynog Dafis. This statement was crucial since it helped to undermine the localized agricultural base of Liberal support within Ceredigion. The second public endorsement came from outside of Wales. Prior to the General Election being called, the Plaid Cymru/Green Party coalition had already organized for Jonathon Porritt of the UK Green Party to address a general public meeting. It was not realized that the meeting might fall within the general election campaign proper. As it turned out, the meeting of Monday, 16 March at the 'Old College', Aberystwyth, attracted an estimated 600 people, and proved to be an electrifying campaign launch evening (see Plate 6.1). It is significant, in this respect, that Porritt himself recalled the meeting when interviewed as part of our research:

> I do remember the meeting very well . . . quite a special meeting. There was a real sense of excitement about something very different . . . I do seem to recall that the Q&A after the talks by Cynog and myself was longer than the actual talks. So probably more happened then, as is often the way, than in the talks themselves.

Alun Williams also emphasized the significance of the public meeting:

> The Jonathon Porritt meeting, as I recall, there were 600 people there. As someone said, it was like an old sort of Welsh revivalist meeting. It was a tremendous atmosphere there. Because Jonathon Porritt is an excellent, entertaining speaker anyway. And Cynog was there of course, and the Old College, the main hall there was absolutely stuffed, people were standing, and it was a wonderful meeting . . . The significance was that, you know, here's Jonathon Porritt, who's I guess the most well-known and the most

articulate Green in the UK, coming from wherever he lived at the time, to west Wales to back what we were doing. It was a fantastic endorsement really, it was saying 'yes, this is OK, I give this my backing'. And I think it convinced the Green supporters in Ceredigion ... this was just a huge endorsement for those sort of people.

There was no doubt that the Jonathon Porritt meeting symbolized a shift in political momentum from the established, agricultural-based networks of Liberal Democrats towards a younger, apparently more vibrant Plaid Cymru/Green Party alliance. On the Saturday prior to polling day, the Plaid Cymru/Green Party campaign set up a campaign stall in the centre of Aberystwyth. They offered day-glo Cynog Dafis stickers and daffodils to passers-by. By this stage, a common assumption (which was remarkable enough in itself) had developed amongst activists that the two main British parties had been effectively eliminated from the contest. It seemed that the battle was now a straight fight between two parties, Plaid Cymru/Green Party and the Liberal Democrats. Cynog Dafis recalls the political tussle at the time as it played out on the streets of Aberystwyth (see Plate 6.2):

> *Ond y diwrnod hwnnw ro'n i yn grwp o bleidwyr ar sgwar Siop y Pethe yn Aberystwyth. A hanner y bobl yn dod i gwrdd â ni, dod i siarad â ni, ac yn cael sticeri ... yn felyn ar ddillad pobl, ein sticeri ni. A jyst lawr yr hewl, yn North Parade, oedd Geraint yn sefyll, Geraint Howells. Dwi'n cofio fe'n sefyll fanna, bron ar ei ben ei hunan, a neb, braidd, yn dod ato fe. Ac oedd e'. . . yn symbolaidd, bron, o'r shifft oedd yn digwydd.*

[That day we were a group of Plaid supporters on the square of Siop y Pethe in Aberystwyth. And half the people coming to meet us, and getting stickers ... our stickers were yellow on people's clothes. And just down the road, on North Parade, Geraint was standing, Geraint Howells. I remember him standing there, almost alone, and hardly anybody noticing him. And it was almost emblematic of the shift that was happening.]

The result of the Ceredigion and Pembroke North constituency was declared in the early hours of the morning on Friday, 10 April (see Table 6.1). A review of UK electoral history demonstrates that the result in Ceredigion and Pembroke North was remarkable in several ways (Dafis 2005b: 182). In the context of the 1992 general election, it was the only constituency where a candidate had moved from fourth to first position in the poll. The 13.3 per cent swing from Liberal Democrat to the Plaid Cymru/Green Party was the highest swing of any seat in the UK (notwithstanding two seats which had held by-elections during the 1987–92 parliament).

Table 6.1 The results of the 1992 General Election in Ceredigion and Pembroke North

Cynog Dafis (Plaid Cymru/Green)	16,020 (31.3%)
Geraint Howells (Liberal Democrat)	12,827 (25.1%)
O. J. Williams (Conservative)	12,718 (24.8%)
John Davies (Labour)	9,637 (18.8%)

Cynog Dafis took every opportunity to announce his arrival on the Westminster scene as the UK's first Plaid Cymru/Green MP. Much of his early work in Westminster centred on promoting environmental issues. Given the timing of his election to Parliament, Dafis was keen, in particular, to draw attention to the significance of the Rio Conference on Sustainable Development, held in 1992 (Dafis 2005b: 186). His maiden House of Commons' speech, too, mentioned Welsh devolution, railway privatization and the Rio Summit, thus addressing respective Welsh, UK and global political scales (NLW PCD 11–12 no date). In more specific contexts, Dafis was also able to play an instrumental role in promoting green bills through the House of Commons. On 20 January 1995, for instance, Cynog Dafis co-sponsored the Home Energy Conservation Bill which became law on 8 June 1995 (Friends of the Earth 1995a; 1995b). On 20 March 1996, too, after the dissolution of the Plaid Cymru/Green Party pact, Cynog Dafis introduced a Road Traffic Reduction Bill to the House of Commons (Friends of the Earth 1996a). This Bill provided a firm parliamentary precedent for the subsequent Liberal Democrat Bill of 13 November 1996 (Friends of the Earth 1996b), which became law on 21 March 1997 (Friends of the Earth 1997). As a result of these efforts, Cynog Dafis won the *Green Magazine* award for best newcomer to parliament in June 1993 (AW Papers, no date, no page). Jonathon Porritt expanded on the further, informal ways in which Cynog Dafis' parliamentary status facilitated new developments in the wider Green movement:

> The idea that we would then have a Green/Plaid MP in parliament was hugely exciting. I suppose most of us probably transferred too much expectation then onto one man . . . At that stage, getting someone with the word 'Green' in, 'MP', was just so overwhelming . . . in terms of the NGOs that are circling the Westminster scene as it were, of which there are many, there wasn't any doubt that Cynog's presence was important, influential. It was a conduit for many of them through to processes going on in parliament. Whether it was a Private Member's Bill or a Select Committee, whatever it might be, he was as assiduous as you could be, really, in terms

of helping to raise voices from outside inside the inner sanctum. And take stuff back out to people, as well . . . I think he did a really good job – a really good job.

Although Dafis spent much of his first term as an MP promoting a green agenda, it is also significant that he did so in a way that was in tune with his own understanding of the purpose of Welsh nationalism. In a House of Commons debate on investment, for instance, Dafis had been able to make a speech outlining the productive links between renewable energy and the Welsh environment. Drawing on previous work conducted by Phil Williams, he was able to argue that Wales, due to its impressive natural resources, could assume an important position within the whole area of renewable energy. In doing so, Wales would also be able to ensure the economic survival of some of its more remote regions (Dafis 2005b: 187). Another example of Dafis' attempts to link nationalist and green discourses can be witnessed in his criticism of the Welsh Office's refusal to formulate a Sustainable Development Strategy for Wales in response to the Rio conference. Through some political lobbying, Dafis was able to occasion a debate within parliament in order to discuss an issue that united nationalist and green concerns (ibid: 197). Once again, Dafis, through his specific contributions within the House of Commons, illustrated the way in which nationalist and green issues could be combined within one unified discourse.

Severing the 'ball and chain of nationalism': ending the Plaid Cymru/Green Party alliance

On 3 July 1995, a Wales Green Party press release was issued by Richard Bramhall, Press Officer for the Wales Green Party, entitled 'Greens welcome end of "Plaid/Green" links in Ceredigion' (NLW PCD 14, no date). The press release maintained further than 'the nightmare is over, at last we can get on with Green Party campaigns free of the ball and chain of nationalism'. The demise of the Plaid Cymru/Green Party alliance was brought about during 1994 and 1995 and involves a high degree of nuanced, localized minutiae, which we do not have the space to discuss in full in this chapter (though see Fowler and Jones 2006; Dafis 2005b: 203–5). We focus, rather, on the key issues that led to the dissolution of the alliance. Many individuals who were supporters of the pact maintained that its demise was brought about by a few disaffected Green Party members who were fiercely opposed to the general idea of nationalism and its practical manifestation in Wales (Dafis 2005b: 203).

The campaign to undermine the pact was conducted on two separate fronts. First, a Green Party member opposed to the pact, Chris Busby, succeeded in gaining the support of the Welsh Green Party for his candidature in the Mid and West Wales seat in the 1994 European elections. His actions, in this respect, put Ceredigion Green Party activists (who were supporting Plaid Cymru) at odds with the UK Green Party. Jonathon Porritt was even expelled from the UK Green Party for his public backing of the Plaid Cymru Candidate, Marc Phillips (Dafis 2005b: 204). Secondly, and more locally, the campaign to undermine the pact between Plaid Cymru and the Green Party also involved establishing an 'Aberystwyth Green Party' in order to provide a base from which disaffected Green Party members could conduct their anti-alliance campaign within Green Party structures. This opposition to joint Plaid Cymru/Green Party candidates was formalized in the context of a local by-election in the Aberystwyth North ward of the former Dyfed County Council. Standing as the 'Aberystwyth Green Party' candidate, Chris Busby polled just eleven votes. It was the second worst result of any Green Party candidate in Welsh electoral history (NLW PCD 14, no date; more broadly, see De-Shalit 2001). Nevertheless, by aligning the 'Aberystwyth Green Party' to the UK Green Party, certain Green Party members within Aberystwyth ultimately succeeded in portraying the Plaid Cymru/Green Party alliance as something that was, once again, opposed to the Green Party at a broader UK scale (Evans 1993).

The key issue, in this regard, was the theoretical reasoning that lay behind the actions of the small band of anti-alliance supporters. In Ceredigion and Pembroke North, those who wanted to undermine the electoral alliance chose to link Plaid Cymru with more unpalatable forms of nationalism. A contemporary document, for instance, claims that certain individuals opposed to the alliance had 'caused extreme offence to many people both in CPNGP [Ceredigion and Pembroke North Green Party] and in Wales by equating support for Cynog Dafis with . . . Serbia, Croatia, Northern Ireland, Hitler's Germany, the Jewish holocaust and ethnic cleansing' (Alun Williams' papers). Richard Bramhall, an opponent of the Ceredigion coalition, also chose to associate Plaid Cymru with more extreme versions of nationalism in a draft document entitled 'Ceredigion local [Green] Party relationship with Plaid Cymru: impact on Wales Green Party' (NLW PCD 14, no date). Bramhall argued in very loose terms that Plaid Cymru's language policy 'points towards exclusively Welsh-medium teaching in schools' (ibid). He made further insinuations about Plaid Cymru's relationship with nationalism:

These days they soft-pedal Nationalism, presenting themselves as a modern element in the 'Europe of 100 flags' . . . In many parts and by many people Plaid is still seen as Nationalist in the worst sense – the sense that is daily making headlines across the world (ibid).

But in addition to these emotive arguments concerning the almost necessary link between Plaid Cymru and more unpalatable forms of nationalism, certain opponents of the alliance sought to draw attention to the inherent incompatibility of nationalist and green discourse. Bramhall, for instance, argued that Plaid Cymru policy ran contrary to Green Party policy in that Plaid Cymru was committed to a traditional growth economy; road building; the Maastricht Treaty; nuclear energy; blood sports; transport of live farm animals; the Criminal Justice Act; and that Plaid Cymru was opposed to a Land Value tax. Moreover, he argued that Plaid Cymru had had a detrimental effect upon the Green Party's development in several constituencies including 'Arfon, Dwyfor, Môn, Llanelli . . . Caerfyrddin and Dinefwr' (ibid). Such statements illustrate the broader tensions that can exist between nationalist and green discourses. The adoption of liberal, or socialist, or green discourses by western nationalist parties will invariably be perceived by many non-nationalists as a secondary consideration. Most will view the ultimate role of a nationalist party as lying in the realm of national self-determination or in safeguarding an ethnic or linguistic minority. In other words, many will argue that it is impossible to reconcile nationalist and environmental discourses. Such were the arguments being propounded by certain disaffected Green Party members in Aberystwyth in 1994 and 1995.

Although the 'Aberystwyth Green Party' was a miniscule group, it did succeed in generating sustained publicity in the local press. Moreover, the movement had persuaded the Green Party at Wales and UK levels to take a dim view of the Plaid Cymru/Green Party alliance. Under these external pressure, Plaid Cymru and the Ceredigion and Pembroke North Green Party formally announced, 'with deep regret', the end of the agreement, at a press conference in the Talbot Hotel, Aberystwyth on 3 July 1995. Their joint press release attempted to put a brave face on the situation: 'New arrangements for Plaid/Green co-operation in Ceredigion', and Cynog Dafis resumed his parliamentary work as a conventional Plaid Cymru MP (NLW PCD 14, no date). Thus, the Plaid Cymru/Green Party partnership joined the lengthening list of partnerships between nationalist and environmentalist groups across Europe, which had withered on the vine after promising a new form of politics (Fowler and Jones 2006).

EXPLICATING AN ELECTORAL POLITICS OF PLACE AND SCALE

The narrative above provides an account of the particular set of circumstances that were crucial to the formation of an electoral pact between Plaid Cymru and the Green Party between 1991 and 1995. A series of personal, temporal and spatial contingencies were necessary for the formation of this alliance (Fowler and Jones 2006). Cynog Dafis' personality and his commitment to both nationalism and environmentalism gave the alliance a certain credibility: he was an individual who succeeded in reconciling the differences that existed between these two contrasting political ideologies. A temporal contingency was also at work here since the 1980s, as has been well documented elsewhere, was a period in which environmental concerns became far more prevalent in popular and political discourse, at least for a while (Porritt and Winner 1988; for a discussion of the 'greening' of more established political parties see Garner 1996; McCormick 1991). In more spatial terms, too, the particularities of the Ceredigion and Pembroke North constituency meant that it was an exceptionally propitious place to forge connections between nationalists and environmentalists. The formation of the alliance between Plaid Cymru and the Green Party, therefore, was dependent on a series of contingent connections or events. In this sense, the narrative account of the formation of the alliance and of its subsequent breakup, provided above, mirrors other work in the social sciences that has sought to elaborate on the theoretical and empirical linkages between nationalist and green ideologies (De-Shalit and Talias 1994; Eckerberg 1994; De-Shalit 1995; Dawson 1995; Podoba 1998; Hamilton 2002). These studies of the association between nationalism and environmentalism, which have been conducted in diverse locations such as eastern European, Israel and Scotland, suggest that territorial identities are far more deeply entrenched than environmental concerns, at least within the context of formal electoral politics. Environmental grievances may well attach themselves to instances of nationalist insurgence at particular times, therefore, but these connections are temporary and highly contingent in character.

We maintain that the empirical themes discussed in this chapter illustrate the need to think about the iterative connections between a localized electoral politics and electoral, policy and parliamentary processes taking place at other geographical scales. Social scientists have been willing to consider how a localized electoral politics may well be the product of processes happening at larger geographical scales and it is clear that the election of Cynog Dafis as the first Plaid Cymru/Green Party fits in well with this conceptual outlook. We witness this top-down influence on localized electoral politics most clearly, of course, in the context of the increased public interest in environmental issues that was emerging at a broader British and, indeed, European scale during this 1980s. This period was characterized by the growing vibrancy of national and international ecological movements and lobbying groups. These succeeded in promoting the significance of environmental issues both to the public at large and to the established political parties. Surveys and opinion polls conducted throughout the western world during the 1980s, for instance, showed that the public was becoming ever-more concerned with the effects of pollution and environmental degradation. This shift signalled a growth in public support towards the policies of green or environmental parties (Porritt and Winner 1988: 19–24; McCormick 1991: 115–21). At the same time, the growth in environmental awareness that took place during the 1980s provided much impetus for the 'greening' of established political parties (McCormick 1991: 28–47; see also McCormick 1991). Both of these broader changes, we contend, helped to promote support for the Green Party within the constituency of Ceredigion and Pembroke North. Green Party policies, at one and the same time, became more popular and palatable for voters within the constituency given the growing engagement of the public and more established political parties with environmental issues.

We contend, however, that we need to augment this conception of a top-down production of localized electoral politics with a viewpoint that acknowledges that small-scale electoral politics can also have (albeit limited) impacts on a broader scale. Cynog Dafis, as a Plaid Cymru/ Green Party MP, contributed to the passing of certain 'environmental' policies, such as the Home Energy Conservation Bill and the Road Traffic Reduction Bill. In both these cases, Cynog Dafis initiated processes that were adopted successfully by the Liberal Democrats. It is certain that his vociferous support of the environment within various Commons' debates testifies to his ability to make green issues more visible than they had previously been within British parliamentary politics. Jonathon Porritt, in this vein, contends that Cynog Dafis 'did several people's worth [of work] in his time in parliament'. He also stated that the increase in the number of green policies being promoted by Plaid Cymru during the 1990s – instigated in no small way by Cynog Dafis – was a cause for celebration (Dafis 2005b: 204).

In addition, we believe that the empirical themes discussed in the previous sections illustrate the complex interplay between a localized politics of place and the scalar politics that helps to reproduce nationalism. We begin by addressing the politics of place. Electoral results in all constituencies are dependent in the last instance on the mix of people residing within them. The politics of place, therefore, informs the manner in which electoral results unfold. It is clear that the cultural, social and political particularities of Aberystwyth and its hinterland in Ceredigion have played an integral role in determining the electoral politics of the constituency of Ceredigion and Pembroke North. As we have already noted, Ceredigion and, indeed, west Wales in general, is characterized by a co-presence of large numbers of nationalist and green voters. The nationalist credentials of the town of Aberystwyth, if not the whole of Ceredigion, have been explored at length in previous chapters of this book. Ceredigion and west Wales, however, also contain key locations for the green movement in Wales. These range from the more official and institutionalized sites, such as the Centre for Alternative Technology and the University of Wales, Aberystwyth to the large number of alternative lifestyle communities dotted throughout the region. The relative strengths of these two distinct cultures within Ceredigion in particular – as evidenced in the results of the European elections of 1989 – provided a justification and springboard for an increased collaboration between the two political ideologies and parties.

The significance of the specific politics of place within Ceredigion and Pembroke North is made clear when compared with the tiny share of votes attained in the other two constituencies, which were contested by a Plaid Cymru/Green Party alliance during the same period (Monmouth, 0.6 per cent; Newport East, 1.7 per cent). But of course, the politics of place is also apparent in another sense. The breakup of the alliance between Plaid Cymru and the Green Party was borne out of a specific set of political geographies within the town of Aberystwyth itself. The relatively painless process through which the electoral pact between Plaid Cymru and the Green Party was formed was, ultimately, called into question in no uncertain terms as a result of emerging tensions both between different factions of the Green Party and between green and nationalist activists. We can also note, in this respect, the significant reticence demonstrated by certain members of Plaid Cymru towards the formation of the electoral alliance in the first place. Those nationalist activists in Ceredigion who had been initially distrustful of the alliance and of its potential long-term electoral harm may well have secretly welcomed the political machinations that led to the severing of the pact in 1995. Cynog Dafis, for instance, notes that he received a piece of

correspondence from a 'cultured' Ceredigion farmer offering 'congratu-
lations' on Plaid's 'divorce' from the Greens in 1995 (Dafis 2005a: 11).
Although this one piece of evidence does not necessarily demonstrate a
broader antipathy towards green ideas amongst Welsh nationalists in
Ceredigion, it suggests that their attitudes were not uniformly supportive of the pact, or of the place of green issues within Welsh nationalism.
Once again, such a contention illustrates the complex electoral politics of
place that were at work in Aberystwyth during the late 1980s and 1990s.

But of course, a key contention of this book is that the politics of place
within Aberystwyth have been implicated in the reproduction of nationalist discourse. We have already discussed how a localized electoral
politics in Aberystwyth contributed to the promotion of environmental
policies and debates at broader geographical scales. More importantly,
we want to argue that the electoral politics of place in Aberystwyth
during the late 1980s and early 1990s also had a bearing on the contours
of Welsh nationalism in subsequent years. It is our contention that the
formation of the alliance between Plaid Cymru and the Green Party in
Ceredigion and Pembroke North had the unintended consequence of
bringing environmental concerns to the forefront of nationalist thinking
throughout Wales. We have already noted the praise that was directed
towards Plaid Cymru by Jonathon Porritt during the mid-1990s as a
result of Cynog Dafis' words and deeds (Dafis 2005b: 204). Plaid Cymru's changing attitudes towards the role that should be played by
environmental issues within its discourse of nationalism is plain to see
during this period. A reading of Plaid Cymru manifestos since the 1987
general election is instructive in this respect. The general election of 1987
was the last British election prior to the explosion of media interest in
environmental issues, and the subsequent European elections of 1989
when the Green Party made substantial progress in the UK. In 1987, the
Plaid Cymru manifesto makes reference to the environment in a superficial, romantic or even naïve manner, and views the environment in a
singularly 'national' sense:

> Wales . . . has a marvellous environment . . . Our environmental heritage is
> among the richest in Europe. We have a unique combination of rural,
> urban and costal landscapes, wildlife and historic buildings. Plaid's
> policies are designed to protect and develop this heritage . . . (Plaid Cymru
> 1987: 2–10)

Just two years later, the Green Party had become a new political force
in time for the 1989 European elections. This is how Plaid Cymru's 1989
manifesto reflected the situation:

The first cornerstone of our programme is our environmental policy . . . Policies to preserve the environment must be given the highest priority. As allies of the Green parties in the European Parliament, Plaid Cymru MEPs would emphasise the over-riding importance of radical policies . . . (Plaid Cymru 1989: 4)

Similar concerns have been apparent in more recent years. In the 2005 UK general election, for instance, Plaid Cymru asserted that it 'will put the environment and tackling climate change at the heart of everything we do in Parliament' (Plaid Cymru 2005: 17). By 2007, in time for the 2007 elections to the National Assembly for Wales, Plaid had come to the conclusion that 'the future of life itself has to be our highest priority' (Plaid Cymru 2007: 5).

What is significant about many of these ecological discourses, however, is the explicit attempt that is made to conjoin them with a discourse of nationalism (). In 1994, for instance, Plaid Cymru's European election manifesto spoke in grand terms of 'an ecological Europe', and emphasized the multi-scalar impacts of climate change in a more sophisticated manner. And yet, in doing so, they sought to reclaim the global debate on environmentalism and position it as a direct external threat to the well-being or – in orthodox nationalist terms – the 'sovereignty' of Wales' communities:

We live in an environment on the edge of a multiple crisis . . . The severe flooding experienced in Europe including the north Wales coastline . . . has demonstrated the devastating effect the threat to the ecological balance of the planet as a whole can have on individual communities. (Plaid Cymru 1994: 23)

The above statement is significant, therefore, since it tried to reconcile the threats posed by environment risks, which were and still are, by definition, global in reach, with the more localized and nationalist context within which Plaid Cymru operated. Global threats, in this sense, were being positioned within these nationalist discourses as challenges that were said to be facing the Welsh nation in particular.

The cynic might argue that such general claims have become commonplace within the manifestos of the majority of political parties over recent years. Furthermore, the cynic might also question the degree to which the emergence of such policies within Plaid Cymru can be traced back to the debates taking place in private and public houses in Ceredigion during the late 1980s and early 1990s. We want to suggest that the incorporation of ecological concerns into Welsh nationalist discourse, as evidenced in Plaid Cymru's policies, strategies and manifestos, was borne out, at least in part, of the detailed negotiations, and subsequent alliance formed, between Plaid Cymru and the Green Party during this period and the key role played by Cynog Dafis within all this. The most apposite example of this rescaling of a localized politics of place into the politics of nationalism appears in the pages of Dafis' recent autobiography (Dafis 2005b: 206–7) in which he discusses his conversations with Dafydd Wigley prior to the latter's first speech as the new President of Plaid Cymru in autumn 1994. As a result of Dafis' encouragement, Wigley had begun to think carefully about the environmental challenges facing Wales and had attended a series of meetings and conferences with Dafis, in which such ideas had been discussed. There, then, followed another meeting between Dafis and Wigley in Gannets Restaurant in Aberystwyth in August 1994, where the two discussed ideas for Wigley's maiden speech as President of Plaid Cymru. The upshot of these discussions was a remarkable speech in which Wigley (quoted in Dafis 2005b: 207) boldly asserted that

> *Mae terfyn ar adnoddau'r hen ddaear hon ac un o flaenoriaethau pennaf ein hoes yw'r rheidrwydd i newid ein cyfundrefn economaidd i ffwrdd o'r ffwlbri sy'n diystyru'r ffactorau hyn.*

> [There is a limit to the earth's resources and one of the main priorities of our age is the necessity to change our economic system away from the idiocy that ignores these factors.]

Wigley, significantly, sought to combine this ecological discourse with the nationalist discourse that had been traditionally promoted by Plaid Cymru, when he stated that Wales required a '*strategaeth ddatblygu cynaliadwy sy'n cydblethu cyfrifoldeb amgylcheddol, cydwybod cymdeithasol, diogelwch cymunedol ac amrywiaeth ddiwylliannol*/sustainable development strategy that interwove ecological responsibility, social conscience, community safety and cultural diversity' (quoted in ibid). Ecological and nationalist ideas were, here, conjoined in one discourse being promoted by Plaid Cymru at the Welsh national scale. Our contention is that the emergence of such a synergy between nationalist and ecological discourses or, in other words, a greening of Welsh nationalist discourse, was very much a product of the specific politics of place that took place in Aberystwyth during the late 1980s and early 1990s.[1]

NOTES

[1]   As another indication of the successful greening of Welsh nationalist discourse that took root during the early 1990s, we can note the demise of the Welsh Green Party since the split from Plaid Cymru in Ceredigion (Griffiths

2004). Green issues in Wales are now promoted by the England and Wales Green Party. The Welsh nationalism of Plaid Cymru, to a certain extent, may well have taken over the mantle of an unofficial Green Party for Wales. An instructive comparison can be made with Scotland, in which the Scottish Green Party has continued to act as a far more significant political player.

7

Nationalism, community and territory: where is Wales?

INTRODUCTION

Our discussion in the preceding chapters has highlighted a number of different discursive contexts within which various groups have sought to define a Welsh nation since the 1960s. In this final empirical chapter, we discuss other important themes relating to issues of community, territory and borders. The need to protect Welsh-speaking communities from the deleterious effects associated with unemployment, lack of services and housing, as well an in-migration of English speakers, has been a source of debate within the nationalist movement over a long period of time. There is no doubt, however, that the discursive significance of such themes has increased in recent years. Different organizations that seek to shape the priorities of Welsh nationalism, especially in the period since the devolution of power in 1999, have engaged in a sometimes heated debate about the character of Welsh-speaking communities and of the threats that are facing them. Interestingly, from a geographical perspective, these debates have also implicitly addressed more fundamental questions about the territorial extent of a Welsh territory; they have, in effect, become debates about the 'where of Wales' (Jones and Fowler 2007a).

This chapter, therefore, seeks to show how ideas relating to community and territory are implicated in the reproduction of nationalist discourse. Of course, Anderson's (1983) work is of especial relevance in this respect. He has famously argued that nations are imagined communities of people. There are many implications of thinking about a nation in such a way. Most oft-cited and discussed is the idea that nations are *imagined*, since 'the members of even the smallest nation will never know most of their fellow-members, meet them, or even hear of them' (ibid: 6). Less discussed perhaps, is the second element within Anderson's conception of the nation as an imagined community, namely that a nation is also imagined as a *community* or, in other words, as a group of people that exhibit a 'deep, horizontal comradeship', (ibid: 7). Following Anderson's lead, we want to suggest that there is a need to think through more systematically two sets of ideas tat arising from Anderson's conception of the nation as an imagined community: community and territory/ border.

In the first place, part of the significance of Anderson's ideas – at least in an implicit sense – is the fact that they are dependent on drawing a distinction between nations as imagined communities and other smaller real communities.[1] These latter types of communities, presumably, are ones in which fellow-members do actually know each other, meet each other and hear of each other. Anderson, perhaps understandably, does not elaborate on these types of small-scale communities or their significance for the reproduction of nationalist discourse. We have been at pains to emphasize throughout this book that individuals, groups of people and organizations located within particular places or, alternatively, small-scale communities, play a key role in shaping nationalist discourse. The use of the term 'community' by Anderson is highly significant, too, for a number of reasons. For much of the twentieth century, the term community evoked notion of solidarity and unity within academia and popular discourse. Stacey (1969), for instance, noted long ago that 'community' was admittedly somewhat of catch-all term, but that it was commonly understood as something that referred to face-to-face social relations within a defined geographical area that were characterized by a sense of belonging, mutual interest and solidarity (see also Cater and Jones 1989: 170). The notion of *gemeinschaft*, namely the dense networks of association that are said to exist in rural communities in particular, and the feelings of solidarity and order that these networks generate, encapsulates these more traditional conceptions of community (Tonnies 1887). Ideas such as these, of course, enable Anderson (1983: 7) to describe a nation as an imagined community of people who share a 'deep, horizontal comradeship'.

By now, however, geographers and others have sought to complicate our understanding of the notion of community. Two interrelated strands have been particularly important and both have a bearing on the arguments that we make in this chapter. First, geographers and others have maintained that even small-scale communities are inherently imagined in character (Rose 1990; Valentine 2001: 124). While face-to-face contact within small-scale communities is far more likely that in the imagined community of the nation, it is clear that an important discursive imagination underpins even the most small-scale communities;

these small-scale communities, therefore, comprise 'a group of people bound together by some kind of belief stemming from particular histori-cal and geographical circumstances' (Rose 1990: 426). Second, and fol-lowing on from the first point, it is also clear that small-scale communities can also be places of tension, contradictions and conflict. If even small-scale communities are imagined in important ways, then it is almost inevitable that different groups of people – differentiated in terms of class, gender, ethnicity, religion, linguistic ability and so on – will imagine that particular community in different ways. Different imagina-tions, in this respect, can highlight different group and individual memories, different cultures and different geographies for that particu-lar community (e.g. Dwyer 1999).

In the second place, Anderson's ideas also draw our attention to the significance of the nation as a territorial and bordered entity. The most instructive aspects of Anderson's argument, in this respect, are his efforts to show how particular technologies – the census, the map and the museum – were used as part of a state-driven process of social and spatial categorization, which underpinned the nation-building process:

> The 'warp' of this thinking was a totalizing classificatory grid, which could be applied with endless flexibility to anything under the state's real or contemplated control: peoples, regions, religions, languages, products, monuments, and so forth. The effect of the grid was always to be able to say of anything that it was this, not that; it belonged here, not there. It was bounded, determinate, and therefore – in principle – countable (Anderson 1983: 184).

The value of Anderson's work is his ability to show how national borders and territories – and nations themselves – are produced through a political act of definition. A nation's territories and borders, therefore, are two sides of the same coin and are crucial geographical elements within the broader nation-defining project. Anderson's work, in this respect, echoes recent work in the social sciences that has sought to show how space, territory and borders are socially produced, as we discussed in Chapter 2 (Murphy 1996; Lefebvre 1991). Paasi's (1991; 1996) work, in this respect, has highlighted the need to view regions or nations as territorial concepts that are continually 'becoming' through varied pro-cesses of 'institutionalization'. Key to this 'becoming' are the interlinked processes of differentiation and integration (Paasi 1996; see also Sletto 2002). Nations and/or regions are differentiated from others through the promotion of a discourse of difference, whereas they are simultaneously subject to a discourse of integration, which highlights their internal homogeneity (see also Dalby 1988; Van Houtum and Van Naerssen

2002). Similar themes emerge in the context of recent attempts to theorize boundaries. Newman and Paasi (1998: 189) maintain that although 'boundary studies have had a long, descriptive and nontheoretical history in geography', they have in recent years undergone a conceptual renaissance. Part of this project has revolved around the need to view borders and boundaries as geographical concepts that are produced in nature. Geographers have drawn inspiration from social and cultural theory to show how boundaries should be viewed as contingent processes in motion or, as Van Houtum and Van Naerssen (2002: 126) put it, 'a social practice of spatial differentiation', while those engaged in critical geopolitics have illustrated the various discourses that help to shape political and popular understandings of boundaries. In this latter context, work by Dalby (1999), for instance, has demonstrated that boundaries are produced by territorialized discourses of power and knowledge.

While we value the contribution that has been made by Anderson and others to our understanding of the way in which national territories and boundaries are produced, we also need to appreciate the fact that state organizations are not the only producers of the territories and borders of the nation. In broad terms, authors such as Newman and Paasi (1998: 187) have maintained that there has been a tendency for social scientists to equate territories and borders with the territoriality of the state. This is a reflection of the existence of a state system that structures the lives of people and, consequently, provides the political and social conditioning that influences the work conducted by academics. There is a growing recognition, nonetheless, particularly within the academic fields of sociology, anthropology and aspects of cultural geography of the multiple territories and borders that help to shape social and spatial life. Part of the impetus for this work has derived from a focus on issues of identity within certain strands of academic research, and especially notions of identity politics (Keating 1998). Identities, and their related borders and territories, in this sense, can be local or transnational in character and can conceivably exist with little reference to state boundaries and territories (see Cohen 1982; Eisenstadt and Giesen 1995). In this respect, we need to take heed of how discourses concerning national territories and borders are multiple in nature and may be derived from a range of state and non-state actors.

In promoting this agenda, we echo Paasi's (1996: 11) attempt to reconcile the relationship between a socio-spatial consciousness, centred on the activities of the state's agents and existing at the national scale, and a social representation, which lies within the domain of more ordinary people within localities, within the production of national borders and territories. More broadly, by showing the ways in which different discourses are implicated in the production of alternative national territories and borders we also seek to illustrate the politics of the group-defining project associated with nationalism. National territories and borders, we contend, rarely exist in the singular. They are, rather, mutable and highly contested social constructs. Or, rather they are social products. Despite the important imagined, discursive and contested aspects of all types of community, we do not think that we should decry their material or physical characteristics. After all, the relative location of a community/nation and the configuration of roads, buildings/towns and so on within it all impact on the possible range of geographical imaginations open to different people living within and outwith its boundaries. Following Lefebvre (1991: 1), we need to examine the complex interplay between different spatialized discourses and the materiality of particular spaces. In this regard, communities, be they small-scale ones or the community of the nation, are comprised of a variety of socio-spatial material practices and organizations, along with dominant and clandestine socio-spatial discourses. The more material aspects of national territories, for instance, are the product of alternative national discourses, while the physicality of national territories also impinges on the types of discourses that can be contemplated.

Our aim in this chapter, therefore, is to examine how such divergent geographical imaginations about the territorial extent of Wales have acted as important themes within Welsh nationalist discourse and to use this empirical material as way of further highlighting the significance of geographical themes for the social construction of the nation. We begin by outlining the historic dimension to these debates about the significance of community and territory of the nation by charting the way in which various organizations, for much of the twentieth century, have sought to promote a nationalist discourse within which an important element has been to defend Welsh-speaking communities from various perceived threats. We then proceed to discuss in detail the more contemporary debates about the significance of Welsh-speaking communities within nationalist discourse. Our main empirical focus is the formation of Cymuned in 2001 and the shockwaves that this event sent throughout the whole of the Welsh nationalist movement. We seek to show in this section how a localized politics of place within the town of Aberystwyth was implicated in this broader debate concerning the territorial extent and scale of the Welsh nation. We contend that an examination of these themes enables us to show how: different organizations have been part of a group-making project associated with the Welsh nation; different geographical visions of the territorial extent of the Welsh nation have been promoted by these organizations; more broadly, issues of place, scale and territory are implicated within nation-building projects.

RURALITY, COMMUNITY AND THE WELSH NATION

As long ago as the 1920s and 1930s, nationalists in Wales advocated a strong connection between the Welsh language and people and its rural areas. For nationalists such as Iorwerth Peate (1931: 2, quoted in Gruffudd 1994: 68), for instance, in the west of Wales in particular could be found:

> folk songs, superstitions, crafts, the gentle bearing of the poor, and a host of other things which are like the fragments of a dream lost in the uproar of industry's juggernaut.

The value of the west of Wales, therefore, derived partly from its distant location from Anglicizing influences and partly from its rurality. Such sentiments became prominent in the official nationalist discourse of Plaid Cymru during the same period. Moses Gruffudd, Plaid Cymru's Chief Agricultural Adviser, for instance, argued that:

> placing the people back on the land is not only appropriate, but is essential if the Welsh nation is to live. The Welsh nation is a nation with its roots in the country and the soil (quoted in D. H. Davies 1983: 92).

The emphasis placed on the moral and linguistic virtues associated with living in rural communities continued within Welsh nationalist circles for much of the inter-war period and drew intellectual sustenance from individuals associated with Aberystwyth, such as H. J. Fleure, head of the Department of Geography in the University College Wales, Aberystwyth and George Stapledon, one-time lecturer in the Department of Agriculture in the same institution and, latterly, Director of the Plant Breeding Station located just outside the town of Aberystwyth (Gruffudd 1994).

Similar debates about the cultural and political significance of Welsh-speaking rural communities emerged during the 1960s and 1970s. Significantly, they offer a foretaste of some of the debates that are discussed at length in the following section. As was discussed in Chapter 4, Cymdeithas yr Iaith was formed as a direct action organization, whose sole purpose would be to promote the status of the Welsh language within Wales. There was a widespread belief at the time – expressed both in critical and more charitable terms – that Plaid Cymru had centred its activities on party parliamentary issues and had, as such, ignored the more fundamental linguistic threat facing the Welsh nation. It was sentiments such as these that inspired Saunders Lewis' (1962) radio lecture on the 'fate of the language' and the formation of Cymdeithas yr Iaith as a separate organization, which would campaign for a higher status for the Welsh language within Wales. As we indicated in Chapter 3, these debates about the need to create a new campaigning organization for the Welsh language were also played out in more geographical terms. There was a geographical tension at work within the nationalist discourse of the 1960s and 1970s, which is highly significant for the empirical work that we discuss at length in the following section of the chapter.

Many of the Society's manifesto pledges and policies reflected a tension between needing to reflect a desire to protect a Welsh-speaking heartland from further social and cultural erosion and to reach out to secure the linguistic future of a broader Wales (Phillips 1998: 145–55). Cymdeithas yr Iaith, in this respect, sought to navigate a difficult 'middle route' between a commitment to the Welsh language within the Welsh-speaking heartland and throughout the whole of the territory of Wales. The distinctiveness of, and difficulties associated with maintaining, this position is made clearer when one considers the discourses being promoted by other nationalist organizations at the same time. The late 1960s and early 1970s witnessed the creation of Adfer (literally Restore), an organization concerned with securing the future of the Welsh language within the Welsh-speaking communities of the heartland. Inspired by the writings of J. R. Jones, Emyr Llewelyn (1972a; 1972b) had sought to challenge members of the nationalist movement to turn their back on 'Britishness' and to create a new Wales within the Welsh-speaking heartland. The creation of Adfer was viewed by Llewelyn as a concrete manifestation of this commitment to energizing Welsh-speaking communities; socially, economically and culturally (Phillips 1998: 148). Adfer itself was subdivided into the Adfer Movement (Mudiad Adfer), which sought to promote Adfer's aims at a more philosophical level, whereas the Adfer Company (Cwmni Adfer) engaged with the practical aspects of ensuring the vitality of Welsh-speaking communities, for instance, through acting as a housing association for Welsh speakers who were unable to buy homes within Welsh-speaking communities. As Phillips (1998: 151) makes clear, the disjuncture between the nationalist (and territorial) discourses promoted by *Adfer* and *Cymdeithas yr Iaith* became ever clearer during the early 1970s and led to open debate and dissent between the two organizations.

At the other extreme, as it were, lay the discourses and concrete policies promoted by Plaid Cymru during the late 1960s and early 1970s. Cynog Dafis (Davies 1973), for instance, has alluded to the increasing policy tensions between Cymdeithas yr Iaith and Plaid Cymru during the 1960s and early 1970s, ones which, at least in part, reflected different geographical imaginations of the 'where of Wales'. Part of the significance of Cymdeithas yr Iaith's policies during the early 1970s, we would argue, is that they were positioned against the alternative nationalist discourse and concomitant geographical imagination being promoted by Plaid Cymru during the same period. Dafis (Davies 1973: 252) refers, for instance, to the:

> tempting heresy that the more rural areas, being economically and socially weakened, might be abandoned in favour of a concentrated effort to recapture the anglicised, urban and industrial, and therefore fashionable, areas of the South East and North East.

As we saw in the previous chapter, part of the refocusing of Plaid Cymru's energies on the south east and north east of Wales derived from its attempts to win parliamentary seats in place such as Rhondda West and Caerffili. Plaid Cymru's alleged abandonment of the Welsh-speaking west of Wales was also said to derive from its economic policy:

> The party's economic plan for Wales . . . described how a free Wales might secure for itself a prosperous niche within the international capitalist system, and its growth-centres strategy implicitly assumed the continued decline of rural society (Davies 1973: 201).

Cymdeithas yr Iaith's nationalist discourse, in this respect, was positioned between the more economic and electoral discourses of Plaid Cymru, which were derived from a geographical imagination that encompassed the whole of Wales, and those of Adfer, which were centred on a perceived need to protect Welsh-speaking communities within 'y Fro Gymraeg'. In general terms, such tensions illustrate the way in which a nationalist movement is inherently fractured from within as different nationalist organizations seek to promote their own visions of nationalist pasts, presents and futures (Brubaker 2004). More specifically, it demonstrates the ways in which the nationalist movement in Wales has been concerned with explicating the link – in descriptive and normative terms – between the Welsh language, communities and the territory of Wales. We turn in the following section to examine such connections in more detail as we focus on the contentious politics of nationalism that was brought about by the formation of the new organization of Cymuned in 2001.

AN IMAGINED WELSH COMMUNITY?

In this section, we want to discuss the way in which recent political debate in Wales has sought to elaborate on the connections between the Welsh language and ideas relating to community and territory. Two interrelated developments helped to bring these issues into sharp focus. First of all, the devolution of power to Wales through the creation of a National Assembly signalled a broad shift in the character of Welsh politics (more broadly see Chaney et al. 2001; Jones and Osmond 2002). The creation of the National Assembly for Wales opened up considerable political and institutional space within Wales, within which issues relating to the Welsh language – and specifically its connections to Welsh-speaking communities, along with its contribution to ideas of Welshness – were able to be debated and politicized (NAfW 2002a; WAG 2002; 2003; see below). Second, the creation of the Assembly fuelled a belief in certain sectors that a Welsh nationalist discourse was becoming irrevocably civic in nature, being based on the bureaucratic state form of the Assembly, rather than being predicated on more ethnic factors associated with language, history and culture. This perceived latter development led to a backlash amongst certain members of the nationalist movement as they sought to reassert the significance of linguistic and cultural factors for ideas of Welshness. We must position the formation of Cymuned – and the linguistic and nationalist debates associated with its emergence – within this broader context.

And yet, while certain national processes acted as the broad context within which demands for a more ethnically orientated form of Welsh nationalism could begin to re-establish itself, it is clear also that other, more localized factors were crucial to its emergence. Not least amongst these more localized factors was the role of a more localized politics of place within the town of Aberystwyth. We begin this section by examining how a place-based politics within Aberystwyth was important for the emergence of Cymuned as an organization, along with the particular brand of nationalist discourse and politics that it espoused. We then proceed to show how the formation of Cymuned led to a series of long-running and acrimonious debates about the link between the Welsh language, Welsh-speaking communities and the territorial extent of a Welsh Wales. Throughout, we seek to show how a place-based politics in

Aberystwyth has been crucial for the contested reproduction of Welsh nationalist discourses in recent years.

Aberystwyth and the emergence of Cymuned

Networks of disaffected nationalists based in Aberystwyth were key to the emergence of Cymuned as an organization during 2001. This is not to say that people based in other locations within Wales were not critical to the development of the organization. Indeed, the first impetus in many ways came from the comments made by Seimon Glyn on BBC radio in response to a perceived unsustainable in-migration into the Welsh heartland, and was followed by other events, such as Ieuan Wyn Jones' memorable performance in response to questions concerning Cymuned's stance on the BBC television programme Question Time, popular protests held in different towns dotted throughout the Welsh heartland and a momentous public meeting held in Mynytho during the same year. The Mynytho meeting, in particular, has attained almost a mythical status within Welsh nationalist circles. Lefi Gruffudd, who attended the meeting, for instance, stated that '*ym Mynytho, does dim cwestiwn bod yna deimlad diwygiad 'na . . . teimlad bod rhaid i rhywbeth ddigwydd a bod rhaid gweithredu*/in Mynytho, there is no doubt that there was a revivalist feeling there . . . a feeling that something had to happen and that one had to act'. And yet, despite these important contributions made by people and places elsewhere, it is also apparent that networks of people within Aberystwyth were key to the emergence of Cymuned, in both organizational and philosophical terms. Some of our respondents drew attention to informal meetings that had taken place in Aberystwyth from February 2001 onwards. Simon Brooks, who has been centrally involved in Cymuned since the outset, argued as follows for instance:

> *Mi sefydlwyd Cymuned yn y lle cynta oherwydd diffyg ymateb gan Gymdeithas yr Iaith a Phlaid Cymru fel ei gilydd . . . Dwi'n cofio cael sgwrs yn nhafarn y Cŵps gydag Elin Haf Gruffydd Jones a gyda Rocet [Arwel Jones] a gyda Robat [Gruffydd] yn trafod hyn. A wedyn penderfynwyd gyda Robat a Rocet wedyn y buasen ni'n dechrau cwrdd yn anffurfiol i drafod y peth, ac oedd hynny ym mis Chwefror.*

> [Cymuned was formed in the first place because of the lack of response by both Cymdeithas yr Iaith and Plaid Cymru . . . I remember having a conversation in the Cŵps with Elin Haf Gruffydd Jones and with Rocet [Arwel Jones] and with Robat [Gruffudd] discussing this. And it was then

decided with Robat and Rocet that we would start meeting informally to discuss the matter, and that was in February.]

Arwel Jones expanded on this theme by stating that more 'informal meetings' were held in venues such as the Black Lion and that these were open to all those individuals that were 'in the know'. Despite being held in public houses, the meetings were held during the day, which testified, according to Arwel Jones, to their sobriety! Interestingly, it is clear that these meetings, from the very outset, were designed with a view to creating a separate organization that would act as a pressure group in opposition to the other more established nationalist movements of Plaid Cymru and, to a lesser extent, Cymdeithas yr Iaith. Nearly all of our respondents, for instance, spoke of a deep sense of dissatisfaction with the way in which Plaid Cymru had handled the transition to a more civic type of politics in Wales, as well as the more ethnically orientated backlash that found their full force in Seimon Glyn's statements. Arwel Jones, in particular, drew attention to the fact that much of the criticism emerging from these early meetings was directed solely towards Plaid Cymru but that this soon expanded into a similar disenchantment with the lack of vigour displayed by Cymdeithas yr Iaith. In this respect, the relationship between Cymuned and Cymdeithas yr Iaith was far more ambivalent that the one that existed between Cymuned and Plaid Cymru. Indeed, it was suggested that Cymuned's increasingly hard-line stance against Cymdeithas yr Iaith was as much driven by the personal feelings of disillusionment displayed by a few key activists within these Aberystwyth meetings as it was from a more widespread sense of dissatisfaction with the Society's policies.

Whatever the debates concerning Cymuned's ideological target, it is evident that increased efforts were made in 2001 to formalize the organization's activities. Significantly, what helped to start this second stage in Cymuned's development was a change of venue for its meetings; from different pubs in Aberystwyth to Talybont, located some 8 miles north of the town. The choice of Talybont was partly due to the presence of Gwasg y Lolfa, a publishing house, within the village and the importance of Robat Gruffudd, its proprietor – along with other members of his family – within the emerging debates about the need for a new nationalist organization, as well as the existence of a congenial pub 'that served food on Sundays'. As well as instigating a gradual formalizing of the nature of the group, it is clear that the move to Talybont also led to a shift in territorial or scalar focus for the emerging organization, most specifically in terms of its membership. Seimon Glyn attended one meeting in Talybont, for instance, and another meeting drew individuals from various parts of Pen Llŷn, the south of Cere-digion and Cardiff. But despite the increasing territorial reach of the organization, some felt that it was still nonetheless an organization whose roots, at least at an intellectual level, lay in Aberystwyth and its hinterland. To a certain extent, the strong focus on Aberystwyth contrib-uted to a certain discord with the emerging organization's other power base in north-west Wales. Jerry Hunter, who has been involved in Cymuned, since its early days, explained this issue as follows:

> *Mae'r grwp yna [yn Nhalybont] wedi bod yn hollbwysig, ynde, efo teulu'r Gruffudd a Gwasg y Lolfa, a Simon Brooks a'r criw yna ynde, a Arwel 'Rocet' yn weithgar iawn yn y dyddiau cynnar yna . . . Mae'n ddiddorol achos 'oedd gyda chi y grŵp yna ac wedyn yng Ngwynedd . . . wedi tyfu'n ganghennau lleol ers hynny, mae gyda chi Ben Llŷn ac wrth gwrs Seimon Glyn wrth gwrs yn ffigwr amlwg ynddo fo, dechreuodd o'r holl beth, ynde. So mae 'na ryw grŵp o gwmpas Seimon Glyn . . . grwpiau Caernarfon, Dyffryn Nantlle, felly oedd y grŵp yna yn Aberystwyth yn gyfrifol i raddau helaeth iawn am ddechrau'r holl beth, fel ymateb i Seimon Glyn. Ond yn fuan iawn, iawn wedyn ar ôl i'r mudiad ddechrau, mi oedd 'na lot o wahaniaethau lleol mewn ffordd.*

[That group [in Talybont] has been crucial, hasn't it, with the Gruffudd family and the Lolfa Press, and Simon Brooks and that crowd, and Arwel 'Rocet' was very lively in those early days . . . It's interesting because you had that group and then in Gwynedd . . . growing in local branches since then, you have Pen Llŷn and, of course, Seimon Glyn has been a prominent figure in that, he started the whole thing, didn't he. So there is a group around Seimon Glyn . . . the Caernarfon, Dyffryn Nantlle groups, so that group in Aberystwyth was responsible for starting the whole thing, in response to Seimon Glyn. But very, very soon after the movement started, there were a lot of differences in a way.]

In this respect, one can perceive a fracturing of the emerging organ-ization into two wings; a first more practical and organic wing based in the rural areas of north and west Wales and the more intellectual wing based in Aberystwyth and its environs. It is interesting to note that Cymuned, after being based for its first few years in Aberystwyth, has relocated to Pwllheli in Pen Llŷn. This shift does not detract from the fact that the organization, for much of its early period of existence, drew its ideological succour and policy direction from networks of people based in Aberystwyth. It was these individuals who helped define Cymuned's nationalist discourse regarding the need to protect Welsh-speaking com-munities from cultural erosion.

Another indication of the close association between Cymuned and Aberystwyth was the establishment of new political party, Llais y Cardi (the voice of the people of Ceredigion), as an offshoot of Cymuned in the period between 2003 and 2004. The broader context for the formation of Llais y Cardi was the publication of Ceredigion's proposed Unitary Development Plan (UDP), in which it was recommended that there should be a concerted programme to build a total of 6,500 new dwellings within the county in order to cater for a massively increased demand for housing envisaged by planning officials. Despite a total of 11,000 objections to the UDP being submitted to Ceredigion Unitary Authority, members of Cymuned believed that there was little hope of changing the minds of a council that they perceived to be wholly undemocratic.[2] It was with this context in mind that Llais y Cardi was formed as a way of increasing the democratic accountability of Ceredigion councillors. The tactics that they sought to employ in order to achieve this aim were somewhat tortuous and consisted of forcing a referendum in which the inhabitants of Ceredigion would be asked whether they wanted to be governed by a democratically elected mayor. Llais y Cardi's hope was that the elected mayor would take heed of the broader feeling in the county concerning the unsustainable in-migration of English speakers that would come about as a result of the adoption of the UDP. The details of the campaign need not detain us at present. Suffice to say that Cymuned's connections with Llais y Cardi – at an ideological and personal level – were extremely close, as this following quote from Gwilym ab Ioan shows:

Does dim raid bod yn ddewin i sylweddoli bod tri sylfaenwr [Llais y Cardi], sef Emyr Hywel, Simon Brooks a fi hefyd yn digwydd bod yn aelodau o bwyllgor gwaith Cymuned . . . meddylfryd Cymuned sydd wedi berwi drosto, fel petai, i'r maes gwleidyddol uniongyrchol yng Ngheredigion. Ond ar ôl dweud hynny, does na ddim cysylltiad swyddogol o gwbl rhwng Llais y Cardi a Chymuned. Ond yn amlwg, y bobl sydd yn cefnogi Llais y Cardi yn weithgar, maen nhw hefyd yn weithgar yng Nghymuned. Ond dyw Cymuned yn dylanwadu dim yn uniongyrchol . . . ar bolisiau Llais y Cardi.

[One doesn't have to be a magician to realise that the three founders [of Llais y Cardi], that is Emyr Hywel, Simon Brooks and I happen to be members of Cymuned's Executive Committee . . . it's Cymuned's mentality that has boiled over, as it were, into the field of direct politics in Ceredigion. But after saying that, there isn't a formal link at all between Llais y Cardi and Cymuned. But clearly, the people that actively support Llais y Cardi, they're also active in Cymuned. But Cymuned doesn't directly influence . . . Llais y Cardi's policies.]

Llais y Cardi was successful in instigating the referendum in Ceredigion but did not succeed in garnering enough support for an elected mayor.[3] Their subsequent decision to contest the Ceredigion elections in 2004 also ended in ignominy and, moreover, served to alienate the supporters of Plaid Cymru within the county and further afield.[4] The broader significance of Llais y Cardi's brief period in existence, we would argue, is that it demonstrates, once again, how Cymuned's nationalist discourse have been informed by networks of people and particular practices within Aberystwyth and a broader Ceredigion.

Withstanding the threat to the Welsh heartland

Cymuned's main aim has been to draw attention to the detrimental processes that are said to be affecting Welsh-speaking communities located within 'y Fro Gymraeg' and to advocate practical ways of ameliorating these problems. The organization, as such can be positioned as the inheritor of the philosophies of J. R. Jones (1966), as well as their more concrete manifestation in the Adfer movement (see above). There is no doubt that the leadership of Cymuned sought to re-affirm commitment to such ideas during 2001. As we showed in Chapter 3, Cymuned criticized the increasing focus within Welsh nationalist politics on civic issues and bemoaned the related lack of attention paid to the perceived ethnic and linguistic core values of the Welsh nation. As part of this development, the leadership of Cymuned developed a series of ideological dichotomies which conceptually delineated 'ethnic' from 'civic' Welsh nationalists (Jobbins 2001; Brooks 2001); 'Welsh speaking' from 'English-speaking' 'ethno-linguistic groups' (Brooks 2001); and 'Y Fro Gymraeg' from the rest of Wales in terms of domestic policy priorities (Cymuned 2001; see also Adfer 1987; Jones 1986; Llewelyn 1986). Significantly, Cymuned has also made extensive use of the language of 'colonisation' and 'colonialism' (Webb 2001), applied specifically to the processes of unsustainable in-migration that were said to be affecting the Welsh heartland (see Plate 7.1).[5] The author of its policy document on the colonization and colonialism said to be affecting Wales, Tim Webb, argued that such a language was an especially pertinent way of conceptualizing an 'unsustainable immigration' taking place in Wales today, being much more powerful that the more neutral term of migration:

> *Wedyn yr hyn wnes i oedd mynd ati i geisio dadansoddi yr hyn oedd yn digwydd mewn ffordd wahanol. Gan gychwyn efo'r gysyniad o wladychu. Sef, yn hytrach na chychwyn efo'r gymhariaeth â phobl du yn symud i mewn i wledydd Prydain,*

*cychwyn efo pobl wyn yn symud i wledydd eraill, gwledydd y trydydd byd ac yn
y blaen. Ac 'o'n i'n teimlo bod hyn yn debycach i'r hyn oedd yn digwydd yng
Nghymru.*

[Then what I did was try to evaluate what was happening in a different
way. Starting with the idea of colonialism. That is, instead of starting with
the comparison of black people moving in to the countries of Britain,
starting with white people moving to other countries, countries in the
third world and so on. And I felt that this was more similar to what was
happening in Wales.]

In this respect, Cymuned drew on a long-standing tradition of using
the language of colonialism within Welsh nationalist discourse. As noted
above, much of J. R. Jones' (1966) philosophy revolved around the need
to reject the sensibilities and processes of Britishness that were corrupt-
ing and undermining Welsh culture. Gareth Miles (1972), too, in his
polemic on the need for a 'Free Wales, Welsh Wales, Socialist Wales',
sought to draw attention to the way in which the Welsh language and
culture was being destroyed by a capitalistic imperialism. Miles, in this
regard, called for a new socialist model for democratic self-government
in Wales, which would ensure the vitality of its language and culture
(Phillips 1998: 152). In this respect, Cymuned's use of the language of
colonialism and colonization is but another manifestation of a long-
running feature of Welsh nationalist discourse. Indeed, these ideas, as
well as their more concrete manifestations and outcomes in various
communities located throughout the Welsh heartland, justified the formation of Cymuned, as was explained to us by Gwilym ab Ioan, a
leading Cymuned activist:

*Y rheswm pennaf dros sefydlu Cymuned oedd sefyllfa druenus y cymunedau
Cymraeg. Y dirywiad oedd yn digwydd oherwydd y mewnlifiad, ac oherwydd yr
allfudiad o bobl ifainc. Ac 'o'n i'n gweld cymunedau'n marw o flaen fy llygaid i
ddweud y gwir, ar raddfa gyflym iawn, iawn. Ro'n i wedi gweld hynny achos es i
ffwrdd o'r ardal 'ma yn '70 a dod nôl yn y 90au. A chael agoriad llygad anhygoel
o weld beth oedd wedi digwydd yn yr ugain mlynedd yna. Ac roedd hynny yn
digwydd ynghynt ac ynghynt o hyd.*

[The main reason for founding Cymuned was the pitiful situation of Welsh
speaking communities. The decline that was happening because of the
in-migration, and because of the out-migration of young people. And I
saw communities dying in front of my eyes to be honest, on a very, very
fast scale. I saw that because I went away from this area in '70 and came
back in the nineties. And had an incredible eye-opener of seeing what had
happened in those twenty years. And it was happening faster and faster
still.]

Gwilym ab Ioan went on to argue that he saw Cymuned's campaign as one that sought to define the Welsh-speaking heartland as a form of *gaeltacht*, within which the Welsh language could thrive and, at a later date, from which it could expand outwards into other parts of Wales.

Cymuned, in this respect, can be viewed as an organization that sought to respond to the gradual Anglicization of Welsh society. In similar ways to Saunders Lewis (1962), J. R. Jones (1966) and others, they have viewed the linguistic threat to a Welsh-speaking heartland as the key focus of nationalist agitation within Wales. In this respect, they have shown far more of a concern with the ethnic credentials of the Welsh nation than some of their counterparts, whom they accuse of being distracted by civic debates (Jobbins 2001; Brooks 2001). Nevertheless, it would be unwise to portray Cymuned's rhetoric with too broad a brush. It is worth emphasizing that Cymuned officially welcomes immigration but deplores an unsympathetic and unsustainable 'colonisation' of rural Welsh-speaking Wales.[6] What has complicated matters, in this regard, is that certain individuals have displayed a more combative attitude towards in-migration in general. It is the attitudes of these individuals, in particular, which has in certain instances led to criticism of Cymuned by members of Cymdeithas yr Iaith and Plaid Cymru.

Whatever the character of the processes that are said to undermine Welsh-speaking communities within the 'Fro Gymraeg', Cymuned strongly assert that these communities will play an important role in the continued reproduction of the Welsh language and the Welsh nation. The main argument propounded, in this regard, is a familiar one, namely that that the Welsh language, in order to survive and thrive, must be rooted in some way in particular communities where it is spoken as a 'natural' language. Cymuned, for instance, officially states that:

> *Y mae gan bobl y Fro Gymraeg hawl i'w chadw fel rhanbarth ac ardaloedd lle y mae'r Gymraeg yn briod iaith, lle y bydd y Gymraeg yn iaith swyddogol, yn iaith naturiol y gymuned, yn brif iaith gweinyddiaeth a masnach a phob agwedd arall ar fywyd, ac yn iaith gyffredin ymhlith mewnfudwyr a rhwng mewnfudwyr a brodorion; ac y mae ganddynt hawl i beidio â dioddef gwladychu na cholli'r boblogaeth gynhenid.*

[The people of 'y Fro Gymraeg' have the right to keep it as a region and areas in which Welsh is the appropriate language, where Welsh is the official language, the natural language of the community, the main language of administration and trade and every other aspect of life, and the common language amongst in-migrants and between in-migrants and indigenous people; and they have the right to suffer neither colonialism nor a loss of the indigenous population.][7]

Tim Webb, who has helped to develop much of Cymuned's policy, reinforced this opinion:

Dwi'n teimlo bod hi yn angenrheidiol i ni geisio cadw y Fro Gymraeg. Er, wrth gwrs, bod y Fro Gymraeg yn llawer gwanach nag oedd hi yn y 90au, heb sôn am yr 80au neu'r 70au. Ond heb bod na gymunedau a broydd lle mae'r Gymraeg yn iaith naturiol y gymuned, dwi ddim yn teimlo bod 'na ddyfodol i'r Gymraeg . . . hynny yw, iaith leiafrifol ym mhob man bydd hi ac yn y diwedd fydd hi ddim yn wahanol iawn i'r Gernyweg er enghraifft. Hynny ydy, hobi i bobl sydd â diddordeb mewn pethau diwylliannol a ieithyddol, ond yn hobi lleiafrifol, yn yr un modd ag yr oedd y Lladin yn hobi tan yn gymharol ddiweddar i leiafrif dysgedig, os liciwch chi.

[I think that it's necessary for us to try to keep the Fro Gymraeg . . . unless there are communities and areas where Welsh is the natural language of the community, I don't feel that there is a future for Welsh . . . that is, it will become a minority language in all areas and in the end it won't be very different from the Cornish, for example. That is, a hobby for people who have an interest in cultural and linguistic things, but a minority hobby, in the same way that Latin was a hobby until fairly recently for an educated minority, if you like.]

Such an argument is acceptable, at one level, since it emphasizes the importance of attempting to preserve certain communities where the Welsh language is spoken on a day-to-day basis. More contentiously, it seems to position those individuals who speak the Welsh language outside the borders of the 'Fro Gymraeg' as ones for whom the language is not 'natural' or for whom the Welsh language is merely a passing interest or hobby. There are clear echoes here of the accusations levelled towards Adfer by members of Cymdeithas yr Iaith and Plaid Cymru during the early 1970s. Dafydd Iwan, for instance, asserted in 1973 in response to Adfer's discourse that he did not believe in the idea that all the inhabitants of Wales beyond 'y Fro Gymraeg' were either foreigners, lost individuals or English people (quoted in Phillips 1998: 151). It seems that members of Cymuned have been wary of being too closely associated with Adfer's philosophy. Tim Webb, too, argued that Cymuned did not want to isolate the Welsh heartland from the rest of Wales. Rather, Cymuned possessed a vision in which the Welsh heartland existed in a symbiotic state with the remaining portions of the Welsh territory. In this way, '*mae'r fro Gymraeg angen gweddill Cymru . . . ond hefyd bod angen y fro Gymraeg . . . er mwyn cynnal y Gymraeg yng ngweddill Cymru*/the 'fro Gymraeg' needs the rest of Wales . . . but also we need the 'fro Gymraeg' in order to maintain Welsh in the rest of Wales'. This is a point that we shall expand on in the following section.

Cymuned's suggestions concerning practical means of achieving this aim have been varied and have focused on issues relating to housing and education. Cymuned advocate the need for affordable housing for the indigenous people of 'y Fro Gymraeg', be they Welsh- or English-speaking. In its presentation to the National Assembly's Local Government and Housing Committee in November 2001, Cymuned argued, among other things, that: the Welsh language should be a material consideration within all planning decisions made within the Welsh heartland; housing decisions made by planning authorities in the Welsh heartland should be made on the basis of research rather than more unscientific forecasting; the Welsh language should be incorporated more fully into the sustainability appraisals conducted on proposed developments within the Welsh heartland; affordable housing should be designated for local residents; welcome packs should be provided by estate agents to housebuyers in order to make them aware of the cultural and linguistic characteristics of the Welsh heartland; council tax rates on second homes should be double those levied on primary dwellings; planning permission be necessary for the re-designation of a dwelling as a second home.[8]

Most interesting, in this respect, have been Cymuned's efforts to try to institutionalize 'y fro Gymraeg' as a meaningful actor in its own right. In a series of policy submissions and presentations, Cymuned has developed the concept of an elected 'Welsh Heartlands Authority' in order to promote the administrative unity of Welsh speaking areas that are currently divided by local authority boundaries (Cymuned 2001; 2003). Under Cymuned's proposals, the Welsh Heartlands Authority would 'take over all executive, representative and advisory responsibilities, at local government level, in the fields of planning, housing, economic development, education and communications' in the territory of its jurisdiction, defined in the first instance by percentages of Welsh-speakers (Cymuned 2003). A new form of politics, and political territory, is therefore being narrated by Cymuned as a way of enabling a more positive engagement with the threat to Welsh-speaking communities. Dylan Foster-Evans, a member of Cymuned, explained the reasoning behind this proposal:

> *Mae 'na ddiffyg ... cyd-weithio rhwng yr awdurdodau lleol ac yn aml dydy'r Gymraeg ddim yn uchel iawn ar eu blaenoriaethau. Wedyn syniad [Cymuned] ... yw creu rhyw fath o uned lle mae'r Gymraeg yn fwy o flaenoriaeth. Nid creu uned sydd 'jest' yn poeni am yr iaith yn unig, ond bod y Gymraeg ar flaen*

feddyliau pobl yn hytrach nag yn cael ei gwasgu a'i gwasgaru ... Doedd demograffeg y Gymraeg ddim yn rhan o sut mae Cymru wedi ei threfnu ... mae'n sefyllfa anffodus fod pethau fel mae nhw.

[There is a lack of cooperation between the local authorities and Welsh often isn't very high amongst their priorities. And so [Cymuned's] idea . . . is to create some sort of unit where Welsh is more of a priority. Not to create a unit that just worries solely about the language, but that Welsh is at the forefront of people's minds rather than being squeezed and dispersed . . . The demography of the Welsh language wasn't part of how Wales has been arranged . . . it's an unfortunate situation that things are as they are.]

The distribution of the Welsh heartland throughout a number of different local authority areas, in this respect, was seen as something that hampered purposive and practical efforts to remedy the problems facing these communities. The emphasis on administrative reform as a means of tackling the problems facing Welsh-speaking communities is novel and may indicate an attempt, within Cymuned's nationalist discourse, to institutionalize a Welsh culture region within the political geography of Wales. This is a point that is taken up at further length in a following section.

Debates concerning migration and access to housing have, therefore, assumed a predominance within Cymuned. But there is a sense, too, at least among the rank and file members of Cymdeithas yr Iaith, that Cymuned's main aim, namely the prioritization of affordable housing for indigenous Welsh speakers, is not particularly novel, being a derivation of the Society's many demands for a Housing Act for Wales (Cymdeithas yr Iaith 1992; 1999; 2005a; Cymdeithas yr Iaith Gymraeg Planning-Economic Group 1989). Dylan Phillips, a key member of Cymdeithas yr Iaith involved in shaping the Housing Act, argued as such in an interview:

Siarada di gyda unrhywun yn Cymuned am beth yw polisi Cymuned mewn gwirionedd, a polisi'r Gymdeithas o Ddeddf Eiddo yw e'. Dy'n nhw ddim wedi dod mewn ag unrhyw syniadau polisi na strategaethau polisi newydd o gwbl, i ddweud y gwir.

[Talk to anyone in Cymuned about what Cymuned's policy actually is, and it is Cymdeithas' policy about a Housing Act. They haven't brought in any new policy ideas or policy strategies at all, to tell the truth.]

Cymuned's main success, it was argued, was its ability to achieve considerable publicity for its activities and policies through a mixture of deft campaigning, inflammatory remarks and the physical inscription of the landscape (see Plate 7.2).

Cymuned's nationalist discourse has drawn heavily, therefore, on the need to protect a Welsh-speaking heartland from alleged processes of colonialism and colonization. At the same time, what has been implicit in their nationalist discourse, we would argue, has been an effort to narrate new types of borders and territories within Wales: ones which can enable Welsh-speaking communities both to withstand the threat arising from an unsustainable in-migration and, in time, to expand outwards into the rest of Wales. Such territorial narratives have increasingly acted as the source of debate between Cymuned and other nationalist organizations within Wales and we turn to focus on these issues in the following section.

Where is Welsh-speaking Wales?

Much academic work, particularly by geographers, has alluded to the existence of a so-called 'Fro Gymraeg' or Welsh-speaking heartland, which is located in the west and the north of the country. Over forty years ago, Bowen (1959: 1) sought to show how Wales was constituted as a 'pays' or a region characterized by specific 'physical or cultural endowments'. The main signifier of the Welsh pays for Bowen was the particular cultural endowment of the Welsh language. Issues to do with language, culture and identity, therefore, were intimately intertwined in his definition of the culture region of Wales. Bowen's paper can be viewed as both a producer of other academic discussions concerning the geography of the Welsh nation or culture region. In many ways, his work was part of a broader academic endeavour to produce in-depth interpretations of the Welsh region (e.g. Thomas 1977). In a more specific context, his paper can be conceived as the inspiration for an ongoing series of books that have sought to chart, using census material, the changing geographies of the Welsh language (Aitchison and Carter 1994; 2004). Indeed, the role of Bowen's legacy within these books is made clear by the authors themselves (see Aitchison and Carter 1994: Preface). Similarly, Bowen's paper can be thought of as a broad-brush interpretation of the geography of the Welsh way of wife, whose finer brush-strokes were witnessed in the sociological studies of particular Welsh communities conducted during the 1950s and 1960s (e.g. Rees 1950).

But despite the volume of this academic work, there been little agreement concerning the exact geographical delineation of the heartland. To a degree, such an ambivalence can be explained by the changing territorial extent of the heartland over time. After all, part of the reasoning behind the formation of both Cymdeithas yr Iaith and Cymuned was the fact that the Welsh heartland, and the Welsh-speaking communities contained within it, were being eroded over time. And yet there is also a more fundamental debate concerning the way in which 'y Fro Gymraeg' should be defined. Our interviews with various key actors in Cymuned, in particular, would seem to indicate a serious attempt to grapple with this process of territorial definition. Tim Webb, in particular, has been heavily involved in resolving this issue:

> *Dan ni'n gweithio ar hyn ar hyn o bryd . . . Y broblem wrth gwrs efo diffinio'r Fro Gymraeg yw oherwydd bod 'na gymaint o bobl wedi mudo i'r Fro Gymraeg, ac yn gwladychu yn yr ystyr bod nhw ddim yn dysgu'r iaith, a'i defnyddio, bod 'na ardaloedd sydd yn froydd Cymraeg yn yr ystyr . . . mai Cymraeg ydy iaith y brodorion . . . eto i gyd, bod y canran o'r boblogaeth gyfan sydd yn medru Cymraeg wedi disgyn yn isel. Felly mae 'na broblem ynghylch diffinio'r Fro Gymraeg.*

> [We're working on this at the moment . . . The problem of course with defining the Fro Gymraeg is because so many people have migrated to the Fro Gymraeg, and are colonizing in the sense that they are not learning the language, and using it, that there are areas which are Welsh-speaking areas in the sense . . . that Welsh is the language of the natives . . . yet, that the percentage of the whole population that speaks Welsh has dropped down low. So there is a problem about defining the Fro Gymraeg.]

There is obviously a recognition in this context that the 'Fro Gymraeg', the key geographical context within which Cymuned propagates much of its political and cultural rhetoric, is not a pre-given territory with defined boundaries. Rather, it is a territorial construct whose exact definition is subject to political debate, and one which can be affected by social and spatial change. This fact has not stopped members of Cymuned, in particular, attempting to develop quasi-scientific interpretations of the territories and boundaries of the 'Fro Gymraeg'. Tim Webb, for instance, tried to outline a relatively sophisticated 'two-tier' model for mapping the extent of the heartland:

> *Mae 'na sawl model posib ar hyn o bryd. Ond mi fydd o, rwy'n meddwl bod rhaid cael dwy lefel o Fro Gymraeg. Dau ddosbarth o froydd mewn ffordd, oherwydd bod cymaint o amrywiaeth. Felly mi fydd yr ardaloedd craidd, Bro Gymraeg craidd, yn rhywbeth fel, bod o leia 80% o'r bobl sy' wedi cael eu geni yng Nghymru, yn medru Cymraeg . . . a hefyd bod dros hanner y boblogaeth gyfan yn medru Cymraeg. Dyna'r ardaloedd craidd. Y Fro Gymraeg ehangach fydd ardaloedd lle mae o leia' hanner y bobl sydd wedi eu geni yng Nghymru yn medru Cymraeg, ac o leia' un rhan o dair o'r boblogaeth gyfan.*

[There are several possible models at the moment ... I think that two levels of Fro Gymraeg are required. Two classes of 'broydd' in a way, because there is so much variance. So the core areas, a core Fro Gymraeg, will be something like, that at least 80% of the people who have been born in Wales, speak Welsh ... also that over half of the total population speak Welsh. Those are the core areas. The wider Fro Gymraeg will be areas where at least half of the population who have been born in Wales speak Welsh, and at least one third of the total population.]

We would suggest that this attempt to articulate a two-tier Welsh heartland (see Plate 7.3) is highly significant, since it reflects three admissions. First, and most clearly, there is an admission that certain parts of Welsh heartland have experienced an in-migration of English speakers and an out-migration of Welsh speakers and have, therefore, suffered a reduction in the proportion of the population with a mastery of the Welsh language. As we have shown, such a process of in-migration into the Welsh 'heartland' is the main *raison d'être* for Cymuned as an organization and echoes both the discourse promoted at various times by organizations such as Cymdeithas yr Iaith and Adfer, and the more general claims that have been made concerning the impact of migration and processes of globalization on territories and regions (see Anderson and O'Dowd 1999; Paasi, 2002). Second, and perhaps more contentiously, we would argue that it also reflects an implicit admission that the construction of a 'Fro Gymraeg' as a 'heartland' in which the Welsh language is a key part of the fabric of community life is merely that: a construction. The 'Fro Gymraeg', *contra* the more bald statements made by various political organizations and commentators in contemporary Wales, is not a homogeneous territory in which the Welsh language acts as the sole or, in some case, even the main means of societal communication and reproduction. To put it simply, the term 'y Fro Gymraeg' masks the existence of a highly variegated culturally-defined territory. Third, and more relevant to the themes discussed in this book, the definition of the 'heartland' used by Cymuned excludes the town of Aberystwyth from the 'inner Fro Gymraeg' (see Plate 7.3). Despite its significance as a key location within which much of Cymuned's nationalist discourse has been formulated, the actual outcome of this discourse has been to relegate the town of Aberystwyth into a second division of Welsh-speaking communities.

The discussions and debates carried out by members of Cymuned, if not the official nationalist discourses that they produce, betray this tension between the actuality of a highly variegated linguistic space within the 'Fro Gymraeg' and the need to portray it as a united linguistic territory. Tim Webb alluded to an interesting debate that took place in Cymuned's annual conference in 2004:

> *Mi gafon ni dipyn o drafodaeth, a honno'n drafodaeth iach a dweud y gwir, yng nghynhadledd Cymuned eleni ynghylch yr union derm ro'n ni am ddefnyddio. Oedden ni eisiau arweiniad gan yr aelodaeth. Ai y term 'y Fro Gymraeg', ynteu 'y Broydd Cymraeg' yn y lluosog oedden nhw yn eu ffafrio? Wel, mi gafwyd pleidlais weddol bendant yn y diwedd o blaid y term 'y Fro Gymraeg'.*

[We had quite a discussion, and a healthy discussion to be honest, in the Cymuned conference this year about the exact term that we were to use. We wanted leadership from the membership. Was it the term 'Fro Gymraeg' [Welsh-speaking area], or 'y Broydd Cymraeg' [Welsh-speaking areas] in the plural which they favoured? Well, we had a fairly decisive vote in the end in favour of the term 'y Fro Gymraeg'.]

A need to portray a united and potentially homogeneous Welsh linguistic territory took precedence in this case over a more nuanced and, perhaps more honest, admission of the existence of a multiplicity of different Welsh-speaking communities within the north and west of Wales. It might have been valuable, we would contend, to offer a more honest appraisal of the character of the 'Fro Gymraeg', one which acceded to notions of unity *and* difference with regard to the linguistic geography of the heartland. And yet, nationalist discourse, in social-cultural and/or geographical contexts, is predicated on the promotion of a narrative of homogeneity. In this regard, Dalby (1999) has demon-strated that territorialized discourses of power and knowledge, associ-ated with nationalism and other political forms, impose a sense of order and homogeneity on the space of the 'us' and a related notion of fragmentation and difference on the space of the 'other'. Cymuned, in this respect, have been following a long-standing tradition within the political realm when they have ascribed a sense of territorial order and homogeneity on the Welsh heartland.

As well as illustrating the difficulties that have been associated with 'scripting' the heartland as an integrated region, it is clear that the above discussion also alludes to more fundamental problems concerning the appropriate relationship that should exist between the Welsh heartland and the remaining political territory of Wales. Cymuned, in this respect, has been chastened by accusations from Plaid Cymru and Cymdeithas yr Iaith, in which it has been portrayed as a xenophobic and reactionary organization, which seeks to promote a 'ghettoised' version of Wales and Welshness within 'y fro Gymraeg'. In this respect, many within Plaid Cymru and Cymdeithas yr Iaith seek to re-inforce the notion that Cymuned are the direct inheritors of Adfer's contentious tradition.

Cymuned have been keen to respond to such accusations and have sought to distance themselves from Adfer's position. In doing so, they have recently attempted to negotiate a difficult middle route between acceding to the linguistic significance of the Welsh heartland whilst still positioning its fortunes within that of a broader Wales. The second article within its 'Statement on 'y Fro Gymraeg', for instance, argues as follows:

> *Yr ydym yn llwyr gefnogol i bob ymdrech i adfer a phoblogeiddio'r Gymraeg yn rhanbarthoedd eraill Cymru (ac hefyd yn gefnogol i ddiwylliant Cymreig y rhanbarthoedd hynny a fynegir trwy gyfrwng y Saesneg neu ieithoedd eraill) ond yn credu bod parhad y Fro Gymraeg yn anhepgor er mwyn sicrhau parhad a datblygiad y Gymraeg yng ngweddill Cymru ac fel iaith genedlaethol, ynghyd â pharhad Cymru fel cenedl.*

> [We are fully supportive of every effort to restore and popularise Welsh in the other regions of Wales (and are supportive too of those regions in which a Welsh culture is expressed through the medium of English or other languages) but believe that the continuation of 'y Fro Gymraeg' is crucial in order to ensure the continuation and development of Welsh in the rest of Wales and as a national language, as well as the continuation of Wales as a nation.][9]

In this respect, Cymuned seeks to position itself as an organization that possesses a similar ideological stance to that occupied by Cymdeithas yr Iaith since the early 1970s (see the discussion above). Yet, both Plaid Cymru and Cymdeithas yr Iaith maintain that Cymuned's discourse and more specific policies give rise to the suspicion that they are, at heart, solely concerned with the linguistic fortunes of the Welsh heartland. In effect, these two organizations seek to draw a distinction between the narratives of Cymuned, which are said to be centred explicitly on the linguistic significance of the 'Fro Gymraeg' and the narratives of Cymdeithas yr Iaith and Plaid Cymru, which are, predominantly, territorial visions that are concerned with the fate of the Welsh language throughout the whole of Wales. In this regard, many within Cymdeithas yr Iaith and Plaid Cymru deem that the exclusive focus on the Welsh heartland – allegedly exhibited within the ranks of Cymuned – is detrimental to the Welsh language, culture and nation. Catrin Dafydd, a young member of Cymdeithas yr Iaith and former President of UMCA (see Chapter 5), for instance, maintained as follows:

> *Rwy'n gweld e'n broblematig pan mae pobl yn sectora Cymru, ac yn dweud bod yr ardal hyn yn fwy Cymreig, a bod yr ardal hyn ddim. Er engrhaifft, mae'r Eisteddfod yng Nghasnewydd ond yw e' eleni, a dwi'n gwybod am ffaith nad yw Cymuned yn cynnal gigs yna, achos y syniad yw falle bod yr ardal ddim yn digon*

Cymreig. A dwi jyst yn meddwl 'wel, sut y'ch chi'n diffinio Cymreig?' Ac i ba raddau y'ch chi'n gallu clymu fe lawr i un ardal bach . . . cyfyngedig. Rwy'n deall bod na wahaniaethau. Ond rwy'n credu beth sy'n rhaid i ni beidio gwneud yw dieithrio ein hunain oddi ar Cymry di-Gymraeg i ddechrau, ardal ddiwydiannol lle mae potensial enfawr i ni ehangu ar Gymreictod. Ie, bydd e'n hollol wahanol i Gymreictod Bethesda, er engrhaifft. Ond dwi'n credu mae rhaid i chi, fel, 'embraco' fe fel gwlad.

[I see it as problematic when people compartmentalise Wales, and say that this is a more Welsh area, and this area isn't. For example, the Eisteddfod is in Newport [in south-east Wales] this year, isn't it. And I know for a fact that Cymuned aren't holding gigs there, because of the idea perhaps that the area isn't Welsh enough. And I just think 'well, how do you define a Welsh area?' And to what extent can you tie it down to one small, restricted area. I understand that there are differences. But I believe that what we mustn't do is alienate ourselves from the non-Welsh speaking Welsh people to start with, an industrial area where there is massive potential for us to expand on Welshness. Yes, it will be totally different from the Welshness of Bethesda [in north-west Wales], for example. But I believe you have to, like, embrace it as a country.]

The criticisms directed by Dafydd Iwan, President of Plaid Cymru, towards Cymuned's conception of the territorial exclusiveness of the Welsh heartland were more explicit and stinging:

Yn sicr, dyna rhan o'u hathroniaeth, lle maen nhw'n trio dweud mai mater tiriogaethol ydy o i'r gorllewin. Ac maen nhw wedi dweud mewn cyfarfod ym Merthyr Tudful, wrth bobl sydd wedi dysgu Cymraeg, ac wedi ymladd i sefydlu ysgolion Cymraeg, dweud nad oedd eu brwydr nhw ddim yn berthnasol i'r iaith o gwbl. Dwi ddim yn deall hwnnw o gwbl, ar wahân i fod yn sarhaus tuag at bobl sydd yn adfer y Gymraeg yn y cymoedd.

[Certainly, that is part of their philosophy, where they try to say that it's a territorial matter for the west. And they have said in a public meeting in Merthyr Tydfil, to people who have learnt Welsh, and who have fought to establish Welsh-medium schools, said that their fight wasn't relevant to the language at all. I don't understand that at all, aside from being an insult towards people who are restoring the Welsh language in the valleys.]

By defining Welshness and the Welsh linguistic territory in such narrow terms, there is a danger, according to some activists, that Welsh cultural identity will only be a meaningful category when ascribed to relatively small groups of individuals living in a few rural communities in the north and west of Wales or, as one long-time language activist put it, '*i lond dwrn o bentrefi ym Mhen Llŷn a Penllyn, cefn gwlad Ceredigion ac yn y blaen*/to a handful of villages in the Llŷn Peninsula, Penllyn [the area around Bala], rural Ceredigion and so on'. In many ways, such comments echo the semi-autobiographical work of Bowie (1993) in which she discusses the cultural and linguistic exclusivity exhibited by certain Welsh nationalists. Importantly, too, Cymuned's discourse runs the risk of alienating the significant efforts made by Welsh speakers and non-Welsh speakers in south-east Wales to promote the Welsh language, either through supporting Welsh-medium education or through attending language classes. Indeed, this is a point that was forcefully made by some of our respondents who possessed strong links with CYD (the Welsh Learners' Council).

However, as we have already shown, Cymuned's attitude towards the relationship between the Welsh heartland and the remaining regions of Wales is quite ambivalent. Perhaps in response to some of the criticism that was levelled towards their earlier territorially exclusive policies, they have sought to reinforce the idea that the fate of the Welsh language throughout the whole of Wales is a matter of concern for them. Such a sentiment emerged in their 'Statement on the Welsh heartland', quoted earlier.[10] We would suggest, nonetheless, that there is a fundamental tension between Cymuned's official rhetoric and the views that have been expressed by certain individuals within the organizations. As we have shown, Cymuned – at an official level at least – seeks to promote the Welsh language throughout the whole of Wales or, as one member put it, '*bod y Gymraeg yn iaith i Gymru gyfan*/that Welsh is a language for the whole of Wales'. At another level, it has made clear time and time again that its main commitment as an organization is to the Welsh-speaking communities that lie within this region. This sense of detachment from the linguistic circumstances of, and problems facing, other areas of Wales was justified as follows by one Cymuned member:

> *Rhywun sydd yn ymgyrchu dros brodorion yn yr Unol Daleithiau, ac yn canolbwyntio ar hawliau ieithyddol pro-Indians ym Montana. Wel, rargian dydych chi ddim yn trafod gwleidyddiaeth yr Unol Daleithiau fel gwlad gyfan. Wel na, un nod sydd gyda nhw, sef ymgyrchu dros hawliau lleiafrifol hwnnw ynde.*

> [Someone who is campaigning for the natives in the United States, and is concentrating on the pro-Indian linguistic rights in Montana. Well, gosh, you don't discuss the politics of the United States as a whole. No, they have one aim, don't they, and that is campaigning for those particular minority rights.]

In this sense, a focus on the more culturally defined territory of the Welsh heartland is said to be justified within Cymuned's nationalist discourse and associated geographical imagination, given the specific problems that are alleged to be facing Welsh-speaking communities within it. Of course, one aspect that the above quote fails to mention is that the Welsh language is an official language throughout the whole of Wales. The comparison with the situation of native American speakers in Montana is, therefore, somewhat misleading since a succession of political narratives and national discourses have ensured that issues relating to the Welsh language have been rescaled to the Welsh national scale (see Chapter 4).

Institutionalizing the nation and national territory

In a previous section, we began to show Cymuned's nationalist discourse had sought to promote an argument concerning the need to institutionalize the Welsh heartland within the political geography of Wales through the creation of a Welsh Heartlands Authority. What is significant is that such arguments, as well as the broader nationalist discourse that Cymuned has espoused, has influenced the emerging organizations being narrated and created in a post-devolution Wales. Part of the reasoning behind the formation of the National Assembly for Wales in 1999 was to bring forms of governance closer to the people of Wales and it is clear that various political and pressure groups within Wales have sought to make full use of this new space of citizenship (e.g. Chaney et al 2001; Jones and Osmond 2002; Morgan and Mungham 2000; Royles 2007; Taylor and Thomson 1999; Williams 2007). Furthermore, it is possible to argue that the National Assembly for Wales has acted in a relatively receptive way to the new demands being placed upon it by these various actors in civil society. This claim is especially pertinent in the context of language policy. The increasing role played by groups from civil society in helping to define a potential new region within Wales, we believe, enables us to qualify Paasi's (2002: 138) claims regarding the lack of voice given to 'ordinary people' in the processes of regionalization taking place within contemporary Europe.

Our interviews with protagonists within the language field, especially Cymuned, indicated a sustained effort to influence the evolution of the linguistic policy agenda. A number of Cymuned's members, for instance, attended meetings and public consultations held at the NAfW, most notably those held under the auspices of the Language and Culture, and Local Government and Housing Committees.[11] Simon Brooks, a key figure within the organization, believed that Cymuned had been successful in its attempt to shape political attitudes towards the Welsh language:

> *Mi lwyddodd Cymuned i rhoi y pwnc o ddyfodol y Gymraeg fel iaith gymunedol ar yr agenda gwleidyddol, does dim dwywaith am hynny. Ac 'oedd hynny yn llwyddiannus iawn. Mae Iaith Pawb yn gwneud hi'n hollol glir fod parhad y Gymraeg fel iaith gymunedol yn bwysig, a dwi ddim yn credu y byddai hynny wedi bod yn wir i'r ffasiwn raddau a mae yn wir yn y ddogfen . . . oni bai am yr awyrgylch gyffredinol a greodd Cymuned yn ystod 2001 a 2002.*

> [Cymuned succeeded in placing the future of the language as a community language on the political agenda, there's no doubt about that. And it was very successful. Iaith Pawb [see below] makes it totally clear that the continuation of Welsh as a community language is important, and I don't think that would have been as true to the degree that it is true in the document . . . but for the general atmosphere that Cymuned created in 2001 and 2002.]

The above quote draws our attention to the belief, among certain members of Cymuned, that they had been able to influence the NAfW's attitude towards language policy and, more broadly, to the discursive reproduction of a Welsh linguistic nation in the period post-devolution. The NAfW has published a number of documents in recent years, which have sought to outline specific policies and strategies that can enable Wales to remain a bilingual country. Most significantly, a key consideration within these strategies and policies is the need to deal with the preservation of Welsh as a community language within the so-called heartland. We can consider firstly a policy statement made by the Welsh Assembly Government, entitled Dyfodol Dwyieithog/A Bilingual Future, and published in July 2002 (WAG 2002). The purpose of this document, as the title indicates, is to outline the Assembly's role in 'revitalizing the Welsh language and creating a bilingual Wales (ibid: 1). A key strand within the policy statement is to invigorate Welsh as a community language. It is accepted at the outset that 'the reduction in the number of primarily Welsh-speaking communities is clearly one of the most serious threats to the future of the Welsh language' (ibid: 11). Two main policy solutions are advocated in order to address this threat. The first is to create economically and socially sustainable communities. This will enable individuals living in these communities to continue to live and work there if they wish. The second policy solution is to encourage planning and housing policies and decisions to take account of the linguistic character of communities.

Further documents reiterate the same commitment to preserving Welsh as a community language within the Welsh-speaking 'Fro Gymraeg'. Iaith Pawb, the Action Plan for the Welsh language, also published by the Welsh Assembly Government (WAG 2003), elaborates on the need for policies that are able to target the particular issues faced by the Welsh-speaking heartland. The policy review of the Welsh language, Our Language: Its Future, conducted by the Culture Committee and the Education and Lifelong Learning Committee of the National Assembly for Wales (NAfW 2002a), too, emphasizes the same need to develop a raft of policies that can address the specific issues facing Welsh-speaking communities within the Welsh heartland. This latter review, in particular, benefited from a lengthy submission from members of Cymuned.[12] While we have no direct evidence to show that Cymuned – either directly or indirectly – was able to shape the linguistic discourses that have emerged within official NAfW and WAG documents, the similarities between the different elements within their discourse and that of the Assembly are striking. A common desire is exhibited in both sets of discourses: to protect communities within the Welsh heartland because of their linguistic and cultural value; to enhance the socio-economic viability of the Welsh heartland; to use the planning system as a way of facilitating more linguistically sensitive decisions on housing issues.

The other significance of NAfW policy documents is the way in which they have begun to imagine a new type of geography for the Welsh linguistic nation. There now exists a set of strategic narratives, in the field of economic development (housing and planning in particular) that are beginning to 'institutionalise' the existence of a new linguistic border and territory within Wales. Interestingly, efforts have been made within governmental circles to define the precise extent of the 'Fro Gymraeg'. Quoting academic research, Our Language: Its Future (NAfW 2002a) states that in 1961 279 communities in Wales (out of a total of 993) recorded that at least 80 per cent of their community could speak Welsh. By 1991, only thirty-two of those communities remained. According to the report, 'this percentage of eighty per cent is extremely important to the future prospects of the Welsh language since it denotes the threshold required by any language to survive as a thriving community language' (NAfW 2002b: 24). On the basis of such concerns, Our Language: Its Future also recommended that only limited in-migration of non-Welsh speakers into the Welsh-speaking heartland should be allowed. This recommendation led to some controversy within Welsh devolved politics, as Cole and Williams (2004: 565) have shown. In advocating the need for such a policy of restrained in-migration to the Welsh heartland, the report has further narrated the existence of the Fro Gymraeg as a specific culture region within Wales, which is said to possess a broader significance for the survival of the Welsh language and, by implication, a Welsh national culture.

Echoing the earlier discussion, it is clear, nonetheless, that these geographical imaginations and nationalist discourse have the potential to create tensions with other, more established linguistic and nationalist discourses in Wales. There is, importantly, a further set of language policies that seek to promote the use of the Welsh language throughout the whole of Wales – the most notable being the Language Act of 1993 (see Cole and Williams 2004: 562–3). As Williams (2000: 31) has noted, the Act's 'chief policy instrument is the refashioned and strengthened Welsh Language Board', whose aim has been:

> (1) to increase the numbers of Welsh speakers; (2) to provide more opportunities to use the language; (3) to change the habits of language use and encourage people to take advantage of the opportunities provided; and (4) to strengthen Welsh as a community language (ibid 32; see also Welsh Language Board 2000).

Interestingly, the Welsh Language Board also sees the Welsh-speaking heartland as being of particular importance to the survival of the Welsh language but, at the same time, their overarching focus, along with the Act of which they are a part, is to promote the status and use of the Welsh a language throughout the whole of Wales.[13] As Williams notes, Welsh language schemes have been adopted by the twenty-two Welsh local authorities as part of the requirements of the Act, thus testifying to the significance of the Welsh language for whole of the political territory of Wales. We would argue that there is the potential for a tension between discourses that connect the Welsh language to the whole of the Welsh territory and those that envision it as a significant cultural feature for a more limited Welsh heartland. This is certainly an issue that is of concern to the Welsh Assembly Government, as the following quote by Jenny Randerson, the Minister for Culture, Sport and the Welsh Language who announced *Iaith Pawb*'s aims in 2002:

> When we consider this document as a whole, and the balance between the areas where Welsh is the language of the majority and where Welsh is the language of the minority, it becomes clear that this is a policy for the whole of Wales. It is one strategy, with different plans for different areas and situations. The emphasis, and the approach taken, may be different in different areas, and that is obvious in the language action plan . . . That approach shows flexibility and is sensitive to local needs.[14]

There is clearly an effort to show here that Iaith Pawb's priority is to support the Welsh language throughout the whole of Wales. In addition, it is an action plan that seeks to take into account the particularities of the condition of the Welsh language in different parts of Wales. And yet, we would argue that the spectre posed by the possibility of the implementation of different linguistic policies in various parts of Wales may well be problematic. The danger, in this respect, is that the Welsh heartland, however it is defined, will be in receipt of a series of policies and strategies that will place it in a relatively favourable position, when compared with other (often Welsh-speaking) communities lying outside it (see also Chaney and Fevre 2001). There is no doubt that such a development could lead to a certain divisiveness within the Welsh-speaking population of Wales, which would be a reflection of the more specific divisions that characterize the relationships between various factions of the Welsh nationalist and linguistic movement. In addition, we believe the emphasis on a territorially delimited interpretation of a Welsh-speaking Wales could lead to the re-emergence of age-old ideas concerning the necessary association between the Welsh language and nation and its more rural areas (see Gruffudd 1994; 1995; 1999).

CONCLUSIONS

The aim of this chapter has been to show certain Welsh nationalist discourses have either implicitly or explicitly been predicated upon the use of particular geographical or territorial imaginations, which act as the spatial manifestation of the community of the nation. While much work within the social sciences has claimed that national discourses make use of the notion of territory as a key motif, our goal in this chapter has to show the contingent and contested nature of this politico-geographical project. Different nationalist organizations in Wales have promoted alternative visions of the 'where of Wales'. The early Plaid Cymru, Adfer and Cymuned have centred their efforts on protecting a geographically circumscribed Welsh heartland whereas the latter-day Plaid Cymru and, to a lesser extent, Cymdeithas yr Iaith have advocated the need to support the Welsh language throughout the whole of Wales. The notion of community, and of Welsh as a community language, has been the main way through which these conflicting discourses have been articulated.

For the past hundred years, there has been considerable concord between different nationalist organizations about the significance of

Welsh-speaking communities for the reproduction of the Welsh language. The debate and division arises, we would argue, when this
linguistic discourse about communities is translated in a nationalist
discourse. Differences of opinion, in this respect, exist when considering
the small-scale communities of the north and west, which are the
repositories of a Welsh-speaking culture. For certain organizations, such
as Adfer and Cymuned, one gets the impression that it is within these
communities that one witnesses the existence of a 'true' Welsh-speaking
national culture; other communities, lying outside this heartland do not
possess the same attributes that make them valuable elements within
nationalist discourse. The impression given in such statements is that
there exist homogeneous and highly localized communities of Welsh-
speakers in certain parts of Wales, whose inhabitants are wholly committed to the future of the Welsh language above all other considerations.
This type of supposition seems naïve at a conceptual level, given the
arguments discussed at the beginning of this chapter concerning contemporary understandings of communities as fractured entities.[15] There
is also scope to question Cymuned's primary focus on the Welsh-
speaking 'heartland' in more empirical terms. We have already noted
that the criteria used to designate the different categories of Welsh
'heartland' would relegate Aberystwyth to a second-tier 'outer Fro
Gymraeg', in spite of the town's significance for the emergence of
Cymuned and other Welsh nationalist organizations. In this respect,
Cymuned's sole focus on the proportion of Welsh speakers living or
born in a particular area might be an important marker of the *number* of
Welsh-medium conversations happening in any one place but it is less
useful as an indicator of the *types* of Welsh-medium conversation occurring within particular places. Although fewer Welsh-medium conversations might well have taken place in Aberystwyth in recent years when
compared with other settlements located within the 'inner Fro Gymraeg', is is clear that conversations within the town have been of the
utmost significance for the reproduction of Welsh nationalist discourse.

More broadly, it is in this context that debates concerning 'the where
of Wales' have taken on a particular significance in recent years. In total,
such themes reinforce the notion that nationalist discourses are plural,
contingent and contested in character, being the product of particular
nationalist organizations (Brubaker 2004). What we have shown in this
chapter is that an examination of the different kinds of geographical and
territorial imaginations that feature within, and help to structure, different types of nationalist discourse is an especially propitious way of
contributing the social constructivist agenda. If territory matters to the

nation, then the aim of a social constructivist account of nationalism should be to show different territories are constructed as being important for particular nations within various nationalist discourses.

NOTES

1   Anderson (1983: 6) comments, almost in passing, that '[i]n fact, all communities larger than primordial villages of face-to-face contact (and perhaps even these) are imagined'. As shown below, we believe that all communities are inherently imagined.
2   See http://news.bbc.co.uk/1/hi/wales/mid/3118890.stm, accessed on 22 November 2006.
3   For Llais y Cardi's success in gaining support for the referendum campaign, see http://news.bbc.co.uk/1/hi/wales/3238767.stm, accessed on 22 November 2006.
4   See http://news.bbc.co.uk/1/hi/wales/mid/3301473.stm, accessed on 22 November 2006.
5   Processes of in-migration have affected Wales over recent years as a result of a variety of factors. In many cases, too, the process of in-migration is at its most acute in the Welsh 'heartland', through a combination of low house prices and attractive scenery. We would argue, nonetheless, that the reality of in-migration is not as important for certain language activists as its perceived or imagined effect on the linguistic constitution of the Welsh 'heartland'.
6   At present, the Office of National Statistics estimates that over the last five years migration into Wales from other countries within the UK was between 55,000 and 62,000 people per year, of which the majority were from England (see www.statistics.gov.uk, accessed 5 April 2007).
7   http://cymuned.net/blog/?p=52, accessed on 22 November 2006.
8   http://cymuned.net/blog/?p=32, accessed on 22 November 2006.
9   http://cymuned.net/blog/?p=52, accessed on 22 November 2006.
10 http://cymuned.net/blog/?p=52, accessed 22 November 2006.
11 Cymuned's submissions to these two committees can be found at http://cymuned.net/blog/?cat=2, accessed 22 November 2006.
12 See, for instance, http://cymuned.net/blog/?p=33, accessed 22 November 2006.
13 The Welsh Language Act's focus, in this respect, has centred on the use of the Welsh language within the public sector and this has been a cause of much criticism by various organizations that are concerned with the fate of the Welsh language.
14 The Official Record of the National Assembly for Wales, 27 November 2002, seehttp://www.cymru.gov.uk/cms/1/ChamberSession/

38034064000E165A000034F700000000/
N0000000000000000000000000004607.html, accessed 15 December 2006.
[15]   Pers. comm., Colin Williams, 5 December 2006.

8

Conclusions: relocating nationalism

In the preceding chapters we have attempted to show how adopting a geographical outlook, specifically through reference to the concepts of place and scale, can help to enliven social constructivist understandings of nationalism. We have tried to justify the validity of these claims in theoretical and more empirical contexts. Our aims in this brief conclusion are to recap some of the main arguments that we have made in the preceding chapters, as well as thinking through the significance of the concepts of place and scale for the reproduction of nationalism in more general terms. We then seek to position our empirical enquiry in a broader context, asking whether we can generalize on the basis of a very specific study of one place located within a single nation. Finally, we make some tentative suggestions concerning the significance of our work for a social constructivist and post-modern project.

We have consistently claimed in this book that we need to examine the importance of the concepts of place and scale for the reproduction of nationalism as a discourse. To date, studies of nationalism have tended to be dominated by either temporal, political or social concerns. The majority of classical theories of nationalism revolve around attempts to time the nation or, in other words, to determine the period of inception. Other studies, conducted by political scientists in the main, seek to demonstrate the way in which nationalism is enlisted as part of a political project; positioned either as a supporter or subverter of state activity. Social constructivists, on the other hand, try to show how various social categories complicate the notions of political and cultural uniformity promoted within nationalist discourse. While each of these intellectual projects is worthwhile, we have argued that there is also a need to take seriously the geographies inherent within the production, circulation and consumption of nationalism. In this respect, while geographers have sought to emphasize the significance of space and place for nationalism, their studies have tended to focus on issues of representation or, in other words, on how nationalist symbols, messages and discourses are transmitted by a variety of media. Geographers, on the whole, have not examined to the same degree how various geographical themes are implicated in the ways in which nationalist discourses are produced, circulated and consumed or, in effect, how they are repro-duced (though see Gruffudd 1994; 1995; 1999). Addressing such an object of enquiry would be of benefit to geography since it would help to expand the number of themes relating to nationalism that are explored within the discipline as well as connecting it more closely to the types of studies of nationalism conducted in other subject areas. More impor-tantly, adopting a geographical perspective would enrich understand-ings – across the humanities and social sciences – of the processes that help to reproduce nationalism. This is especially apparent in the context of social constructivist understandings of nationalism as discourse.

We have argued that a consideration of the concepts of place and scale is an ideal way of beginning to demonstrate the potential synergy between geographical themes and a social constructivist understanding of nationalism (see Brubaker 2004: 11–18). Focusing on these two con-cepts, for instance, can enable us to show how the groupness of nations is a dynamic social and spatial process. Rather than being pre-given social identities, particular places may contribute in different ways to the reproduction of nationalist discourse and these, too, are connected in complex ways to a range of discourses, practices and organizations that exist at the national scale. A focus on place and scale can also help to emphasize the contingency of the group-making project associated with nationalism. Certain places play a more significant role than others in producing nationalist discourse. At the same time, particular places and scales may be enlisted as rhetorical devices within nationalist discourses while others may well be marginalized or omitted. In another context, a focus on places and scales can also enable us to question the alleged homogeneity of a national project. Organizations that are located in particular places and that possess a particular scalar reach may well promote a nationalist discourse that is at odds with the one promoted by an alternative organization (based in another location and possessing a different scalar reach). In this way, issues of place and scale should lie at the heart of all considerations of how nationalist discourse are produced, circulated and consumed.

We attempted to demonstrate the veracity of these claims in the empirical chapters of the book. In Chapter 4, we discussed the signifi-cance of Aberystwyth for the reproduction of a linguistic nation-building project in Wales, particularly during the 1960s. A series of political practices and discourses located within the confines of the town were crucial for the production of a Welsh nationalist discourse at this time and these shaped, and were shaped by, an emerging set of nationalist discourses and organizations that were concerned with the fate of the Welsh language. The local and national scales with regard to a discourse of linguistic nationalism, therefore, existed in a state of mutual interdependency. Similar themes were discussed in Chapter 5, where we focused on the efforts that were made from the mid-1960s to establish a Welsh-medium hall of residence within the University College of Wales, Aberystwyth. The campaign was driven forward by a combination of local discourses and practices and a broader nationalist debate at the national scale. The significant upshot of this campaign was the designation of Pantycelyn Hall as a Welsh-medium hall of residence in 1973–4. Importantly, students resident within the Hall since this time have been in the vanguard of the production of nationalist discourse within Wales in a variety of different contexts. Demands for a greater support of the Welsh language within higher education in Wales have featured heavily within this nationalist politics and, indeed, students within the University have been successful in shaping the politics of higher education throughout the whole of Wales. Once again, nationalist discourses, practices and organizations influenced, and were influenced by, networks of people within the town of Aberystwyth.

Our final two case studies examined alternative nationalist themes. In Chapter 6, we focused on the electoral significance of Aberystwyth. Electoral politics, of necessity, is played out in both local and national contexts and it is clear that such themes were important in the successful electoral campaigns conducted by the Welsh nationalists in the constituency of Aberystwyth and Ceredigion North during the early 1990s. To a large degree, the creation of a successful electoral pact between Plaid Cymru and the Green Party was predicated on a series of highly localized factors, including the existence of strong networks of trust between the two camps within the town and the presence of a significant individual, Cynog Dafis, who was able to embody the electoral pact. We also argued that the success of the pact at the local scale was tied in with some of the broader trends affecting nationalist politics during this period. Key, in this respect, was the gradual emergence of a greener kind of nationalist politics at the Welsh national scale (and, indeed, further afield in Westminster) at this time which was both a product, and producer, of the similar changes that were taking place in Aberystwyth and Ceredigion North. In Chapter 7, we explored the significance of Welsh-speaking communities and a Welsh-speaking homeland within Welsh nationalist discourse. Over a number of years, various nationalist organizations and individuals have argued about the importance of particular communities as repositories of the Welsh language and Welsh way of life. At the same time, others have maintained that there is a need to protect and enhance the status of the Welsh language throughout the whole of Wales. In this way, a particular contested geographical imagination has been enrolled within Welsh nationalist discourse. What is significant for the purposes of this book is the way in which a politics of place within Aberystwyth has been crucial in the context of the emergence of this nationalist debate. The localized politics of place of Aberystwyth, in this respect, has been connected in important ways to an emerging nationalist discourse at the national scale.

Taken together, this empirical material emphasizes some of the central claims that we have sought to make in this book, namely that a focus on the concepts of place and scale may serve to enrich and enliven our understandings of nationalism. In effect, a geographical perspective can help to illustrate the numerous variegated and contested themes that help to make up the broader discourse of Welsh nationalism. Despite the value of such an approach, we anticipate that one criticism of this book will centre around its tendency to focus overmuch on the production of Welsh nationalist discourse, without paying sufficient heed to the circulation and consumption of this discourse. To an extent, such a criticism is warranted. The empirical focus on Aberystwyth has meant that we have tended to elaborate on the significant events and networks within the town, which contributed to the emergence of a broader Welsh nationalist discourse. Less attention has been directed on the ways in which these discourses were communicated to a broader Welsh population; less still on how these discourses were consumed and contested by groups of people in different parts of Wales. We would argue, nonetheless, that examining the production of Welsh nationalist discourse within the town of Aberystwyth, its circulation to, and consumption by, different groups of people living in different regions of Wales would have been far beyond the scope of our study. At the same time, we would maintain that we have been able to discuss some instances of this recursive association between the production, circulation and consumption of nationalist discourse. In Chapter 5, for instance, we were able to show the campaign for the establishment of a Welsh-medium hall of residence was predicated on a series of connections between a high localized politics of place and the broader circulation of nationalist discourses through the Welsh mass media. In a similar way, the more ecological kind of nationalist politics adopted by Plaid Cymru in the early 1990s in Aberystwyth and throughout Wales was based, to a large extent, on a perceptible shift in broader public attitudes towards both Welsh nationalism and green politics. In this way, the production of a different kind of Welsh nationalist politics during this period was affected by and impacted on the nationalist and ecological attitudes of the Welsh electorate.

In broader terms, we need to question the degree to which it is possible to generalize from the current study. In other words, to what extent is the experience of Aberystwyth unique with a Welsh and, indeed, international context? The town's location and its internal geography is certainly significant in this respect and marks it out as somewhere that was ideally placed to act as a hub and generator of Welsh nationalist discourse. As we discussed in Chapter 3, it is clear that the town's location has contributed to its status as a crucible of Welsh nationalism. In this respect, it is worthwhile contrasting Aberystwyth's experience with that of Bangor, another medium-sized town located within the 'Welsh heartland' containing a large university. The main difference between the two towns, of course, is their relative location within Wales. Aberystwyth, in this respect, has been able to act as a literal meeting place for people from different parts of Wales. John Davies, for instance, stated that Aberystwyth's cultural and political significance was determined, at least in part, by the fact that its central location within Wales had enabled it to facilitate a mixing of different kinds of people. In contradistinction to Bangor, whose population, according to many of our respondents, was said to be more uniform in cultural, social and political terms, Aberystwyth's population has been characterized by a greater sense of variety and difference, the value of which has been to generate (political) debate. A similar theme was taken up by Siôn Jobbins, a member of Cymuned and former mayor of the town, when he stated that there was '*cawl arbennig o bobl yn yr ardal yma sydd yn codi ar un ystyr rhyw fath o* "think tank" *anffurfiol, gwleidyddol yn sicr*'/a special mixture [literally soup] of people in this area that creates in one sense some sort of informal, certainly political "think tank"'. As a result of this mixture of educated and politicized people within the town, Jobbins maintained that a 'lot of ideas were flying around/lot o syniadau yn hedfan o gwmpas'.

Of course, another question revolves around Aberystwyth's ability to maintain its status as a key location for the reproduction of Welsh nationalism in the future. This question is especially pertinent given Cardiff's increasing role as a key space for civil society in a devolved Wales (Royles 2007). A number of the individuals interviewed as part of the project bemoaned the cultural and political brain drain that was being experienced in Wales as talented and politicized individuals were being lost to Cardiff from Welsh-speaking areas such as Aberystwyth. Such a demographic shift raises the interesting proposition that Cardiff could take over as an alternative site for the reproduction of Welsh nationalist discourse. Although it is difficult to foretell the possible role that might be played by Cardiff as a hotbed of Welsh nationalism, the city's location and large size might hamper the development of organic networks of Welsh nationalists. This argument was made forcefully by Simon Brooks, a member of Cymuned:

> *Ond mae gofod daearyddol yn bodoli ac mae'n bwysig ... Dyna lle mae Aberystwyth wedi bod yn llwyddiannus, sydd ddim yn wir am lot o lefydd eraill. Sydd ddim, i ddweud y gwir, yn wir am Gaerdydd. Er gwaetha'r holl Gymry Cymraeg, siaradwyr Cymraeg sy'n byw yng Nghaerdydd yn eu degau o filoedd, heblaw am y capeli, does gyda chi ddim gofodau o Gymraeg fel y cyfryw, sydd yn gallu caniatáu datblygiad math o gymdeithas sifil Gymraeg ei iaith sy'n bodoli yn Aberystwyth.*

> [But geographical space exists and it's important ... That's where Aberystwyth has been successful, that's not true about a lot of other places. That's not, to tell the truth, true of Cardiff. Despite all the Welsh speakers, Welsh speakers that live in Cardiff in their tens of thousands, apart from the chapels, you don't have spaces of Welshness as such, that are able to allow the development of the type of Welsh-language civil society that exists in Aberystwyth.]

Brooks, in the above quote, illustrates the way in which the location and scale of Aberystwyth, as well as the various sites within it, have impacted positively on its ability to maintain a pre-eminent position within the reproduction of Welsh nationalist discourse. The recent student protests about the need to support the Welsh language within higher education, discussed in Chapter 5, would seem to add some empirical weight to this claim. Aberystwyth, in this sense, is distinctive and different. As such, it may well be difficult to generalize more broadly from the themes discussed in this book. We would argue, nonetheless, that an important aspect of a social constructivist project must be to chart the differential impact of various places to the reproduction of (Welsh) nationalism. All types of places are able to contribute to the reproduction of nationalist discourse and practice, as recent research in Wales has shown (e.g. Fevre et al. 1999; Thompson and Day 1999). The challenge must be to show how people living, working and socializing in a *range* of different places are implicated – in various ways – in the reproduction of nationalist discourses.

Following on from this point, some might contend that Wales is particularly distinctive in this respect, thus making it difficult to use the conceptual and methodological framework promoted in this book when studying other kinds of nationalism. It is true that Graham Day (2002) has maintained that Wales should be thought of as a community of communities. If this is the case, then Wales' socially and geographically fractured character may well make it a particularly apposite country to portray nationalist discourse as something that is produced and consumed differently in different places. It may be difficult to sustain an argument concerning the distinctiveness of Wales in this respect since it is likely that all nations, despite the pretension to homogeneity, are ultimately fractured in character. Taylor's (1993) work, for instance, shows how people living in the towns and cities of the north of England have to negotiate their own localized understandings of the dominant (southern and rural) geographical imaginations contained within English nationalist discourse. There is a very real sense in his work of the way in which people in different parts of England are involved in the reproduction of alternative understandings of the characteristics of Englishness. Place, in this respect, will influence the reproduction of nationalist discourse within all nations. To think otherwise would merely reinforce a nationalist article of faith, concerning the alleged socio-cultural and territorial homogeneity of nations, which has been disproved in a number of empirical studies (e.g. Mikesell 1983).

On that note, it seems that a geographical perspective may have much to contribute to social constructivist understandings of nationalism. If nationalist discourses are produced, circulated and consumed in different ways by various categories of people then, by the same token, the same is true in more geographical contexts. The danger, in this sense, is that we ascribe a uniformity to particular places in terms of the role that they play in the reproduction of nationalist discourse. But of course, if we are right to question the conception of a nation and a national territory as a homogeneous territorial entity, then we must also be suspicious of work that portrays more localized places in equally uniform ways. It is important, in this respect, to focus on the politics of more localized places and the ways in which these are reworked into broader nationalist discourses and organizations. Localized places, such as Aberystwyth, are inherently plural in nature and, as we argued above, it is likely that this heterogeneity provides much of the heat that helps to generate political debate. We witnessed this clearly in the context of the early protests conducted in Aberystwyth concerning the legal status of the Welsh language and the need for a Welsh-medium hall of residence.

In many ways, it was the localized conflict that took place in these instances that encouraged certain individuals to promote a more emphatically politicized Welsh nationalist discourse.

At another level, we want to argue that a focus on the more localized contexts within which nationalist discourse is reproduced may also draw our attention to the material practices that are part and parcel of this process. The construction of nationalist discourse is never something that occurs solely within the discursive realm but is rather something that is grounded within the networked practices of individuals and the materialities of particular places. Part of the significance of the campaigns for the establishment of a Welsh-medium hall of residence, for instance, was the designation of a physical building that would, in subsequent years, facilitate the mixing of students from different parts of Wales and politicize them into nationalist and linguistic activists. In addition, we have demonstrated that a focus on practice and the materiality of the nation gives added weight to a conception of the nation as something that exists at the national scale. In addition to the nationalist discourses that may be circulated and consumed by groups and individuals throughout the territory of the nation, the nation is also embedded in a series of practices (e.g. bilingual registration of births) and more material forms (e.g. bilingual road signs). In this sense, nationalist discourse is never merely the product of localized discourses but may also be rescaled into, and embedded within, a series of discourses, practices and material forms that exist at the national scale. This process is not pre-determined in any way but is rather contingent on the 'success' of the group-building project contained within nationalist discourses (see Brubaker 2004).

As well as contributing to the social constructivist project with regard to nationalism, we maintain that the themes discussed in the book possess a relevance to current debates in the discipline of geography about the character of territories in the contemporary world. Recent work in human geography has sought to elaborate on a different relational and topological way of conceptualizing space and territory within the social sciences. Relational and topological accounts of space start from the premise that the world is and, indeed, has always been characterized by numerous and intricate connections between people and places, which succeed in undermining bounded and territorial conceptions of space. Although this global inter-connectedness has always existed to some extent, it has experienced a fundamental increase in its significance over recent years. Amin et al. (2003: 6), for instance, argue that 'an era of increasingly geographically extended spatial flows' and an 'an intellectual context where space is frequently being imagined as a product of networks and relations' is, increasingly, challenging 'an older topography in which territoriality was dominant' (see also Massey 1994). Significantly, a focus on the way in which global connections help to constitute places and territories, as illustrated by Massey (2004: 6), immediately 'combat[s] localist or nationalist claims to place based on eternal essentialist, and in consequence exclusive, characteristics of belonging'. While such work is laudable and can be viewed as something that is clearly in tune with social constructivist understandings of nationalism, we would argue that the sole focus on the (more) recent *global* inter-connections that purportedly undermine essentialist understandings of territory fails to take sufficient heed of the inherent plurality of the territories that have always been produced within nationalist discourses. Territories, even when considered in a relatively bounded way, have never been homogeneous or isomorphic in character. An examination of the role of place and scale in reproducing nationalism, as advocated in this book, clearly illustrates the multiple portrayals of national territory contained within nationalist discourse.

More generally, we believe that our work is also reflective of the broader post-modern project, in which efforts have been made to deconstruct the various grand theories and meta-narratives that seek to structure our lives. As we discussed in Chapter 2, post-modern ideas underpin social constructivist accounts of nationalism, as various scholars have sought to demonstrate the variegated, plural and contested character of nationalism. Geographers, over a number of years, have also sought to contribute to the broader post-modern project by showing how space and place may enable scholars to question the certainties presented within particular ontologies and epistemologies (for modernity as a whole, see Ogborn 1998; for urbanism, see Graham and Marvin 2001; for the spaces of poverty, see Yapa 1996). We have been at pains in this book to illustrate how a focus on the places and scales of nationalism can enable us to portray it as something that is essentially plural in character; produced through a range of different discourses and practices. If this is the case, then there is some scope to envisage a more emancipatory form of nationalism that incorporates a number of different voices from within the space of the nation. While more of the more extreme nationalist organizations in Wales and beyond may seek to promote exclusionary conceptions of the nation (see Borland et al. 1992; Fevre et al. 1997), in theory, all members of a nation – wherever they live, work and socialize – possess the potential to produce alternative national discourses. By the same token, all members of the nation can, theoretically, alter or resist the various tenets promoted within particular nationalist discourses so that they reflect more closely their own personal desires and social mores. Of course, these alternative and more localized takes on nationalism need not necessarily be more egalitarian or progressive in nature. Indeed, it is possible that these more localized interpretations of nationalist discourse may be far more exclusionary and destructive than those being promoted by a national elite. And yet, thinking about nationalism in such plural terms removes some of its oppressive and homogenizing tendencies and gives hope to those individuals who seek to question some of its more dubious claims (see also Bhabha 1990a; Soja 1996). This point is especially pertinent in a contemporary period in which many nationalist practices and discourses, seemingly, posit far more exclusionary claims to existence. Thinking about the multiple places and scales of nationalism, we would argue, offers some hope for producing nationalist discourses and projects that are far more inclusionary and liberating in character.

Bibliography

Adfer (1987). *Manifesto Adfer*, Adfer, Penrhosgarnedd.

Agnew, J. (1987). *Place and Politics: The Geographical Mediation of State and Society*, Allen and Unwin, London.

Agnew, J. (1996). 'Mapping politics: how context counts in electoral geography', *Political Geography* 15: 129–46.

Agnew, J. (1997). 'The dramaturgy of horizons: geographical scale in the "reconstruction of Italy" by the new Italian political parties, 1992–1995', *Political Geography* 16: 99–121.

Agnew, J. (2002). *Place and Politics in Modern Italy*, University of Chicago Press, Chicago, IL.

Agnew, J. (2004). 'Nationalism' in J. S. Duncan, N. C. Johnson and R. H. Schein (eds) *A Companion to Cultural Geography*, Blackwell, Oxford, pp. 223–37.

Aitchison, J. A. and Carter, H. A. (1994). *A Geography of the Welsh Language*, University of Wales Press, Cardiff.

Aitchison, J. A. and Carter, H. A. (2000). 'The Welsh language 1921–1991: a geolinguistic perspective', in G. H. Jenkins and M. A. Williams (eds) *'Let's Do Our Best for the Ancient Tongue': The Welsh Language in the Twentieth Century*, University of Wales Press, Cardiff, pp. 29–107.

Aitchison, J. A. and Carter, H. A. (2004). *Spreading the Word: The Welsh Language 2001*, Y Lolfa, Talybont.

Amin, A., Massey, D. and Thrift, N. (2003). *Decentering the Nation: A Radical Approach to Regional Inequality*, Catalyst, London.

Anderson, B. (1983). *Imagined Communities: Reflections on the Origin and Spread of Nationalism*, Verso, London.

Anderson, J. (1986). 'Nationalism and geography', in J. Anderson (ed.) *The Rise of the Modern State*, Harvester Press, Brighton, pp. 115–42.

Anderson, J. (1988). 'On theories of nationalism and the size of states', *Antipode* 18: 218–32.

Anderson, J. and O'Dowd, L. (1999). 'Borders, border regions and territoriality: contradictory meanings, changing significance', *Regional Studies* 33: 593–604.

Anderson, K. (1991). *Vancouver's Chinatown: Racial Discourse in Canada, 1875–1980*, McGill-Queen's University Press, Montreal.

Applegate, C. (1990). *A Nation of Provincials: The German Idea of Heimat*, University of California Press, Berkeley.

Appleton, L. (2002). 'Distillations of something larger: the local scale and American national identity', *Cultural Geographies* 9: 421–47.

Armstrong, J. (1982). *Nations Before Nationalism*, North Carolina University Press, Chapel Hill, NC.

A. W. Papers (no date). 'The Plaid/Green pact in Ceredigion: key dates', copy available from Alun Williams, no page numbers.

Azaryahu, M. and Kellerman, A. (1999). 'Symbolic places of national history and revival: a study in Zionist mythical geography', *Transactions of the Institute of British Geographers* 24: 109–23.

Azaryahu, M. and Kook, R. (2002). 'Mapping the nation: street names and Arab-Palestinian identity: three case studies', *Nations and Nationalism* 8: 195–213.

Baker, A. R. H. (1998). 'Military service and migration in nineteenth-century France: some evidence from Loir-et-Cher', *Transactions of the Institute of British Geographers* 23: 193–206.

Barn (1967). 'Neuadd breswyl Gymraeg yn Aberystwyth', May: 165 (written under the pseudonym Isambard).

Barn (1968). 'Y Cymry dan eu pwn yn ein colegau Saesneg', April: 144 (written under the pseudonym Isambard).

Bhabha, H. (1990a). 'DissemiNation: time, narrative, and the margins of the modern nation', in H. Bhabha (ed.) *Nation and Narration*, Routledge, London, pp. 291–322.

Bhabha, H. (1990b). 'Interview with Homi Bhabha: the third space', in J. Rutherford (ed.) *Identity: Community, Culture, Difference*, Lawrence and Wishart, London, pp. 207–21.

Billig, M. (1995). *Banal Nationalism*, Sage, London.

Bondi, L. and Peake, L. (1988). 'Fending for ourselves: women as teachers of geography in higher education', *Journal of Geography in Higher Education* 12: 216–18.

Borland, J., Fevre, R. and Denney, D. (1992). 'Nationalism and community in north-west Wales', *Sociological Review* 40: 49–72.

Bourdieu, P. (1977). *Outline of a Theory of Practice*, Cambridge University Press, Cambridge.

Bourdieu, P. (1996). *The State Nobility: Elite Schools in the Field of Power*, Polity Press, Oxford.

Bowen, E. G. (1959). 'Le Pays de Galles', *Transactions and Papers of the Institute of British Geographers* 26: 1–23.

Bowie, F. (1993). 'Wales from within: conflicting interpretations of Welsh identity', in S. MacDonald (ed.) *Inside European Identities*, Berg, Oxford, pp. 167–93.

Boyle, M. (2002). 'Edifying the rebellious Gael: uses of memories of Ireland's troubled past among the West of Scotland's Irish Catholic diaspora', in D. Harvey, R. Jones, N. McInroy and C. Milligan (eds) *Celtic Geographies: Old Culture, New Times*, Routledge, London, pp. 173–91.

Brenner, N. (1998). 'Global cities, "glocal" states: global city formation and state territorial restructuring in contemporary Europe', *Review of International Political Economy* 5: 1–37.

Brenner, N. (2001). 'The limits to scale? Methological reflections on scalar structuration', *Progress in Human Geography* 25: 591–614.

Breuilly, J. (1993). *Nationalism and the State*, Manchester University Press, Manchester.

Brooks, S. (2001). 'Hawl foesol i oroesi', *Barn* 463: 6–8.

Brooks, S. (2002). 'The living dead', *Agenda*, Spring, pp. 10–12.

Brubaker, R. (1996). *Nationalism Reframed: Nationhood and the National Question in the New Europe*, Cambridge University Press, Cambridge.

Brubaker, R. (2004). *Ethnicity Without Groups*, Harvard University Press, Cambridge, MA.

Buechler, S. M. (1995). 'New social movement theories', *Sociological Quarterly* 36: 441–64.

Burgess, J. P. and Hyvik, J. J. (2004). 'Ambivalent patriotism: Jacob Aall and Dano-Norwegian identity before 1814', *Nations and Nationalism* 10: 619–37.

Butler, D. and Kavanagh, D. (1992). *The British General Election of 1992*, Basingstoke, Macmillan.

Butler, D. E. and Stokes, D. E. (1969). *Political Change in Britain: Forces Shaping Electoral Choice*, Macmillan, London.

Calhoun, C. (1997). *Nationalism*, Open University Press, Buckingham.

Cambrian News (1963). 'Asking for arrest!', 5 February, p. 1.

Carter, N. (1992). 'Whatever happened to the environment? The British General Election of 1992', *Environmental Politics* 1: 442–8.

Cater, J. and Jones, T. (1989). *Social Geography: An Introduction to Contemporary Issues*, Edward Arnold, London.

Chaney, P. and Fevre, R. (2001). 'Welsh nationalism and the challenge of "inclusive" politics', *Research in Social Movements Conflict and Change* 23: 227–54.

Chaney, P., Hall, T., and Pithouse, A. (eds) (2001). *New Governance, New Democracy? Post-Devolution Wales*, University of Wales Press, Cardiff.

Chatterjee, P. (1993). *The Nation and its Fragments*, Cambridge University Press, Cambridge.

Chatterjee, P. (1986). *Nationalist Thought and the Colonial World*, Zed Books, London.

Cloke, P., Goodwin, M., and Milbourne, P. (1998). 'Cultural change and conflict in rural Wales: competing constructs of identity', *Environment and Planning A* 30: 463–80.

Cohen, A. P. (1982). *Belonging: Identity and Social Organisation in British Rural Cultures*, Manchester University Press, Manchester.

Cole, A. and Williams, C. H. (2004). 'Institutions, identities and lesser-used languages in Wales and Brittany', *Regional and Federal Studies* 14: 554–79.

Collinge, C. (2005). 'The *différance* between society and space: nested scales and the returns of spatial fetishism', *Environment and Planning D: Society and Space* 23: 189–206.

Combs, T. (1977). *The Party of Wales, Plaid Cymru,*. Unpublished Ph.D. Thesis, The University of Connecticut.

Confino, A. (1997). *The Nation as a Local Metaphor: Würtemberg, Imperial Germany and National Memory, 1871–1918*, University of North Carolina Press, Chapel Hill.

Confino, A. and Skaria, A. (2002a). 'The local life of nationhood', *National Identities* 4: 7–24.

Confino, A. and Skaria, A. (2002b). 'Viewed from the locality: the local, national and global', *National Identities* 4: 5–6.

Connor, W. (1990). 'When is a nation?', *Ethnic and Racial Studies* 13: 92–103.

Connor, W. (1994). *Ethno-nationalism: The Quest for Understanding*, Princeton University Press, Princeton, NJ.

Connor, W. (2004). 'The timelessness of nations', *Nations and Nationalism* 10: 35–47.

Conversi, D. (1995). 'Reassessing current theories of nationalism: nationalism as boundary maintenance and creation', *Nationalism and Ethnic Politics* 1: 73–85.

Cosgrove, D. and Daniels, S. (eds) (1988). *The Iconography of Landscape: Essays on the Symbolic Representation of Landscape*, Cambridge University Press, Cambridge.

Crang, M. (1999). 'Nation, region and homeland: history and tradition in Dalarna, Sweden', *Ecumene* 6: 447–70.

Cresswell, T. (1996). *In Place/Out of Place*, Minnesota University Press, Minneapolis, MN.

Cresswell, T. (2004). *Place: A Short Introduction.=*, Blackwell, Oxford.

Curtice, J. (1989). 'The 1989 European Election: protest or green tide?', *Electoral Studies* 8: 217–30.

Cymdeithas yr Iaith Gymraeg (1972). *Maniffesto Cymdeithas yr Iaith Gymraeg*, Cymdeithas yr Iaith Gymraeg, Aberystwyth.

Cymdeithas yr Iaith Gymraeg (1992). *The Property Act Handbook*, Cymdeithas yr Iaith Gymraeg, Aberystwyth.

Cymdeithas yr Iaith Gymraeg (1999). *Property Act Handbook: The Right to a Home, Community and Language – The Responsibility of Cynulliad Cenedlaethol Cymru*, Cymdeithas yr Iaith Gymraeg, Aberystwyth.

Cymdeithas yr Iaith Gymraeg (2005a). *Y Llawlyfr Deddf Eiddo: Drafft Ymgynghorol*, Cymdeithas yr Iaith Gymraeg, Aberystwyth.

Cymdeithas yr Iaith Gymraeg (2005b). *Deddf Iaith Newydd i'r Gymraeg Dyma'r Cyfle! Cynigion ar gyfer Deddf Iaith Newydd*, Cymdeithas yr Iaith Gymraeg, Aberystwyth.

Cymdeithas yr Iaith Gymraeg Planning-Economic Group (1989). *Homes Migration Prices: Community Control of the Property Market*, Cymdeithas yr Iaith Gymraeg, Aberystwyth.

Cymuned (2001). *Housing, Work and Language*, Cymuned, Aberystwyth.

Cymuned (2003). *Cymuned's Proposals to the Richards' Commission*, Cymuned, Aberystwyth.

Dafis, C. (2005a). 'Plaid Cymru and the Greens: flash in the pan or a lesson for the future?', 4 November, lecture presented at the National Library for Wales.

Dafis, C. (2005b). *Mab y Pregethwr*, Talybont, Y Lolfa.

Daily Herald (1963). 'They fight for the language of heaven', 4 February, p. 5.

Dalby, S. (1988). 'Geopolitical discourse: the Soviet Union as Other', *Alternatives* 13: 415–42.

Dalby, S. (1999). 'Globalization or global apartheid? Boundaries and knowledge in postmodern times' in D. Newman (ed.) *Boundaries, Territory and Postmodernity*, Frank Cass, London, pp. 132–50..

Daniels, S. (1993). *Fields of Vision: Landscape Imagery and National Identity in England and the United States*, Princeton University Press, Princeton.

Davies, C. (1973). 'Cymdeithas yr Iaith Gymraeg', in M. Stephens (ed.) *The Welsh Language Today*, Gwasg Gomer, Llandysul, pp. 248–63..

Davies, C. A. (1989). *Welsh Nationalism in the Twentieth Century: The Ethnic Option and the Modern State*, Praeger, New York.

Davies, C. A. (1999). 'Nationalism, feminism and Welsh women: conflicts and accommodations', in R. Fevre and A. Thompson (eds) *Nation, Identity and Social Theory: Perspectives from Wales*, University of Wales Press, Cardiff, pp. 90–108.

Davies, D. H. (1983). *The Welsh Nationalist Party 1925–1945*, University of Wales Press, Cardiff.

Davies, G. P. (2000). 'The legal status of the Welsh language in the twentieth century', in G. H. Jenkins and M. A. Williams (eds) *'Let's Do Our Best for the Ancient Tongue': The Welsh Language in the Twentieth Century*, University of Wales Press, Cardiff, pp. 217–48.

Davies, J. (Janet) (1993). *The Welsh Language*, University of Wales Press, Cardiff.

Davies, J. (John) (1976). 'Blynyddoedd cynnar Cymdeithas yr Iaith Gymraeg', in A. Eirug (ed.) *Tân a Daniwyd.* Cymdeithas yr Iaith Gymraeg, Aberystwyth, pp. 13–27.

Davies, J. (John) (1993). *A History of Wales,* Penguin, London.

Davies, J. (John) (2000). *Lecture to Commemorate the 75th Anniversary of Plaid Cymru – The Party of Wales*, Plaid Cymru, Cardiff.

Davies, R. (1999). *Devolution: A Process not an Event*, Institute of Welsh Affairs, Cardiff.

Dawson, J. (1995). 'Anti-nuclear activism in the USSR and its successor states: a surrogate for nationalism?', *Environmental Politics* 4: 441–66.

Day, G. (2002). *Making Sense of Wales: A Sociological Perspective*, University of Wales Press, Cardiff.

Delaney, D. and Leitner, H. (1997). 'The political construction of scale', *Political Geography* 16: 93–7.

Denver, D. T. and Hands, G. (1997). 'Challengers, incumbents and the impact of constituency campaigning in Britain', *Electoral Studies* 16: 175–93.

Desforges, L. and Jones, R. (2000). 'The production of national identity in Wales: higher education and the Welsh language', *Contemporary Wales* 13: 27–45.

Desforges, L. and Jones, R. (2001). 'Bilingualism and geographical knowledge: a case study of students at the University of Wales, Aberystwyth' *Social and Cultural Geography* 2: 333–46.

Desforges, L. and Jones, R. (2004). 'Learning geography bilingually', *Journal of Geography in Higher Education* 28: 411–24.

De-Shalit, A. (1995). 'From the political to the objective: the dialectics of Zionism and the environment', *Environmental Politics* 4: 70–87.

De-Shalit, A. (2001). 'Ten commandments of how to fail in an environmental campaign', *Environmental Politics* 10: 111–37.

De-Shalit, A. and Talias, M. (1994). 'Green or blue and white? Environmental controversies in Israel', *Environmental Politics* 2: 327–33.

Dicks, B. and van Loon, J. (1999). 'Territoriality and heritage in south Wales: space, time and imagined communities', in R. Fevre and A. Thompson (eds) *Nation, Identity and Social Theory: Perspectives from Wales*, University of Wales Press, Cardiff, pp. 207–32.

Dilthey, W. (1924 [1907]). 'Das Wesen der Philosophie', in W. Dilthey *Gerammelte Schriften V*, B. G. Teubner, Leipzig.

Dwyer, C. (1999). 'Contradictions of community: questions of identity for young British Muslim women', *Environment and Planning A* 31: 53–68.

Eckerberg, K. (1994). 'Environmental problems and policy opptions in the Baltic states: learning from the west?', *Environmental Politics* 3: 445–70.

Edensor, T. (1997). 'National identity and the politics of memory: remembering Bruce and Wallace in symbolic space', *Environment and Planning D: Society and Space* 29: 175–94

Edensor, T. (2002). *National Identity, Popular Culture and Everyday Life*, Berg, Oxford.

Edwards, H. T. (1987). 'Y Gymraeg yn y bedwaredd ganrif ar bymtheg', in G. H. Jenkins (ed.) *Cof Cenedl II*, Gwasg Gomer, Llandysul, pp. 119–52.

Eisenstadt, S. N., and Giesen, B. (1995). 'The construction of collective identity', *European Journal of Sociology* 36: 72–102.

Ellis, E. L. (1972). *The University College of Wales Aberystwyth 1872–1972*, University of Wales Press, Cardiff.

England, K. (1999). 'Sexing geography, teaching sexualities', *Journal of Geography in Higher Education* 23: 94–101.

Enloe, C. (1989). *Bananas, Beaches, Bases: Making Sense of International Politics*, Pandora, London.

Evans, D (forthcoming). '"How far do you have to be across the border to be, to be considered Welsh?" National identification at the local level', *Contemporary Wales*.

Evans, D. G. (1989). *A History of Wales 1815–1906*, University of Wales Press, Cardiff.

Evans, G. (1993). 'Hard times for the British Green Party', *Environmental Politics* 2: 327–33.

Evans, W. G. (2000). 'The British state and Welsh-language education, 1914–1991' in G. H. Jenkins and M. Williams (eds) *Let's Do our Best for the Ancient Tongue: The Welsh Language in the Twentieth Century*, University of Wales Press, Cardiff, pp. 343–69.

Express, The (1963). 'Arrest plea: but Silyn and 70 other "criminals" just stay free', 3 February, p. 4.

Fairclough, N. (2003). *Analysing Discourse: Textual Analysis for Social Research,*. Routledge, London.

Fevre, R., Borland, J. and Denney, D. (1997). 'Class, status and party in the analysis of nationalism: lessons from Max Weber', *Nations and Nationalism* 3: 559–77.

Fevre, R., Borland, J. and Denney, D. (1999). 'Nation, community and conflict: housing policy and immigration in North Wales', in R. Fevre and A. Thompson (eds) *Nation, Identity and Social Theory: Perspectives from Wales*, University of Wales Press, Cardiff, pp. 129–48.

Ffransis, M. (1985). *S4C: Pwy Dalodd Amdano?*, Cymdeithas yr Iaith Gymraeg, Aberystwyth.

Foucault, M. (1969). *The Order of Things: An Archaeology of the Human Sciences*, Routledge, London.

Foucault, M. (1970 [1966]). *The Order of Things: An Archaeology of the Human Sciences*, Random House, New York.

Foucault, M. (1977). *Discipline and Punish: The Birth of the Prison*, Allen Lane, London.

Foucault, M. (1991). 'Governmentality' in G. Burchell, C. Gordon and P. Miller (eds) *The Foucault Effect: Studies in Governmentality*, University of Chicago Press, Chicago, IL, pp. 87–104.

Fowler, C. and Jones, R. (2006). 'Can environmentalism and nationalism be reconciled? The Plaid Cymru/Green Party alliance, 1991–1995', *Regional and Federal Studies* 16: 315–31.

Friends of the Earth (1995a). 'Home Energy Conservation Bill returns to House of Commons', press release, 19 January 1995.

Friends of the Earth (1995b). 'Maddock's Energy Bill succeeds', press release, 8 June 1995.

Friends of the Earth (1996a). 'Road Traffic Reduction Bill introduced to Commons', press release, 20 March 1996.

Friends of the Earth (1996b). 'Don Foster MP to introduce Road Traffic Reduction Bill as Private Members Bill', press release, 13 November 1996.

Friends of the Earth (1997). 'Road Traffic Reduction Bill becomes law', press release, 20 March 1997.

Garner, R. (1996) *Environmental Politics*, Prentice Hall, London.

Gellner, E. (1973). 'Scale and the nation', *Philosophy of the Social Sciences* 3: 1–17.

Gellner, E. (1983). *Nations and Nationalism*, Basil Blackwell, Oxford.

Giddens, A. (1985). *The Nation-State and Violence*, Polity Press, Cambridge.

Graham, S. and Marvin, S. (2001). *Splintering Urbanism: Networked Infrastructures, Technological Mobilities and the Urban Conditio*, Routledge, London.

Gregory, D. (1994). *Geographical Imaginations*, Blackwell, Oxford.

Gregory, D. (2000). 'Discourse', in R. J. Johnston, D. Gregory, G. Pratt and M. Watts (eds) *The Dictionary of Human Geography*, Blackwell, Oxford, pp. 80–81.

Griffith, R. E. (1971–73). *Urdd Gobaith Cymru*, 3 vols, Cwmni Urdd Gobaith Cymru, Aberystwyth.

Griffiths, I. (2004). 'The Wales Green Party and the National Assembly of Wales Elections 2003', *Regional and Federal Studies* 5: 197–210.

Gruffudd, I. (2004). *Achos y Bomiau Bach*, Gwasg Carreg Gwalch, Llanrwst.

Gruffudd, P. (1994). 'Back to the land: historiography, rurality and the nation in interwar Wales', *Transactions of the Institute of British Geographers* 19: 61–77.

Gruffudd, P. (1995). 'Remaking Wales: nation-building and the geographical imagination', *Political Geography* 14: 219–39.

Gruffudd, P. (1999). 'Prospects of Wales: contested geographical imaginations', in R. Fevre and A. Thompson (eds) *Nation, Identity and Social Theory: Perspectives from Wales*, University of Wales Press, Cardiff, pp. 149–67.

Gruffydd, A. (2004). *Mae Rhywun yn Gwybod*, Gwasg Carreg Gwalch, Llanrwst.

Habermas, J. (1981). 'New social movements', *Telos* 49: 33–7.

Hamilton, P. (2002). 'The greening of nationalism: nationalising nature in Europe', *Environmental Politics* 11: 27–48.

Hartshorne, R. (1939). *The Nature of Geography: A Critical Survey of Current Thought in the Light of the Past*, The Geographical Association, Lancaster, PA.

Hechter, M. (1975). *Internal Colonialism: The Celtic Fringe in British National Development, 1536–1966*, Routledge and Keegan Paul, London.

Heffernan, M. (1995). 'For ever England: the Western Front and the politics of remembrance in Britain', *Ecumene* 2: 293–324.

HMSO (1847). *Report of the Royal Commission on Education in Wales*, 3 vols, London.

HMSO (1927). *Welsh in Education and Life*, London.

HMSO (1993). Welsh Language Act 1993, London.

Herb, G. (1999). 'National identity and territory', in G. Herb and D. Kaplan (eds) *Nested Identities: Nationalism, Territory, and Scale*, Rowman & Littlefield, Lanham, MD, pp. 9–30.

Herb, G. and Kaplan, D. (1999a). *Nested Identities: Nationalism, Territory, and Scale*, Rowman & Littlefield, Lanham, MD.

Herb, G. and Kaplan, D. (1999b). 'Introduction: a question of identity', G. Herb and D. Kaplan (eds) *Nested Identities: Nationalism, Territory, and Scale*, Rowman & Littlefield, Lanham, MD, pp. 1–8.

Herod, A. (1997). 'Labor's spatial praxis and the geography of contract bargaining in the US east coast longshore industry', *Political Geography* 16: 145–69.

Herod, A. and Wright, M. (2002). 'Placing scale: an introduction', in A. Herod and M. Wright (eds) *Geographies of Power: Placing Scale*, Blackwell, Oxford, pp. 1–14.

Hobsbawm, E. (1983). 'Introduction: inventing traditions', in E. Hobsbawm and T. O. Ranger (eds) *The Invention of Tradition*, Cambridge University Press, Cambridge, pp. 1–14.

Hobsbawm, E. and Ranger, T. O. (eds) (1983). *The Invention of Tradition*, Cambridge University Press, Cambridge.

Hooson, D. (1994). *Geography and National Identity*, Blackwell, Cambridge, MA.

Howitt, R. (1998). 'Scale as relation: musical metaphors of geographical scale', *Area* 30: 49–58.

Hroch, M. (1985). *Social Preconditions of National Revival in Europe*, Cambridge University Press, Cambridge.

Hutchinson, J. (1987). *The Dynamics of Cultural Nationalism: The Gaelic Revival and the Creation of the Irish Nation State*, Allen and Unwin, London.

Ignatieff, M. (1993). *Blood and Belonging: Journeys into the New Nationalism*, Chatto & WIndus, London.

Iwan, D. (1969). 'Anadl einioes cenedl', *Y Faner*, 4 December.

Iwan, D. (1992). *Holl Ganeuon Dafydd Iwan*, Y Lolfa, Talybont.

Jenkins, G. H. (1993). *Prifysgol Cymru: Hanes Darluniadol*, University of Wales Press, Cardiff.

Jenkins, G. H. and Williams, M. A. (2000). 'The fortunes of the Welsh language 1900–2000: introduction', in G. H. Jenkins and M. A. Williams (eds) *'Let's Do Our Best for the Ancient Tongue': The Welsh Language in the Twentieth Century*, University of Wales Press, Cardiff, pp. 1–27.

Jobbins, S. (2001). 'D. J.', *Barn* 461: 16–17.

Johnson, N. C. (1995). 'Cast in stone: monuments, geography and nationalism', *Environment and Planning D: Society and Space* 13: 51–65.

Johnson, N. C. (1997). 'Making space: Gaeltacht policy and the politics of identity', in B. Graham (ed.) *In Search of Ireland: A Cultural Geography*, Routledge, London, pp. 151–73.

Johnson, N. C. (2003). *Ireland, the Great War and the Geography of Remembrance*, Cambridge University Press, Cambridge.

Johnston, R. J. and Pattie, C. (2004). 'Electoral geography in electoral studies: putting voters in their place', in C. Barnett and M. Low (eds) *Spaces of Democracy: Geographical Perspectives on Citizenship, Participation and Representation*, Sage, London, pp. 45–66.

Jonas, A. (1994). 'The scale spatiality of politics', *Environment and Planning D: Society and Space* 12: 257–64.

Jones, B. (1999). *Etholiadau'r Ganrif: Welsh Elections 1885–1997*, Y Lolfa, Talybont.

Jones, D. G. (1973). 'The Welsh-language movement', in M. Stephens (ed.) *The Welsh Language Today*, Gwasg Gomer, Llandysul, pp. 264–318.

Jones, G. E. (1982). *Controls and Conflicts in Welsh Secondary Education 1889–1944*, University of Wales Press, Cardiff.

Jones, J. B. (1988). 'The development of Welsh territorial institutions: modernization theory revisited', *Contemporary Wales* 2: 47–61.

Jones, J. B. (1997). 'Welsh politics and changing British and European contexts', in J. Bradbury, and J. Mawson (eds) *British Regionalism and Devolution*, Jessica Kingsley, London, pp. 55–73.

Jones, J. B. and Osmond J. (eds) (2002). *Building a Civic Culture: Institutional Change, Policy Development and Political Dynamics in the National Assembly for Wales*, Welsh Governance Centre and the Institute of Welsh Affairs, Cardiff.

Jones, J. G. (1992). *Concepts of Order and Gentility in Wales 1540–1640*, Gomer Press, Llandysul.

Jones, J. G. (2000). 'The attitude of political parties towards the Welsh language', in G. H. Jenkins and M. A. Williams (eds). *'Let's Do Our Best for the Ancient Tongue': The Welsh Language in the Twentieth Century*, University of Wales Press, Cardiff, pp. 249–76.

Jones, J. R. (1966). *Prydeindod*, Llyfrau'r Dryw, Llandybïe.

Jones, J. R. (1970). *Gwaedd yng Nghymru*, Cwmni Cyhoeddiadau Modern, Liverpool.

Jones, R. (1999). 'Foundation legends, *origines gentium* and senses of ethnic identity: legitimising ideologies in early medieval Celtic Britain', *Environment and Planning D: Society and Space* 17: 691–703.

Jones, R. and Desforges, L. (2003). 'Localities and the reproduction of Welsh nationalism', *Political Geography* 22: 271–92.

Jones, R. and Fowler, C. (2007a). 'Where is Wales? Narrating the territories and borders of the Welsh linguistic nation', *Regional Studies* 41: 89–101.

Jones, R. and Fowler, C. (2007b). 'Placing and scaling the nation', *Environment and Planning D: Society and Space* 25: 332–54.

Jones, R. and Fowler, C. (2007c). 'National *élites*, national masses: oral history and the (re)production of the Welsh nation', *Social and Cultural Geography* 8: 417–32.

Jones, R. O. (1997). *Hir Oes i'r Iaith: Agweddau ar Hanes y Gymraeg a'r Gymdeithas*, Gwasg Gomer, Llandysul.

Jones, R. T. (1986). 'The shadow of the swastika', in I. Hume and W. T. R. Pryce (eds) *The Welsh and their Country*, Gomer Press, Llandysul, pp. 234–43..

Jones, R. W. (2001a). 'Coleg Cymraeg – Yr Unig Ateb', *Barn* November.

Jones, R. W. (2001b). 'Iaith a hunanlywodraeth', *Barn*, No. 464: 10–11.

Jones, R. W. (2004). *Methiant Prifysgolion Cymru/The Failure of the Universities of Wales*, Institute of Welsh Affairs, Cardiff.

Jones, R. W. and Trystan, D. (1999). 'The 1997 Welsh Referendum Vote', in B. Taylor and K. Thomson (eds) *Scotland and Wales: Nations Again?*, University of Wales Press, Cardiff, pp. 65–93.

Kaplan, D. (1999). 'Territorial identities and geographic scale', in G. Herb and D. Kaplan (eds) *Nested Identities: Nationalism, Territory, and Scale*, Rowman & Littlefield, Lanham, MD, pp. 31–49.

Kaufmann, E. and Zimmer, O. (1998). 'In search of the authentic nation: landscape and national identity in Canada and Switzerland', *Nations and Nationalism* 4: 483–510.

Keating, M. (1998). *The New Regionalism in Western Europe*, Elgar, Cheltenham.

Kedourie, E. (1960). *Nationalism*, Hutchinson, London.

Kedourie, E. (ed.) (1971). *Nationalism in Asia and Africa*, Weidenfeld and Nicolson, London.

Knopp, L. (1999). 'Queer theory, queer pedagogy: new spaces and new challenges in teaching geography', *Journal of Geography in Higher Education* 23: 77–9.

Kong, L. (2005). 'Religious schools: for spirit, (f)or nation', *Environment and Planning D: Society and Space* 23: 615–31.

Kornprobst, M. (2005). 'Episteme, nation-builders and national identity: the re-construction of Irishness', *Nations and Nationalism* 11: 403–21.

Labour Party (1997). *New Labour: Because Britain Deserves Better*, Labour Party, London.

Labour Party (2001). *Ambitions for Britain: Labour's Manifesto 2001*, Labour Party, London.

Lefebvre, H. (1991). *The Production of Space*, Blackwell, Oxford.

Lewis, S. (1926). *Egwyddorion Cenedlaetholdeb*, Plaid Genedlaethol Cymru, Caernarfon.

Lewis, S. (1962). *Tynged yr Iaith*, British Broadcasting Corporation, London.

Lewis, W. J. (1980). *Born on a Perilous Rock: Aberystwyth Past and Present*, Cambrian News, Aberystwyth.

Liverpool Daily Post (1963). 'Police ignore billposting, so use-Welsh campaigners block roads', 4 February, p. 1.

Llais y Lli (12 January 1965). 'Hostel Gymraeg i Aberystwyth?', *Llais y Lli*, 12 January, p. 1.

Llais y Lli (2 October 1965). 'Croeso i Goleg Aber', *Llais y Lli*, 2 October, p. 2.

Llais y Lli (15 November 1965). 'Ehangu! Ond beth am y Cymry', *Llais y Lli*, 15 November, p. 1.

Llais y Lli (13 December 1965). 'Ymweliad D. J. Williams', *Llais y Lli*, 13 December, p. 1.

Llais y Lli (28 February 1966). 'Ewch rhagoch yn eofn: dywedwch yn groyw', *Llais y Lli*, 24 February, p. 1.

Llais y Lli (15 November 1966). 'Pwyllgor i argymell: Neuadd 'nawr', *Llais y Lli*, 15 November, p. 1.

Llewelyn, E. (1972a). *Areithiau*, Y Lolfa, Talybont.

Llewelyn, E. (1972b). *Y Chwyldro a'r Gymru Newydd*, Y Lolfa, Talybont.

Llewelyn, E. (1986). 'What is Adfer', in I. Hume and W. T. R. Pryce (eds) *The Welsh and their Country*, Gomer Press, Llandysul, pp. 244–52.

Lorimer, H. (1999). 'Ways of seeing the Scottish Highlands: authenticity, marginality and the curious case of the Hebridean blackhouse', *Journal of Historical Geography* 25: 517–33.

Lynch, P. (1995). 'From red to green: the political strategy of Plaid Cymru in the 1980s and 1990s', *Regional and Federal Studies* 5: 197–210.

McAllister, L. (2001). *Plaid Cymru: the Emergence of a Political Party*, Seren, Bridgend.

McCormick, J. (1991). *British Politics and the Environment*, Earthscan, London.

McDowell, L. and Bowlby, S. (1983). 'Teaching feminist geography', *Journal of Geography in Higher Education* 7: 97–107.

MacLaughlin, J. (2001). *Reimagining the Nation-State: The Contested Terrains of Nation-Building*, Pluto Press, London.

Mann, M. (1995). 'A political theory of nationalism and its excesses', in S. Periwal (ed.) *Notions of Nationalism*, Central European University Press, Budapest, pp. 44–64.

Marston, S. (2000). 'The social construction of scale', *Progress in Human Geography* 24: 219–42.

Marston, S., Jones, J. P. and Woodward, K. (2005). 'Human geography without scale', *Transactions of the Institute of British Geographers NS* 30: 416–32.

Marston, S. and Smith, N. (2001). 'States, scales and households: limits to scale thinking? A response to Brenner', *Progress in Human Geography* 25: 615–19.

Martin, C. T. (ed.) (1884). *Registrum Epistolarum Fratris Johannis Peckham*, Longman, London.

Massey, D. (1984). *Spatial Division of Labour*, Macmillan, London.

Massey, D. (1994). *Space, Place and Gender*, Polity Press, Cambridge.

Massey, D. (2004). 'Geographies of responsibility', *Geografiska Annaler* 86B: 5–18.

Melucci, A. (1980). 'The new social movements: a theoretical approach', *Social Science Information* 19: 199–216.

Mikesell, M. W. (1983). 'The myth of the nation state', *Journal of Geography* 82: 257–60.

Miles, G. (1972). *Cymru Rydd, Cymru Gymraeg, Cymru Sosialaidd*, Cymdeithas yr Iaith, Aberystwyth.

Miller, B. A. (2000). *Geography and Social Movements: Comparing Antinuclear Activism in the Boston Area*, University of Minnesota Press, Minneapolis, MN.

Miller, W. L. (1977). *Electoral Dynamics*, Macmillan, London.

Mitchell, J. (1996). *Strategies for Self-Government*, Polygon, Edinburgh.

Monk, J. (2000). 'Looking out, looking in: the "other" in the Journal of Geography in Higher Education', *Journal of Geography in Higher Education* 24: 163–77.

Morgan, K. and Mungham, G. (2000). *Redesigning Democracy*, Seren, Bridgend.

Morgan, K. O. (1980). [1963] *Wales in British Politics 1868–1922*, University of Wales Press, Cardiff.

Morgan, K. O. (1982). *Rebirth of a Nation: Wales 1880–1980*, Oxford University Press, Oxford.

Morgan, K. O. (1995) [1966]. 'The campaign for Welsh disestablishment' in K. O. Morgan (ed.) *Modern Wales: Politics, Places and People*, University of Wales Press, Cardiff, pp. 147–65.

Morgan, P. (1997). *The University of Wales 1939–1993*, University of Wales Press, Cardiff.

Morris, J. (2003). 'Yn fy meddwl i', *Gwreiddiau* 1: 4.

Morton, M. (2002). *Hanes Barn, 1962–1991*, unpublished Ph.D. thesis, University of Wales, Aberystwyth.

Mulligan, A. (2001). 'Ties that b(l)ind: marginal sites of creative intervention in the development of Irish nationalism', paper presented at the Association of American Geographers annual conference, New York.

Murphy, A. B. (1996). 'The sovereign state system as political-territorial ideal: historical and contemporary considerations', in T. Biersteker and C. Weber (eds) *State Sovereignty as Social Construct*, Cambridge University Press, Cambridge, pp. 81–120.

Murphy, A. B. (2002). 'National claims to territory in the modern state system: geographical considerations', *Geopolitics* 7: 193–214

NAfW (2002a). *Ein Hiaith: Ei Dyfodol/Our Language: Its Future*, National Assembly for Wales, Cardiff.

NAfW (2002b). *A Winning Wales: National Economic Development Strategy*, National Assembly for Wales, Cardiff.

Nairn, T. (1977). *The Break-up of Britain: Crisis and Neo-Nationalism*, Verso, London.

Nash, C. (1996). 'Men again: Irish masculinity, nature, and nationhood in the early twentieth century' *Ecumene* 3: 427–53.

Nash, C. (1999). 'Genealogies of Irishness: ancestor searching and diasporic identities', paper presented at the Royal Geographical Society (with the Institute of British Geographers) annual conference, Leicester.

Nations and Nationalism (2004). 'Special issue on "History and national destiny"' *Nations and Nationalism* 10: 1–209.

Nelmes, G. V. (1979). 'Stuart Rendel and Welsh Liberal political organization in the late-nineteenth century', *Welsh History Review* 9: 469–85.

Newman D. and Paasi, A. (1998). 'Fences and neighbours in a postmodern world: boundary narratives in political geography', *Progress in Human Geography* 22: 186–207.

NLW PADR A13/3 (no date). 'Student petition in support of the establishment of a Welsh-medium hall of residence', National Library of Wales, Papers of Alwyn D. Rees: A13/3.

NLW PADR A13/36 (no date). 'Senate letter to Council', National Library of Wales, Papers of Alwyn D. Rees: A13/36.

NLW PCD 10 (no date). 'Wales Green Party press release, 3 July, 1995' [the National Library of Wales' papers of Cynog Dafis (Folder 14)].

NLW PCD 11–12 (no date). 'Draft of Cynog Dafis' maiden speech to the House of Commons, 11 May, 1992' [the National Library of Wales papers of Cynog Dafis (Folder 11–12)].

NLW WPE BA 4/13. 'Green Wales – Green Planet! . . .Speakers Jonathon Porritt and Cynog Dafis', Ceredigion Green Party/Plaid Cymru General Election poster, 1992 [the National Library of Wales' 'Welsh Political Ephemera' (Folder BA 4/13)].

Ogborn, M. (1998). *Spaces of Modernity: London's Geographies 1680–1780*, Guilford Press, London.

Özkırımlı, U. (2000). *Theories of Nationalism*, Macmillan, Basingstoke.

Paasi, A. (1991). 'Deconstructing regions: notes on the scales of spatial life', *Environment and Planning A* 23: 239–56.

Paasi, A. (1996). *Territories, Boundaries and Consciousness: The Changing Geographies of the Finnish-Russian Border*, John Wiley, Chichester.

Paasi, A. (2002). 'Bounded spaces in the mobile world: deconstructing "regional identity"', *Tijdschrift voor Economische en Sociale Geografie* 93: 137–48.

Page, E. (1977). *Michael Hechter's internal colonial thesis: some theoretical and methodological problems*, Centre for the Study of Public Policy, University of Strathclyde, Glasgow.

PCGPC&PN (1993). *Towards a Green Welsh Future*, Plaid Cymru and Green Party Ceredigion, Aberystwyth.

Peate, I. (1931). *Cymru a'i Phobl*, University of Wales Press, Cardiff.

Penrose, J. (2002). 'Nations, states and homelands: territory and territoriality in nationalist thought', *Nations and Nationalism* 8: 277–97.

Philippou, S. (2005). 'Constructing national and European identities: the case of Greek-Cypriot pupils', *Educational Studies* 31: 293–315.

Phillips, D. (1998). *Trwy Ddulliau Chwyldro. . . ? Hanes Cymdeithas yr Iaith 1962– 1992*, Gwasg Gomer, Llandysul.

Plaid Cymru (1989). *Cynhadledd '89 Conference*, Plaid Cymru, Cardiff.

Plaid Cymru (1990). *Cynhadledd '90 Conference*, Plaid Cymru, Cardiff.

Plaid Cymru (1994). *Plaid Cymru European Election Manifesto*, Plaid Cymru, Aberystwyth.

Plaid Cymru (2005). *We Can Build a Better Wales: Westminster Election Manifesto 2005*, Plaid Cymru, Cardiff.

Podoba, J. (1998). 'Rejecting green velvet: transition, environment and nationalism in Slovakia', *Environmental Politics* 7: 129–44.

Porritt, J. and Winner, D. (1988). *The Coming of the Greens*, Fontana, London.

Pred, A. (1984). 'Place as historical contingent process: structuration and the time-geography of becoming place', *Annals of the Association of American Geographers* 74: 279–97.

Prescott, J. R. V. (1972). *Political Geography*, Methuen, London.

Pryce, W. T. R., (1975). *Migration and the Evolution of Culture Areas: Cultural and Linguistic Frontiers in north-east Wales 1750 and 1851*, Institute of British Geographers, London.

Purcell, M. (2003). 'Islands of practice and the Marston/Brenner debate: toward a more synthetic human geography', *Progress in Human Geography* 27: 317–32.

Radcliffe, S. (1999). 'Embodying national identities: mestizo men and white women in Ecuadorian racial-national imaginaries', *Transactions of the Institute of British Geographers* 24: 213–26.

Rees A. D. (1950). *Life in a Welsh Countryside: A Social Study of Llanfihangel yng Ngwynfa*, University of Wales Press, Cardiff.

Relph, E. (1976). *Place and Placelessness*, Pion, London.

Reynolds, S. (1984). *Kingdoms and Communities in Western Europe, 900–1300*, Oxford University Press, Oxford.

Richter, M. (1978). 'The political and institutional background to national consciousness in medieval Wales' in T. W. Moody (ed.) *Nationalism and the Pursuit of National Independence*, Appletree Press, Dublin, pp 37–55..

Roberts, O. (2001). '"A very ordinary, rather barren valley": argyfwng Tryweryn a gwleidyddiaeth yr amgylchedd yng Nghymru', in G. J. Jenkins (ed.) *Cof Cenedl* 16, Gomer Press, Llandysul, pp. 155–90.

Rokkan, S. (1970). *Cities, Elections, Parties*, McKay, New York.

Rose, G. (1990). 'Imagining Poplar in the 1920s: contested concepts of community', *Journal of Historical Geography* 16: 425–37.

Rough Guides (2003). *The Rough Guide to Wales*, Rough Guides, London.

Royles, E. (2007). *Revitalising Democracy? Devolution and Civil Society in Wales*, University of Wales Press, Cardiff.

Sahlins, P. (1989). *Boundaries: The Making of France and Spain in the Pyrenees*, University of California Press, Berkeley.

Said, E. (1978). *Orientalism*, Penguin, London.

Saigol, R. (2005). 'Enemies within and enemies without: the besieged self in Pakistani textbooks', *Futures* 37: 1005–55.

Sassen, S. (1991). *The Global City*, Princeton University Press, Princeton, NJ.

Scott, J. C. (1998). *Seeing Like a State: How Certain Schemes to Improve the Human Condition Have Failed*, Yale University Press, New Haven, CT.

Scourfield, J. and Davies, A. (2005). 'Children's accounts of Wales as racialized and inclusive', *Ethnicities* 5: 83–107.

Sharp, J., Routledge, P., Philo, C. and Paddison, R. (eds) (2000). *Entanglements of Power: Geographies of Domination/Resistance*, Routledge, London.

Shields, R. (1991). *Places on the Margin: Alternative Geographies of Modernity*, Routledge, London.

Sidorov, D. (2000). 'National monumentalization and the politics of scale: the resurrections of the Cathedral of Christ the Savior in Moscow', *Annals of the Association of American Geographers* 90: 548–72.

Sletto, B. (2002). 'Boundary making and regional identities in a globalized environment: rebordering the Nariva Swamp, Trinidad', *Environment and Planning D: Society and Space* 20: 183–208.

Smith, A. D. (1982). 'Nationalism, ethnic separatism and the intellegentsia' in C. H. Williams (ed.) *National Separatism*, University of Wales Press, Cardiff, pp. 17–41.

Smith, A. D. (1986). *The Ethnic Origins of Nations*, Blackwell, Oxford.

Smith, A. D. (1991). *National Identity*, Penguin, London.

Smith, A. D. (1998). *Nationalism and Modernism*, Routledge, London.

Smith, A. D. (2003). 'The poverty of anti-nationalist modernism', *Nations and Nationalism* 9: 357–70.

Smith, D. (1984). *Wales! Wales?*, Allen and Unwin, London.

Smith, D. (2001). *Out of the People: A Century in Labour*, National Library of Wales, Aberystwyth.

Smith, N. (1987). 'Dangers of the empirical turn: some comments on the CURS initiative', *Antipode* 19: 59–68.

Smith, N. (1992a). 'Geography, difference and the politics of scale', in J. Doherty, E. Graham and M. Malek (eds) *Postmodernism and the Social Sciences*, Macmillan, London, pp. 57–79.

Smith, N. (1992b). 'Contours of a spatialized politics: homeless vehicles and the production of geographical scale', *Social Text* 33: 55–81.

Smith, N. (1993). 'Homeless/global: scaling places', in J. Bird, B. Curtis, T. Putnam, G. Roberston and L. Tickner (eds) *Mapping the Futures: Local Cultures, Global Change*, Routledge, New York, pp. 87–119.

Smith, N. (1996). 'Spaces of vulnerability: the space of flows and the politics of scale', *Critique of Anthropology* 16: 63–77.

Smith, N. (2000). 'Scale', in R. J. Johnston, D. Gregory, G. Pratt and M. Watts (eds) *The Dictionary of Human Geography*, Blackwell, Oxford, pp. 724–7.

Soja, E. (1989). *Postmodern Geographies*, Blackwell, Oxford.

Soja, E. (1996). *Thirdspace*, Blackwell, Oxford.

Stacey, M. (1969). 'The myth of community studies', *British Journal of Sociology* 20: 134–47.

Swyngedouw, E. (1992). 'The Mammon quest: glocalisation, interspatial competition and monetary order: the construction of new spatial scales', in M. Dunford and G. Kafkalas (eds) *Cities and Regions in the New Europe: The Global-Local Interplay and Spatial Development Strategies*, Belhaven Press, London, pp. 39–67.

Swyngedouw, E. (1996). 'Reconstructing citizenship, the rescaling of the state and the new authoritarianism: closing the Belgian mines' *Urban Studies* 33: 1499–521.

Swyngedouw, E. (1997a). 'Neither global nor local: 'glocalisation' and the politics of scale', in K. Cox (ed.) *Spaces of Globalization: Reasserting the Power of the Local*, Guilford Press, London, pp. 137–66.

Swyngedouw, E. (1997b). 'Excluding the other: the production of scale and scaled politics', in R. Lee and J. Wills (eds) *Geographies of Economies*, Arnold, London, pp. 167–76.

Swyngedouw, E. (2000). 'Authoritarian governance, power, and the politics of rescaling', *Environment and Planning D: Society and Space* 18: 63–76.

Swyngedouw, E. (2003). 'Scaled geographies: nature, place and the contested politics of scale', in E. Sheppard and B. McMaster (eds) *Scale and Geographic Inquiry: Nature, Society and Method*, Blackwell, Oxford, pp. 129–53.

Taylor, B. and Thomson, K. (eds) (1999). *Scotland and Wales: Nations Again?*, University of Wales Press, Cardiff.

Taylor, P. J. (1991). 'The English and their Englishness', *Scottish Geographical Magazine* 107: 146–61.

Taylor, P. J. (1999). *Modernities: A Geohistorical Interpretation*, Polity, Cambridge.

Taylor, P. J. and Flint, C. (2000). *Political Geography: World-Economy, Nation-State and Locality*, Prentice-Hall, London.

Taylor, P. J. and Johnston, R. J. (1979). *Geography of Elections*, Penguin, Harmondsworth.

Thomas, B. (1959). 'Wales and the Atlantic economy', *Scottish Journal of Political Economy* 6: 181–92.

Thomas, D. (1977). *Wales: A New Study*, David and Charles, London.

Thompson, A. (2001). 'Nations, national identities and human agency: putting people back into nations' *Sociological Review* 49: 18–32.

Thomson, A. and Day, G. (1999). 'Situating Welshness: "local" experience and national identity', in R. Fevre and A. Thompson (eds) *Nation, Identity and Social Theory: Perspectives from Wales*, University of Wales Press, Cardiff, pp. 27–47.

Thompson, A. and Fevre, R. (2001). 'The national question: sociological reflections on nations and nationalism', *Nations and Nationalism* 7: 297–315.

Thrift, N. (1983). 'On the determination of social action in space and time', *Environment and Planning D: Society and Space* 1: 23–57.

Tilly, C. (ed.) 1975 *The Formation of National States in Western Europe*, Princeton University Press, Princeton, NJ.

Times, The (1963). 'Summonses in Welsh: group's campaign in Aberystwyth', 4 February, p. 6.

Tonnies, F. (1887, reprinted 1963). *Community and Association*, Harper and Row, New York.

Tuan, Y. (1977). *Space and Place: The Perspective of Experience*, Edward Arnold, London.

Tudur, G. (1987). *Wyt Ti'n Cofio?: Chwarter Canrif o Frwydr yr Iaith*, Y Lolfa, Talybont.

UCWA (1965). University College of Wales Aberystwyth Council Minutes, 14 December 1965.

UCWA (1967a). University College of Wales Aberystwyth Council Minutes, 21 June 1967.

UCWA (1967b). University College of Wales Aberystwyth Council Minutes, 1 November 1967.

UCWA (1967c). University College of Wales Aberystwyth Council Minutes, 18 December 1967.

UCWA (1968a). University College of Wales Aberystwyth Council Minutes, 18 March 1968.

UCWA (1968b). University College of Wales Aberystwyth Council Minutes, 21 June 1968.

UCWA (1973). University College of Wales Aberystwyth Council Minutes, 7 November 1973.

UCWA (1975). University College of Wales Aberystwyth Senate's Halls' Committee Minutes, 2 February 1975.

Valentine, G. (2001). *Social Geographies: Space and Society*, Prentice-Hall, London.

Van Houtum, H., and Van Naerssen, T. (2002). 'Bordering, ordering and othering', *Tijdschrift voor Economische en Sociale Geografie* 93: 125–36.

WAG (2002). *Dyfodol Dwyieithog/A Bilingual Future*, Welsh Assembly Government, Cardiff.

WAG (2003). *Iaith Pawb: A National Action Plan for a Bilingual Wales*, Welsh Assembly Government, Cardiff.

Wales Labour Party (1992). *It's Time to Get Wales Working Again*, Wales Labour Party, Cardiff.

Wallerstein, I. (1974). *The Modern World System I. Capitalist Agriculture and the Origins of the European World Economy in the Sixteenth Century*, Academic Press, New York.

Wallerstein, I. (1980). *The Modern World System II. Mercantilism and the Consolidation of the European World Economy, 1600–1750*, Academic Press, New York.

Wallerstein, I. (1989). *The Modern World System III. The Second Era of Great Expansion of the Capitalist World Economy, 1730–1840*, Academic Press, New York.

Webb, T. (2001). *Colonization, Colonialism and Anti-colonialism*, Cymuned, Aberystwyth.

Weber, E. (1977). *Peasants into Frenchmen: The Modernization of Rural France 1870–1914*, Stanford University Press, Stanford, CA.

Welsh Language Board (2000). 'Language revitalization: the role of the Welsh Language Board' in C. H. Williams (ed.) *Language Revitalization: Policy and Planning in Wales*, University of Wales Press, Cardiff, pp. 83–115.

Welsh Nation (1963). 'The inside story of Trefechan Bridge', March 1963, p. 1.

Welsh Office (1965). *Legal Status of the Welsh Language: Report of the Committee Under the Chairmanship of Sir David Hughes Parry*, HMSO, London.

Whelan, Y. (2003). *Reinventing Modern Dublin: Streetscape, Iconography and the Politics of Identity*, University College Dublin Press, Dublin.

Whitehead, M. (2003). 'Love thy neighbourhood: Rethinking the politics of scale and Walsall's struggle for neighbourhood democracy', *Environment and Planning A* 35: 277–300.

Whitehead, M., Jones, R. and Jones, M. (2007). *The Nature of the State: Excavating the Political Ecologies of the Modern State*, Oxford University Press, Oxford.

Wiebe, R. (2002). *Who We Are: A History of Popular Nationalism*, Princeton University Press, Princeton, NJ.

Wigley, D. (1992). *O Ddifri*, Gwasg Gwynedd, Caernarfon.

Williams, C. (1999). 'Passports to Wales? Race, nation and identity', in R. Fevre and A. Thompson (eds) *Nation, Identity and Social Theory: Perspectives from Wales*, University of Wales Press, Cardiff, pp. 69–89.

Williams, C. H. (1977). 'Non-violence and the development of the Welsh Language Society 1962–c.1974', *Welsh History Review* 8: 426–55.

Williams, C. H. (1982). 'Separatism and the mobilization of Welsh national identity', in C. H. Williams (ed.) *National Separatism*, University of Wales Press, Cardiff, pp. 145–202.

Williams, C. H. (2000). 'On recognition, resolution and revitalization', in C. H. Williams (ed.) *Language Revitalization: Policy and Planning in Wales*, University of Wales Press, Cardiff, pp. 1–47.

Williams, C. H. (ed.) (2007). *Language and Governance*, University of Wales Press, Cardiff.

Williams, C. H. and Smith, A. D. (1983). 'The national construction of social space', *Progress in Human Geography* 7: 502–18.

Williams, G. and Morris, D. (2000). *Language Planning and Language Use: Welsh in a Global Age,*. University of Wales Press, Cardiff.

Williams, J. L. (1973). 'The Welsh language in education', in M. Stephens (ed.) *The Welsh Language Today*, Gwasg Gomer, Llandysul, pp. 92–109.

Williams, M. (1991). *Hanes UCAC: Cyfrol y Dathlu*, Adran Lenyddiaeth UCAC, Aberystwyth.

Y Cymro (1963). 'Protest iaith yn enyn llid rhai o bobl Dolgellau: dyrnu, cicio a thynnu gwallt' (Language protest attracts the vitriol of some of Dolgellau's residents: punching, kicking and hair-pulling), 2 December, p. 1.

Y Faner (1969). 'Anadl einioes cenedl', Dafydd Iwan, 4 December.

Yapa, L. (1996). 'What causes poverty? A postmodern view', *Annals of the Association of American Geographers* 86: 707–28.

Yuval-Davies, N. (1997). *Gender and Nation*, Sage, London.

Zimmer, O. (2003). 'Boundary mechanisms and symbolic resources: towards a process-oriented approach to national identity', *Nations and Nationalism* 9: 173–93.

Index

source of nationalist activities, as
125
  Cymdeithas yr Iaith, and 125–6
  Meibion Glyndŵr 126
  roadsigns campaign 125
  role of students 126
  Welsh television channel
    campaign 125
  University's Welsh-language
    scheme, and 128
  protests against 128
Welsh-medium education, and
123–31
  campaigns for 124
  national agenda, and 129
  national campaign for 130
  national support for 131
Welsh-medium education
  campaigns, and 127–8
place
  definitions 21–2
  electoral politics of
    see electoral politics
  focus on concept of 202
  localized places 23
    active role of 26
    ethnography of locality 24
    group-making processes 28
    metonyms, use as 24
    reproduction of nationalism, and
    23
    scalar connections, significance
    29
  meaning 6
  meaning of notion 21
  national identities, and 24
  particularities of 21
  politics of 21, 27
    rearticulation of 27
  role in electoral politics 135
  socio-spatial networks 22
  spatial categories, as 22
  study of 21
  triple dialectic 27
    'common stock of knowledge' 27
  types of 22–3
Plaid Cymru 52–6

abandonment of west Wales by 172
electoral politics, and 138–41
  Aberystwyth, in
    see Aberystwyth
  consolidation of political gains
    140
  direct action, and 138
  home-rule 139
  National Assembly, and 140
  political reach 140
  pressure group, whether 139
  relationship between 138
  status of party, and 138
electoral support 53
  1960s 53
  1979–99 55
  'heartland' constituencies 55
  post-war 53
Green Party alliance 143–7
  1989 formal debate 146
  1992 election results 153
  benefits 146
  election of first MP 150–4
  end of 154–6
  formal agreement of coalition
    146
  impact of 147
  intellectual roots of 143
  interaction in 1980s 144
  joint programme for Ceredigion
    147–50
  polling data 146
  public support for each party 145
  sustainable development, and
    143
manifestos 160–1
  ecological concerns 161
nationalist discourse of 52–3
platform 53
pressure group, as 54, 139
  political party, and 54
Welsh institutions, and 53
Welsh language, and 54
Welsh nationalism, and 52–6
Welsh Office, and 54
'where of Wales' 172
Pont Trefechan 84–92